REGIONAL PATHWAYS TO NUCLEAR NONPROLIFERATION

# STUDIES IN SECURITY AND INTERNATIONAL AFFAIRS

SERIES EDITORS

Sara Z. Kutchesfahani
Senior Policy Analyst, Center for Arms Control and Non-proliferation
Senior Program Coordinator, Fissile Materials Working Group

Amanda Murdie
Dean Rusk Scholar of International Relations and Professor of International Affairs, University of Georgia

SERIES ADVISORY BOARD

Kristin M. Bakke
Associate Professor of Political Science and International Relations, University College London

Jeffrey Knopf
Professor and Program Chair, Nonproliferation and Terrorism Studies, Middlebury Institute of International Studies at Monterey

Fawaz Gerges
Professor of International Relations, London School of Economics and Political Science

Deepa Prakash
Assistant Professor of Political Science, DePauw University

Rafael M Grossi
Ambassador of Argentina to Austria and International Organisations in Vienna

Kenneth Paul Tan
Vice Dean of Academic Affairs and Associate Professor of Public Policy, The National University of Singapore's (NUS) Lee Kuan Yew School of Public Policy

Bonnie D. Jenkins
University of Pennsylvania Perry World Center and The Brookings Institute Fellow

Brian Winter
Editor-in-chief, Americas Quarterly

Regional Pathways to Nuclear Nonproliferation

Wilfred Wan

The University of Georgia Press
Athens

Paperback edition, 2023
© 2018 by the University of Georgia Press
Athens, Georgia 30602
www.ugapress.org
All rights reserved
Set in Minion Pro by Graphic Composition, Inc., Bogart, Georgia

Most University of Georgia Press titles are available from popular e-book vendors.

Printed digitally

Library of Congress Cataloging-in-Publication Data

Names: Wan, Wilfred, author.
Title: Regional pathways to nuclear nonproliferation / Wilfred Wan.
Description: Athens, Georgia : The University of Georgia Press, [2018] | Series: Studies in security and international affairs | Includes bibliographical references and index.
Identifiers: LCCN 2018003944 | ISBN 9780820353302 (hardcover : alk. paper) | ISBN 9780820353296 (ebook)
Subjects: LCSH: Nuclear nonproliferation. | Nuclear arms control. | Regionalism (International organization)
Classification: LCC JZ5675.W37 2018 | DDC 327.1/747—dc23
LC record available at https://lccn.loc.gov/2018003944

Paperback ISBN 978-0-8203-6492-6

CONTENTS

Acknowledgments   ix
List of Abbreviations   xi

CHAPTER 1. Nuclear Frustrations   1
CHAPTER 2. Global Nuclear Order at a Crossroads   16
CHAPTER 3. Foundations for Regional Nuclear Order   28
CHAPTER 4. Established Orders: Western Europe and Latin America   44
CHAPTER 5. Northeast Asia   60
CHAPTER 6. Southeast Asia   78
CHAPTER 7. The Middle East   95
CHAPTER 8. Elusive Orders: Africa and South Asia   112
CHAPTER 9. The Future of Nonproliferation   127

Notes   143
Bibliography   165
Index   183

ACKNOWLEDGMENTS

This book stands at the intersection of many of my recent lives.

The idea of writing this book came from my friend Hannah Cooper, who, upon hearing about my hazy fellowship plans, asked pointedly: "Why not a book?" She does not recall this conversation. Hannah, John de Boer, Alexandra Ivanovic, Lee Schrader, Basilio Valdehuesa, and Anthony Yazaki were colleagues who provided much valued encouragement during my time at the United Nations University Centre for Policy Research (UNU-CPR), when the bulk of the work for this project was undertaken. Any expression of thanks is woefully insufficient for Louise Bosetti, the best friend I could ever ask for. Some Pop Rocks will have to suffice.

The genesis for the ideas outlined in this book dates back many years. They are intimately linked to my work on the nuclear nonproliferation regime conducted as a graduate student at the University of California, Irvine under Etel Solingen, Patrick Morgan, and Erwin Chemerinsky, and as a Stanton Nuclear Security Fellow with the Belfer Center for Science and International Affairs under Matthew Bunn, Martin Malin, and Steven Miller. I remain thankful for their guidance; Etel's influence especially is evident across these pages and far beyond.

The book was finalized during my time as a researcher with the United Nations Institute for Disarmament Research (UNIDIR). John Borrie and Tim Caughley, among others, have been fantastic to work with and have been incredibly supportive of all my research projects undertaken in my personal capacity—including this one. I am thrilled to be a part of UNIDIR and the important work it does. I do want to stress that the views expressed in this publication are my sole responsibility and do not reflect the views or opinions of the United Nations, UNIDIR, its staff members or sponsors, or those of any other institute listed in these pages.

Too many others—animals included—have provided one form of support or another over the course of this project, only some of whom were aware that it even existed. For instance, both Nobu Akiyama and Sebastian von Einsiedel graciously granted me a great deal of autonomy during my fellowship years. The list also contains friends and scholars like Sungyeol Choi, Anne-Sophie Darier, Elena Finckh, Courtney Fung, Koji Enomoto, Amy Grubb, Kei Koga, Tom Le, and Valerie Wright. I look forward to spending time with each far away from conference halls in the near future and apologize for not providing them their own sentences here. My mom Fina and sister Cordia (a neurologist and the proper Dr. Wan) deserve much more.

Of course, I am indebted to the University of Georgia Press and the hard work of Lisa Bayer, Walter Biggins, Jane M. Curran, Katherine La Mantia, and Thomas Roche in particular. A special thanks to Jeffrey W. Knopf, whose 2015 edited volume initially drew me to the press, and who later provided words of encouragement on my project. The reviewers involved in the publication process—including the Studies in Security and International Affairs series editors as well as other anonymous individuals—helped move this book to a much better place. I am also grateful for institutional support from the UNU-CPR, Hitotsubashi University, the Japan Society for the Promotion of Science, the Social Sciences Research Council, and the Pacific Forum Center for Strategic and International Studies.

Finally, this book would not exist without the help of the bevy of academics, experts, and current and former officials who agreed to talk to me formally and informally about issues spanning the nuclear landscape. The countless individuals who are not directly quoted in these pages still provided indispensable material that informs this work. Any misanalyses can be laid squarely at my feet.

ABBREVIATIONS

ABACC	Brazilian-Argentine Agency for Accounting and Control of Nuclear Materials
ACRS	Arms Control and Regional Security
ADMM	ASEAN Defence Ministers' Meeting
ADMM-Plus	ASEAN Defence Ministers' Meeting–Plus
AFCONE	African Commission on Nuclear Energy
APEC	Asia-Pacific Economic Cooperation
APT	ASEAN Plus Three
ARF	ASEAN Regional Forum
ASEAN	Association of Southeast Asian Nations
ASEANTOM	ASEAN Network of Regulatory Bodies on Atomic Energy
BRICS	Brazil, Russia, India, China, and South Africa
CARICOM	Caribbean Community
ECOWAS	Economic Community of West African States
EDC	European Defence Community
EPC	European Political Cooperation
EU	European Union
Euratom	European Atomic Energy Community
G-77	Group of 77
GCC	Gulf Cooperation Council
IAEA	International Atomic Energy Agency
ISIS	Islamic State
JCPOA	Joint Comprehensive Plan of Action
NAM	Non-Aligned Movement
NAPCI	Northeast Asia Peace and Cooperation Initiative
NATO	North Atlantic Treaty Organization
NEAPSM	Northeast Asia Peace and Security Mechanism
NPT	Nuclear Non-Proliferation Treaty
OAU	Organisation of African Unity
OPANAL	Agency for the Prohibition of Nuclear Weapons in Latin America and the Caribbean
SAARC	South Asian Association for Regional Cooperation
SAGSI	Standing Advisory Group on Safeguards Implementation
SCCC	Common System of Accounting and Control

SEANWFZ	Southeast Asia nuclear-weapon-free zone
SSOD	Special Session on Disarmament
START	Strategic Arms Reduction Treaty
SWIFT	Society for Worldwide Interbank Financial Telecommunications
THAAD	Terminal High Altitude Area Defense
UN	United Nations
UNIDIR	United Nations Institute for Disarmament Research
WMD	Weapons of mass destruction

REGIONAL PATHWAYS TO NUCLEAR NONPROLIFERATION

CHAPTER 1

Nuclear Frustrations

> The Treaty [on the Non-Proliferation of Nuclear Weapons] has served us well for 35 years. But unless we regard it as part of a living, dynamic regime capable of evolving to match changing realities, it will fade into irrelevance and leave us vulnerable and unprotected.
> —MOHAMED ELBARADEI, May 2, 2005

A little over a decade ago, the director general of the International Atomic Energy Agency (IAEA) sounded an alarm for the global nuclear nonproliferation regime. This was a period of turmoil for the international community. North Korea had suspended its participation in Six-Party Talks, and its Foreign Ministry had claimed that the regime was no longer bound by its five-year-old moratorium on long-range missile testing.[1] Meanwhile, reports from the *New York Times* and the *Washington Post* placed uranium hexafluoride suspected to be of North Korean origin in Libya, rekindling concerns in the West about an active black market proliferation ring—just over a year after the uncovering of the Abdul Qadeer Khan network.[2] Concerns about the Iranian nuclear program had reached an apex too. Tehran's tepid cooperation with the IAEA failed to improve the tense situation that had lingered since revelations in 2003 of its undeclared nuclear facilities; Mohamed ElBaradei of the IAEA was unable to confirm the absence of clandestine activity and referred to the "confidence deficit" in place.[3] Safeguards reporting failures in Libya, South Korea, and Egypt between 2003 and 2005, moreover, were disturbing works on their own accord, yet the inconsistent response by the IAEA flirted with the "danger of setting bad precedents based on arbitrary criteria or judgments informed by political considerations."[4]

At the outset of the 2005 Review Conference of the Nuclear Non-Proliferation Treaty (NPT), Director General ElBaradei delivered a stark warning about the precariousness of the global nuclear order and its cornerstone treaty. His warning was intended as a call to action, an appeal for the then-188 states parties to reinforce their commitment to the treaty, redress its shortcomings, and move toward achieving its lofty aspirations. Instead, his words went unheeded. The 2005 conference in fact marked the nadir for both the NPT and its surrounding regime. The 153 states in attendance bickered over procedural details for the majority of the nearly month-long conference, with political maneuvering preventing any discussion of the substantive issues and challenges that dominated the global security landscape. The end result was a final document that provided only the barest technical details about the proceedings themselves. Any momentum from the successful conference five years earlier was effectively derailed. The disaster left the nuclear nonproliferation regime without even a blueprint to guide them in tackling contemporary challenges.

Ten years later, the situation appeared all too familiar. Expectations for a strengthened nuclear order were heightened following a successful treaty review conference in 2010. There was a much-heralded action plan, with concrete steps designated to be taken across the treaty's so-called three pillars of nonproliferation, disarmament, and development for peaceful use. Parties had even outlined a process and timeline toward the establishment of a weapons of mass destruction (WMD)-free zone in the Middle East, which had long been on the agenda. Yet, enthusiasm dissipated over the course of the intervening five years. The movement executed against the action plan was negligible in the eyes of most non–nuclear weapon states. The 2015 NPT Review Conference marked an exercise in futility. Questions about commitment to the NPT were raised, underlining the animosity and resentment that had built against the five recognized nuclear weapon states—the United States, United Kingdom, Russia, China, and France. Joint statements from Austria on behalf of 159 states, and Australia on behalf of 26 states, explicitly criticized the group for lack of disarmament progress.[5] Again, the conference concluded with no consensus on a substantive outcome document—despite negotiations that continued into the eleventh hour. The status of the 2010 action plan was left in limbo.

With states parties again unable to sustain progress across successive conferences, the health of both the treaty and its surrounding regime has come into question. The frustrations of the review process suggest the threat of the NPT being reduced to the role of a paper tiger, with not enough accountability on promises made and agreements concluded. Even the 2015 NPT Review Conference was somewhat overshadowed by nuclear negotiations between Iran and the permanent five members of the UN Security Council plus Germany (P5+1). While the resulting Joint Comprehensive Plan of Action (JCPOA) was a major victory for the nuclear nonproliferation regime, provisions on monitoring and verification went beyond those in the NPT, while conditions set on uranium enrichment clearly restricted Tehran's rights in a manner in opposition to NPT principles—both deviations arguably undermining the treaty in the long run.[6] Since the conference, a number of nonproliferation and disarmament goals remain stuck in neutral: entry into force of more Additional Protocols, ratification of the Comprehensive Test Ban Treaty, negotiation of the proposed Fissile Material Cut-Off Treaty, among others. Meanwhile, the North Korea threat continues unabated, with nuclear tests in 2016 and 2017 and rumors of miniaturization. With familiar flashpoints, and the nature of nuclear proliferation itself evolving, the NPT—and, by extension, the global nuclear nonproliferation regime—needs a jolt to avoid becoming an anachronism, one unable to address myriad challenges present and future.

ARGUMENT

This book makes the case for a more specialized, decentralized, and localized nuclear nonproliferation regime.[7] The coherence and robustness of global nuclear order—defined broadly as the framework of rules and norms in place governing the possession and use of nuclear weapons—will be enhanced if the NPT is supplemented by more concerted nonproliferation and disarmament efforts below the global level.[8] In particular, the book posits that the nature of challenges across the nuclear landscape demands enhanced cooperation at the regional level, cooperation that includes but extends beyond the nuclear-weapon-free zones in existence. The most prominent concerns on the agenda not only expose the shortcomings of the existing global nuclear order but are inextricably linked to the security environment, energy policies, and other dynamics and characteristics at the regional level. These include the lingering status of treaty nonparties India, Pakistan, and Israel, the burgeoning North Korean weapons program, and the nuclear security and safety infrastructures. At the same time, patterns of regionalism in the post–Cold War era have contributed to stronger institutional foundations upon which stronger regional nuclear orders appear feasible in many instances. Regional institutions—ranging from organizations to dialogues to ad hoc arrangements—have gradually become more involved across economic, environmental, and human security domains; the nuclear arena presents another frontier for multilateral cooperation.

The encompassing power of nuclear weapons can belie the distinctive nature of proliferation threats across the various regions of the world.[9] Northeast Asia is understandably consumed by developments in the North Korean nuclear program, which poses an existential threat to those in its immediate vicinity, with ramifications for the United States and China. In the Middle East, many skeptical eyes continue to watch the implementation of the JCPOA, especially those of Israeli prime minister Benjamin Netanyahu—whose state's own policy of nuclear ambiguity remains a source of great consternation for its neighbors. Yet, proliferation and disarmament issues seem far removed for other regions. Southeast Asia and Africa, for instance, appear often detached from such concerns. Yet, with states there in the embryonic stages of peaceful nuclear development, issues of safety and security culture will factor soon. That these regions may represent the preeminent theaters in the war against illicit trafficking and the nuclear black market underscores the ubiquity—if not universality—of nuclear proliferation concerns.

The utility of stronger regional nuclear orders thus appears quite apparent. This is reinforced by the tumultuous state of the current global geopolitical landscape, with the potential for a leadership vacuum given escalating tensions between Russia and the West, America's turn toward isolationism under the Donald J. Trump administration, and Britain's in-progress exit from the European Union. Yet, what is the possibility that strengthened regional nuclear orders will emerge? What are the pathways toward their establishment? And given the diverse nature of the nuclear threat, what organizational and substantive form might these orders take in different regions? These are the central questions explored in this book, which advances an analytical framework aimed to assess the conditions for regional nuclear order centering on (1) commonalities in issue definition, (2) patterns of regionalism, and (3) existing nuclear cooperation (detailed in chapter 3). As subsequent chapters indicate, ideal conditions for regional nuclear orders do not exist. Yet, by analyzing how different geopolitical groupings of states perceive their commonalities both broadly and within the context of the nuclear sphere, this book highlights avenues toward greater nuclear nonproliferation cooperation at that level.

The NPT has served as the centerpiece for global nuclear order since it entered into force in 1970, and it has become one of the most long-lasting and widely adhered-to cooperative arrangements at the international level. But its longevity and near universality can obscure fundamental shortcomings. The 2005 and 2015 Review Conference outcomes reveal widespread discord. Especially concerning is the possibility that states parties have lost faith in the treaty's ability to prevent nuclearization, enhance transparency in nuclear programs, facilitate development for peaceful use, and delegitimize nuclear weapons. This book argues that changes across the nuclear and security landscapes have challenged the sufficiency of the NPT in these core matters. States parties continue to be frustrated by "legacies, reiterations or reincarnations of problems that the regime has failed over many years to tackle effectively."[10] The 2017 UN General Assembly negotiations that concluded the Treaty on the Prohibition of Nuclear Weapons reveal the depths of this discontent. The limitations of the NPT are impediments to its adaptive prowess, its very structure and scope breeding stagnation and resentment. Yet, the treaty and the order it upholds are not unsalvageable. Rather, actions to supplement the NPT can preserve it and maintain the whole of the nuclear nonproliferation regime.

EXISTING WORKS

There exists a plethora of work on nuclear weapons, touching on some of the themes discussed in this book. There are three problems with the existing works, however.

1) *The majority of the literature is centered on proliferation, not nonproliferation.* Scholars have tended to examine and reexamine the reasons why states might seek to acquire or forgo nuclear weapons. The state-centric character of the literature is a product of the evolution of the field itself; the study of proliferation, in fact, is largely grounded in the major approaches in International Relations. For instance, the conventional explanation for proliferation is informed by neorealist theory, with nuclear weapons seen as the ultimate means of protection in a world marked by competition and uncertainty. This security-based model of nuclear motivation underlines the impact of external threats in determining behavior.[11] Even those who examine institutions do so with the question of impact on the state. For instance, social constructivists credit the nuclear nonproliferation regime with establishing an "internalized belief among its participants that [nuclear weapons are] illegitimate and abhorrent."[12] The exclusion and ostracism of India, Pakistan, Israel, and North Korea from the nuclear community helps to dispel proliferation as a viable option for others.[13] While a number of recent works engage in supply-side analyses, examining technical capability and accessibility in the surrounding environment, for instance, these scholars too engage nuclear weapons from the perspective of state decisions to proliferate.[14]

2) *Works that incorporate the region generally lack a comparative dimension.* The link between nuclear weapons and regional dynamics is hardly uncharted territory. However, scholars tend to limit their analysis to the predominant proliferation threat in a region. Some works confine their scope to a single geographic area—for instance, focusing on the India-Pakistan arms race, the Brazil-Argentina rivalry, or the North Korean program.[15] A smaller group broaden their perspectives beyond an individual region and provide invaluable insight as to the impact of regional security concerns on the nuclear policies of states.[16] Yet, they still project from the level of the preeminent state, in effect examining how the decisions of those states are made and how their decisions will affect the texture of regional and international politics. Notably, there are several works that do engage in the kind of regional comparative analysis pursued in this book, featuring the region as subject. In two prominent instances, however, these compare and contrast only East Asia and the Middle East and do so only as a framing device for other arguments: drawn on role perceptions of "global rogues" North Korea and Iran, or on domestic coalitions and their integration into the global economy.[17] Across the board, then, existing works eschew broader regional trends and processes from analysis. In this manner, they echo the focus on individual state threats and state decision making.

3) *Works that impose an institutional (nonproliferation) approach generally neglect regional-level analysis.* Given the prominence of neoliberal institutionalism in international relations, it is surprising that the nuclear nonproliferation

regime has so rarely featured as an empirical case.[18] After all, the regime perpetuates mutual understandings about the nuclear weapon threat, promotes information sharing and transparency, and constrains deviant behaviors through accountability mechanisms and regularized dialogue. These reflect the positive externalities of institutions.[19] Yet, scholars readily acknowledge that the actual impact of the rules and promised benefits remains understudied as it pertains to the nuclear arena.[20] The small sample of works that feature an institutional perspective instead stay focused on particular policies and particular actors and campaigns. They include volumes that delve deep into the UN machinery, the various multilateral nonproliferation arrangements, and the assorted challenges to such tools.[21] Still, these works on nuclear order underplay regional dimensions. Even the exceptions linger again on the North Korea and Iranian cases, or strictly on the utility of nuclear-weapon-free zones.[22] A 2016 piece on "regional nuclear regimes" offers much insight but still poses these institutions as the primary byproduct of a regional power seeking to provide leadership in that arena—the statist, neorealist perspective.[23]

FOCUS OF THE BOOK

The topics tackled in the following pages are not unfamiliar to nuclear proliferation scholars. They include the state of the nuclear nonproliferation regime, the regional nature of challenges, the future of nuclear order, and the interplay between these various elements.[24] However, this book seeks to address the aforementioned gaps in the existing literature on nuclear weapons in three distinct ways.

First, it employs an expressly institutional lens on the nuclear issue, moving away from the well-trodden territory of state decisions to acquire nuclear weapons. Accordingly, it does not confine analysis to the security landscapes of individual countries but instead moves to capture the multidimensionality of nuclear proliferation risk and threat across regions. This includes arms control and disarmament issues, but also nuclear safety and security concerns. While the latter two are topics often segregated from discussion of nuclear proliferation, the vulnerability of facilities has become increasingly relevant from the proliferation lens in the post–Cold War era, as one primary threat scenario "envisions the construction of a crude nuclear bomb by non-state actors using special nuclear materials."[25] Thus, issues such as nuclear waste and radioactive source management also cannot be overlooked. It is both revealing and instructive that the IAEA has sought in the twenty-first century to employ a nonproliferation approach that integrates safety and security with traditional safeguards issues.

Second, in its examining of nonproliferation, the book infuses the nuclear issue with an emerging theoretical perspective. The regionalism literature offers insights that can complement the longstanding International Relations approaches that undergird existing nuclear scholarship. This is an essential addition given the altered nature of international order in the post–Cold War era. Patterns of regional activity have emerged that are not limited to trade and investment; they have come to encompass political and even security issues. For all the work done in the past two decades on regionalism processes, for all the literature that has traced the contributions of regional organizations, it is striking that there remains a lack of systematic analysis of regional nuclear orders, real or potential, that extends beyond the five nuclear-weapon-free zones in existence. Again, while the two are not mutually exclusive concepts, this book makes a key distinction between those zones and the more encompassing notion of regional nuclear order.

Third, and interrelated, because the empirical chapters pivot on regions, not singular states or threats, this book presents a thorough analysis of the character of nuclear nonproliferation cooperation at the regional and subregional levels. Again, it argues that a regional reorientation presents the most effective means with which the international community can bolster the NPT and existing global nuclear order. This can be contrasted to approaches that stress the role of domestic legislation (as with UN Security Council Resolution 1540), limited-term political forums (the Nuclear Security Summit series), and focused multilateral campaigns (the Cooperative Threat Reduction Program and the Global Partnership), for instance. Strengthened regional nuclear orders do not, and should not, preclude state participation in such arrangements. At the same time, they require multilateral mechanisms exclusive to the grouping of states in question.

THE REGIONAL NUCLEAR ORDER AT A GLANCE

As mentioned, the notion of nuclear order at the regional level has been synonymous with nuclear-weapon-free zones in the existing literature, and understandably so. These arrangements have after all been part and parcel of the global nuclear nonproliferation regime since its very beginning, with the 1967 Treaty of Tlatelolco negotiated among states in Latin America in the same timeframe as the NPT.[26] That the two texts set forth many of the same obligations for states only underscored the close nature of their relationship, the idea that the regional treaty would complement the global treaty. Contracting parties to the Latin America nuclear-weapon-free zone agreed to prevent the "testing, use, manufacture, production or acquisition of . . . any nuclear weapons, directly or indirectly."[27] They also agreed to conduct timely negotiations for IAEA safeguards agreements and to provide regular compliance reports to that entity. A year later, the NPT featured identical text on state obligations, while its centerpiece article specified that safeguards agreements were to be negotiated and concluded by all non-nuclear-weapon states parties with the IAEA.[28] Notably, the Treaty of Tlatelolco established an additional intergovernmental verification mechanism in the form of the Agency of the Prohibition of Nuclear Weapons in Latin America and the Caribbean (OPANAL). As chapter 4 details, OPANAL remains the backbone of regional nuclear order in that region.

The Latin America zone presented a model for regional nuclear order for the world, in a manner that outstripped even the European Atomic Energy Community (Euratom) founded in 1957; after all, the latter's jurisdiction was confined to nuclear energy in the civilian sector. OPANAL gained observer status at the first NPT Review Conference in 1975, which reaffirmed the value of nuclear-weapon-free zones in its outcome document, recognizing that they represented "an effective means of curbing the spread of nuclear weapons."[29] A number of states sought to incorporate binding security assurances from the nuclear weapon states within the context of zone treaties and also called for studies pursuant to the possibility of establishing regional fuel cycle centers—underscoring the emphasis placed on strengthening regional nuclear order. Proposals for zones came in the Middle East, South Asia, and the South Pacific in the 1970s, with the final emerging through the 1985 Treaty of Rarotonga. A 1975 special report commissioned by the UN General Assembly noted nuclear-weapon-free zones were "not to be seen as an alternative to the [NPT], but rather as a potentially powerful instrument to supplement that Treaty."[30]

Ample opportunities for regional nuclear nonproliferation cooperation emerged with the end of the Cold War. In 1991, Argentina and Brazil signed the Guadalajara Accord for the Use of Nuclear Energy for Peaceful Purposes, which established the Brazilian-Argentine Agency for Accounting and Control of Nuclear Materials (ABACC). In 1992, North and South Korea signed the Joint Declaration of the Denuclearization of the Korean Peninsula, which committed each party to joint inspections and established a Joint Nuclear Control Commission. Some felt that the declaration could even serve as a stepping stone for a Northeast Asian nuclear-weapon-free zone.[31] The period of transformation was marked by states moving "beyond the traditional emphasis on denial" of weapons-usable materials and equipment, looking beyond nonproliferation, and adopting a proactive "antiproliferation" mentality.[32] Support for nuclear-weapon-free zones continued; they were "encouraged as a matter of priority."[33] With treaties in Southeast Asia, Central Asia, and Africa all coming since 1995, nuclear-weapon-free zones have come to encompass 115 states, including the entirety of the Southern Hemisphere, as well as Mongolia, which was recognized as a one-state zone (see table 1.1). The convening of two Conferences of States Parties and Signatories to Treaties That Establish Nuclear-Weapon-Free Zones since 2005 further solidifies their growth.

TABLE 1.1   Nuclear-Weapon-Free Zones in Populated Areas

Region	Treaty	States	Entry into Force
Latin America and the Caribbean	Tlatelolco	33	4/25/1969
South Pacific	Rarotonga	13	11/12/1986
Southeast Asia	Bangkok	10	3/28/1997
Mongolia		1	2/28/2000
Central Asia	Semipalatinsk	5	3/21/2009
Africa	Pelindaba	53	7/15/2009

Source: United Nations Office for Disarmament Affairs, "Nuclear-Weapon-Free Zones," https://www.un.org/disarmament/wmd/nuclear/nwfz/.

The importance of nuclear-weapon-free zones should not be dismissed. They represent clearly the most visible manifestation of existing regional nuclear order. The specification of localized initiation and voluntary participation as hallmarks highlight the unique agency afforded to developing countries in such arrangements. At least in principle, they not only set forth invaluable norms of behavior but also stand as instruments with which states can manage the inequalities of the system, obliging global powers to their terms in the nuclear arena. Furthermore, the treaty texts reflect the unique histories of each region with the nuclear issue. This includes tweaks in the jurisdictions of some nuclear-weapon-free zones, with bans on the disposal of radioactive waste, explicit prohibitions on weapons research and development, and mentions of environmental rehabilitation. Some attached expanded legal requirements, including accession to existing multilateral agreements. Treaties have demonstrated structural variation as well, with the Latin America and Africa zones opting to create new organizations, while those in Southeast Asia and the South Pacific formed commissions composed of foreign ministers that met in conjunction with existing regional forums.

Still, the different forms taken by nuclear-weapon-free zones underscore the larger point that they represent but one manifestation of regional nuclear order.[34] Because of the impact of the Treaty of Tlatelolco, these treaties remain susceptible to many of the shortcomings faced by the global nuclear nonproliferation regime (discussed further in chapter 2). They remain tethered to the NPT and IAEA safeguards agreements, their scope largely confined to proliferation through state diversion. While several treaties have made mention of global nuclear safety and security instruments, they have not sought to engage states in formalized cooperation on those subjects, or any others. Their absence altogether in several critical regions—notably, Northeast Asia, the Middle East, and South Asia—further illustrates the shortcomings of what has heretofore been an "all or nothing" approach. There is no doubt that nuclear-weapon-free zones can provide the foundation for robust regional nuclear order, as such a zone has provided in Latin America. However, because of an altered international landscape, because of the wave of economic and security regionalisms, and because the "[United Nations'] role of encouraging, supporting and legitimating regional organizations in the provisions of security should not be underestimated," it would be remiss to consider alternative outcomes.[35] As this book examines the viability of strengthened regional nuclear orders, it does not restrict itself to the form in which such an order would likely take place.

RESEARCH DESIGN

The immense reach of the global nuclear nonproliferation regime necessitates a broad approach in considering the possibility of its regional reorientation. In deploying the analytical framework outlined earlier, this book utilizes a multiple case study methodology that encompasses select geopolitical regions across the world. Each chapter draws upon a spectrum of resources: this includes close readings of primary documents such as NPT Review Conference proceedings, treaty texts, and reports from governments and international organizations; extensive scholarly and policy analyses on regional political, economic, and security relations; contemporary sources such as national and international newspapers and interview transcripts, primarily to represent policy thinking of leaders and governments; and approximately twenty-five personal interviews (of officials and subject experts) conducted in and around the 2015 NPT Review Conference.[36]

Case Selection

The bulk of the empirical section in this book is devoted to Northeast Asia, Southeast Asia, and the Middle East. This is because each region represents potential crucial cases in nonproliferation, each to some degree housing the spectrum of threat across the nuclear landscape past, present, and future.[37] Northeast Asia and the Middle East fall under least-likely cases for regional nuclear orders, as the relevant independent variables stand "at values that only weakly predict an outcome or predict a low-magnitude outcome."[38] Nuclear politics in both instances are intertwined with hostile geopolitical and security landscapes, with the general absence of institutional structures and shared identities. Still, nuclear threats loom large in each instance. In contrast, Southeast Asia presents a curious case in the opposite direction. There exists a dominant institutional presence—the Association of Southeast Asian Nations (ASEAN)—that has sought to expand further into the security realm.

In addition, the region has become a key battleground for illicit trafficking of weapons-usable materials, while the planned development of nuclear energy programs in the near future will fundamentally alter the nature of threat. But there exists no urgent existential threat, and the presence of a nuclear-weapon-free zone remains. In each of these three scenarios, then, in which areas has regional nuclear cooperation taken hold? To what degree is a more coherent nuclear order possible?

Surrounding the three crucial cases are four shadow cases that serve as invaluable points of comparison. The first two cases involve an examination of the mature, functioning regional nuclear orders that have taken hold in Western Europe and Latin America. It is these two largely historical cases that this book examines first, following the birth of nuclear cooperation in each case, and the subsequent establishment of two forms of fairly comprehensive order: the former centered on Euratom, the latter on the Treaty of Tlatelolco and OPANAL. Following chapters devoted to each of the three crucial cases above, the empirical section then concludes with a chapter on the far-off cases of Africa and South Asia. Despite the presence of a nascent nuclear-weapon-free zone, Africa presents a case in which regionalism processes are too immature, and nuclear threats not prioritized enough, for a true nuclear order to have broached the agenda. South Asia, meanwhile, remains a stubborn case of regional nuclear disorder, dominated by the security rivalry on the peninsula. The chapter peruses both regions for the conditions that will allow for cooperation in the long run, while underlining the fact that regional nuclear order—as with global nuclear order—ultimately stands as a function of broader geopolitical dynamics.

A Basis for Comparative Analysis

Given the comparative regional and institutional perspective this book imposes on the study of nuclear nonproliferation, it appears that the diversity of history, context, and challenges across the globe offer roadblocks to any attempt to make even shallow connections between cases. The regions selected for this book stand in many ways in stark contrast from one another. Even when one examines only the three crucial case studies, Northeast Asia houses some of the most advanced economies in the world and represents a potential battleground for global conflict, housing a resurgent Russia and an emerging China, with increasing questions about the future presence of the United States. Meanwhile, the Middle East is marked by ongoing political and social turbulence, much of it linked to the so-called Arab Winter, while the conflict between Israel and Palestine continues to simmer. The Islamic State caliphate adds another dimension of the challenge to a region long ill at ease with colonially demarcated boundaries. Finally, Southeast Asia is notable for the ambitious—if messy—

order imposed by ASEAN. Of course, as suggested, there exist vast differences across regions in the nuclear arena too. No states in Southeast Asia even house nuclear power plants. Northeast Asia, meanwhile, features two recognized nuclear weapon states in China and Russia, two more protected by the U.S. nuclear umbrella, and a rogue nuclear possessor in North Korea. In scratching the surface of these various regions, there are a number of seemingly irreconcilable differences that renders any singular approach futile.

Yet in many ways, the difference across regions is precisely what provides the rationale undergirding this book. The existing global nuclear nonproliferation regime has conglomerated all aspects of the nuclear issue under one umbrella, the scope of its centerpiece NPT leaving nearly no stone unturned. Because of its three pillars, and its near universality, a counterproductive interconnectivity has taken hold. Discussions to strengthen safeguards through a wider, mandatory application of the Additional Protocol do not exist separate from a call for the UK, France, and China to take more concrete disarmament action. Progress toward a WMD-free zone in the Middle East includes quid pro quo parsing how precisely nuclear weapon states should facilitate the fullest exchange of information and equipment for peaceful use. Discussions about consequences attached to NPT noncompliance cannot take place because of the existence of disparate obligations with varying specificity of language. It has become difficult to compartmentalize different aspects of the nuclear issue. And it is precisely because of these struggles that scholars, analysts, and policymakers should examine beneath the global level.

Moreover, there exist key commonalities among the regions examined in this book that make comparative regional analysis fruitful. First, for all its imperfections, the near-universality of the NPT suggests a base level of commitment to nuclear nonproliferation and disarmament principles. The notion that the further spread of nuclear weapons represents a stabilizing force for international order remains a strictly academic exercise; any policymaker who suggests movement in that direction is quickly rebuked.[39] The common perception regarding the undesirability of nuclear weapons proliferation thus offers an impetus for multilateral cooperation, for strengthening nuclear order overall. Accordingly, it serves as a baseline for comparison among regions. Second, to reiterate, the latest wave of regionalism is not a transient or selective phenomenon. The complex relations between neighbors increasingly serve as significant determinants of interstate affairs. While there are clear differences in the pace and scope of regionalism processes, that every region is experiencing this—as represented by formal organizations, trade patterns, common identity, and so on—provides another point of comparison. It is precisely the manifestation of that regionalism that allows comparative analysis, presenting insight both on existing regional nuclear orders and on potential areas of growth.

BOOK LAYOUT

In order to execute this analysis, the first section of this book pursues the interplay between regionalism and nuclear cooperation separately.

Chapter 2 tracks the past trajectory of the global nuclear nonproliferation regime, dating back to the entry into force of the centerpiece NPT. It lays the foundation for the book by reassessing the very purpose of the regime. It also makes the case that the durability and near universality of the treaty belie its limited adaptability and innovation across each of its three pillars and suggests that the NPT-centered regime must be supplemented by a regional approach if global nuclear order is to address the challenges of post–Cold War threats.

Chapter 3 examines the other half of the equation. It analyzes the character of regionalism in the post–Cold War era, drawing a particular distinction with the previous 1970s wave—and diving into the accompanying "new regionalist" strand of literature in the process.[40] The chapter pinpoints the economic origins of the phenomenon and then traces its growth to new domains, including political and security realms. It concludes by setting forth a framework with which to study the potential for regional nuclear order.

The remainder of the book connects the disparate lines of discussion, one on patterns in regionalism, the other on the evolution of global nuclear order, in shifting to a systematic examination of the nuclear landscape across empirical cases. Without adhering to a singular structure, the book deploys the framework detailed in chapter 3 to each case study. It gauges the shape of regionalism, identifies the nuclear challenges present, and then considers elements of nuclear cooperation present. Each chapter then projects a way toward a strengthened regional nuclear order.

Chapter 4 commences the empirical section with the relative success stories of Western Europe and Latin America. It adopts a historical overview, examining critical moments that defined the functioning nuclear orders in those regions. The examination of Western Europe considers the unique postwar environment in which the 1957 Euratom Treaty emerged. It then chronicles the development of European nuclear order, which has come to incorporate nonproliferation concerns outside the civilian boundaries of Euratom—a process linked intimately to regional integration dynamics. Meanwhile, the analysis of Latin America discusses the two-stage construction of Latin America's current nuclear order: first with the signing of the 1967 Treaty of Tlatelolco, second with the creation of the ABACC and the accession of Brazil and Argentina to Tlatelolco in the early 1990s.

Chapter 5 turns to the case of Northeast Asia, arguably the epicenter of activity for the nuclear issue in the present and the future. The unresolved crisis on the Korean peninsula, debate over Japan's nuclear restart, and force modernization plans from China are all emblematic of nuclear proliferation challenges that the existing regime has struggled to address. The chapter acknowledges the divergence between economic and security regionalism trends but suggests that these differences are slightly overplayed. The region may benefit because of a relatively strong consensus on common "soft" concerns in the nuclear arena. An encompassing regional nuclear order cannot be expected, but technical cooperation on nuclear safety and security issues—especially among the triumvirate of China, Japan, and South Korea—can contribute to an atmosphere of confidence building and information exchange that could propel movement.

Chapter 6 delves into a study of Southeast Asia. On the surface, Southeast Asia does not seem quite relevant to proliferation considerations. However, as a hotbed of piracy and trafficking, a home to terrorist activity, and with power plant development on the horizon, it represents the next frontier of nuclear nonproliferation. The chapter centers on the regional institutional architecture dominated by ASEAN and its related venues. Tracing ASEAN's meager forays into the security arena, it finds that its presence inhibits regional nuclear order, as such issues directly challenge core principles of noninterference and sovereignty. Unless security concerns related to the South China Sea spark significant change, only the development of nuclear energy programs (on the horizon in Indonesia and Malaysia) will address the palpable lack of urgency in the region, allowing a realistic nuclear order to develop on friendlier, "nontraditional security" terms.

Chapter 7 analyzes the frustrating case of the Middle East. For decades, the vision of regional nuclear order in that region has coalesced around the nuclear-weapon-free zone/WMD-free zone espoused by many policymakers. However, an alternative vision is necessary. While acknowledging the major upheaval that continues to destabilize the region, the chapter parses processes of regionalism—and subregionalism—that contribute to the order present in the Middle East. It considers the viability of identity politics in the proposal of security and nuclear orders; this includes an extensive breakdown of the WMD-free zone process and a consideration of the impact of the 2015 JCPOA on the nuclear and security landscapes. Basic conditions in the region render this highly unlikely in the near future, but subregional cooperation could provide a promising alternative and a key first step.

Chapter 8 concludes the case study section by examining Africa and South Asia. If previous chapters draw upon regionalism trends to identify some hope (however modest) for strengthened regional nuclear order, these cases provide outcomes on the other end of the spectrum. The presence of a nuclear-weapon-free zone in Africa belies the general lack of interest on nuclear issues. The chapter analyzes how that order came to be, and how it has come to wither away. The development of security regionalism through the African Union in the past decade portends well, but without external assistance, Africa looks likely to remain a weak link on the global supply chain. The second half of the chapter turns to South Asia, which remains overrun by a deterrence-based nuclear order between India and Pakistan. The failures of even economic regionalism among South Asian states, despite the presence of the South Asian Association for Regional Cooperation (SAARC), suggest that this regional nuclear disorder is likely to remain. From a proliferation perspective, a Cold War–like détente might be the best possible outcome given existing conditions.

The concluding chapter takes a step back, offering a global perspective. It highlights the nuclear proliferation scenarios of most relevance in the current landscape and the manner in which different threats challenge the existing global nuclear order. It considers the future of that order, given current trends. Then, the chapter returns to the specific notion of intensified activity at the regional level to supplement the NPT. It draws comparisons between a regional approach to ones that emphasize action at the global, multilateral, and national levels. A final section offers a series of policy prescriptions toward strengthened regional nuclear orders, in the service of a strengthened global nuclear order.

CHAPTER 2

Global Nuclear Order at a Crossroads

States parties continue to view the nearly universal Nuclear Non-Proliferation Treaty (NPT) as indispensable, and as the proper tool with which to navigate the complexities of the nuclear threat. Former U.S. president Barack Obama's watershed Prague speech on disarmament in April 2009 emphasized the NPT as the foundation for the global nuclear nonproliferation regime, declaring that "the basic bargain is sound"—echoing a frequent message from the 190 states parties to the treaty.[1] Former International Atomic Energy Agency (IAEA) director general Hans Blix has referred to the treaty as the "central instrument" not only for nuclear nonproliferation but "for global disarmament."[2] The most ardent critics of the global nuclear nonproliferation regime do not question the content of the treaty nor its place in international order, instead lambasting the commitment of individual parties.

While the text of the NPT has been unchanged since it opened for signatures in 1968, the architecture around it has grown, with the elaboration of the IAEA safeguards system, the convening of the Zangger Committee and Nuclear Suppliers Group, the establishment of the Standing Advisory Group on Safeguards Implementation (SAGSI), and the release of Safeguards Implementation Reports.[3] The 1993 Programme 93+2 and the 1997 voluntary Additional Protocol encompassed a host of actions that increased the IAEA's access to information surrounding the nuclear programs of NPT states parties.[4] In extending the treaty indefinitely in 1995, states parties also decided upon structural alterations aimed to strengthen the review process and enhance its substantive focus, including through the establishment of subsidiary bodies for the three main committees and the extension of the Preparatory Committees process. Overall, then, the NPT has become the purveyor for a complex global nuclear nonproliferation regime.

Notably, however, the nature of the nuclear proliferation threat has shifted dramatically in the post–Cold War era, moving out from the narrow confines of the NPT's legal jurisdiction. The treaty's targeted pathway of state diversion in technology and material from peaceful programs to weapons programs now presents but one avenue to nuclearization; even the general theme of state-to-state horizontal proliferation has been joined by the newfound challenge of nonstate actors. The current reality of nuclear challenges is reflected in the rise of new multilateral venues and ad hoc agreements, suggesting that states—for all their high praise and continued devotion to the NPT—also recognize the need to address the blind spots of the nuclear nonproliferation regime.[5] The centerpiece NPT stands in danger of being relegated to the sidelines without supplementary action; the state of global nuclear order, upon deeper examination, stands at a crossroads.

CHAPTER OVERVIEW

This chapter connects the past, present, and future of the global nuclear nonproliferation regime. It begins by examining the order that was put into place with the 1970 entry into force of the NPT. A close examination of the treaty reveals the limited character of its jurisdiction and hints at the need for supplementary action in light of the evolution of the proliferation threat outlined above. To underline the point, the chapter then revisits notions of adaptability and flexibility of the existing order. Indeed, treaty parties have consistently resisted addressing issues left ambiguous or ignored by the original text. Despite the enormous scope and ambition expressed in parts of the text, the NPT has never in fact shifted from its fundamental character, containing the authority and detail to tackle a narrow pathway to proliferation. Thus, the chapter concludes by suggesting a greater innovation in global nuclear order—one that will bolster the NPT and its surrounding regime. Regional nuclear order, while building upon that global foundation, represents a necessary supplement to preserve the overall effort.

THE GLOBAL NUCLEAR NONPROLIFERATION REGIME

References to a global nuclear nonproliferation regime are ubiquitous among works that examine the NPT.[6] The treaty has been alternately called the anchor, centerpiece, and cornerstone of an entity that some refer to in shorthand as the NPT regime. Still, further and more consistent identification of the regime is elusive—due in part to the absence of a centralized organizational form around the treaty, the numerous related formal treaties and agreements, and the inherently uneven manner in which the treaty is structured to address its so-called three pillars: nonproliferation, disarmament, and development for peaceful uses of nuclear energy. Ultimately however, even taking into account the regime's dynamic and fluid qualities, the NPT stands as its clear core component. Examining it is the key to identifying both the limits of the adaptive prowess of the current global regime and the necessity of a regional reorientation.

The Treaty and Regime

As constructed, the NPT was an instrument first, foremost, and almost solely aimed to deter horizontal proliferation. The desire to freeze the number of nuclear weapon states in existence originated among the global superpowers and became widespread as the 1962 Cuban Missile Crisis and China's 1964 test explosion represented harbingers of global catastrophes. That a number of industrialized countries in regions of strife—prominently, West Germany, Japan, and India—neared the capability for weapons development further raised the specter of nuclear war. The United States and the Soviet Union moved to decisive action; along with the UK, their role as primary agenda setters led to the treaty's imbalanced focus on nonproliferation.[7] UN General Assembly Resolution 2028, which paved the way for treaty negotiations, cited as its first principle the need for the treaty to be "void of any loopholes which might permit nuclear or non-nuclear Powers to proliferate, directly or indirectly, nuclear weapons in any form."[8]

The goals of the treaty and regime became manifestly clear in the layout and text of the treaty. The very first articles in the text specify the principles of nonproliferation, with the third denoting specific obligations to that end for both nuclear weapon states and non-nuclear weapon states. Article III's length, substance, and technical detail are unmatched by any other section of the NPT. Non-nuclear weapon states were to negotiate safeguards agreements with the IAEA within 180 days of the treaty's inception and to conclude and enter into force those agreements within eighteen months. It specified the purpose of safeguards as verifying NPT obligations "with a view to preventing diversion of nuclear energy from peaceful uses to nuclear weapons or other nuclear explosive devices."[9] The IAEA fleshed out the technical components of the system in 1972 with Information Circular 153—also known as the blue book, the model agreement, or full-scope and comprehensive safeguards.[10] Those agreements remain the foundation of the global nuclear nonproliferation regime.

In contrast, there is no elaboration on the means of verification regarding the rest of the treaty. With respect to development for peaceful uses, no specific mechanisms are discussed that would ensure the "fullest possible exchange of equipment, materials, and scientific and technological information."[11] The IAEA's only mention in the NPT concerns its role in safeguards, despite its obvious relevance in the field of energy promotion. Similarly on the disarmament issue, detail regarding the "effective measures" agreed upon is altogether lacking.[12] The lack of concrete disarmament obligations is evident as Article VI is one of the shortest and most abstract articles in the treaty, underscored by its clear delineation between the NPT and a future disarmament treaty. U.S. negotiator Gerard Smith did not hesitate to point out that the text "does not require us to achieve any disarmament agreement."[13] Overall, the system was designed to prevent unverifiable access to nuclear materials by one group of treaty parties. It was not designed for much else.

Reassessing Transformation

It would be difficult to argue that the NPT has experienced much fundamental transformation since its entry into force. Despite enduring two significant shocks to the system—the May 1974 "peaceful" test explosion from nonparty India and the 1991 uncovering of Iraq's clandestine nuclear program—parties moved only to adjust the parameters around the existing system upheld by the comprehensive safeguards agreements.[14] Even with the emergence of nuclear suppliers' networks that allowed those states to control transfers at the pass, and even with the IAEA shifting from a primarily authenticating role to more actively accounting for the possibility of obstruction and willful deception, diversion remained the proliferation pathway that the global nuclear nonproliferation regime was best equipped to tackle. That remains the case to this day. Deeper inspection of each of the pillars of the NPT further illustrates this characteristic institutional rigidity, underscoring the need for supplementary action.

Enforcement of Nonproliferation Safeguards: The aforementioned shocks resulted in the further definition of the safeguards system. Yet, an India- and Iraq-centric narrative belies the institutional stasis in place since the NPT entered into force. For instance, questions about safeguards' effectiveness long predated the discoveries of the 1991 joint UN-IAEA mission in Iraq. A decade earlier, Israel had bombed Iraq's Osirak nuclear reactor (purchased from the French), specifically expressing misgivings about the reliability of safeguards in justifying its attack. Former IAEA inspector Roger Richter even attested to a loophole centered on undeclared materials when he testified that "the most sensitive facilities in [Osirak] could remain outside the purview of the IAEA as long as Iraq did not declare that they contained either plutonium or uranium metal or uranium oxide."[15] Perhaps because of Israel's status as non-NPT party, perhaps because the attack overshadowed the justification, no safeguards review commenced at that time.[16] Instead, the bombing inspired only limited measures regarding the physical protection of nuclear facilities. It was an incident that revealed the high bar for policy change then and since.

Indeed, even while Programme 93+2 and the Additional Protocol came as a response to Iraq, the issue of enforcement has been largely sidestepped. After all, the noncompliance ruling reached in that case came under exceptional circumstances, with the discoveries emanating from the highly empowered joint UN-IAEA mission in the post–Gulf War landscape.[17] The veracity of the "normal" safeguards system remains questionable, as the NPT provides no details on how monitoring should be executed on a case-by-case basis, nor on how the IAEA Board of Governors is expected to arrive at a noncompliance ruling.[18] This has rendered inconsistency the norm, as witnessed when the board deliberated over a series of noncompliance cases in the new millennium: Iran and Libya in 2003, South Korea in 2004, and Egypt in 2005. Each was in the vein of Iraq (involving the discovery of undeclared materials, facilities, or fuel cycle activities), yet only Egypt and South Korea were permitted to take corrective actions prior to "final" rulings from the Security Council. The discrepancy instigated accusations of Western bias. The lack of uniformity in the regime encompasses not only the aftermath of safeguards violations but the very act thereof, with no official definition provided for noncompliance, nor any distinction made regarding the severity of breaches (for instance, obstruction of inspections versus evidence of diversion). Still, the status quo persists.

The drawn-out saga in North Korea provides another naked example of the constraints of the NPT. In 2003, IAEA director general Mohamed ElBaradei declared the country to be in "chronic non-compliance with its safeguards agreement since 1993."[19] This followed a Board of Governors resolution in January that year that reached the same conclusion, citing as its rationale the country's continued uranium enrichment activity and expulsion of inspectors.[20] When North Korea responded by withdrawing from the NPT, the UN Security Council took no action. It was unable to pass any resolution condemning the country either on the violation of its safeguards agreement or the breach of the required three months' notice for treaty withdrawal. The series of events contributed to a "fundamental lack of faith" in the system.[21] However, to this date, parties have left that flawed enforcement mechanism in place, failing to clarify muddled procedures even after the aforementioned wave of noncompliance deliberations. Efforts to revise the withdrawal clause also did not garner widespread support. The regime's blind spots remain and seemingly are subject to political maneuvering. A similar phenomenon can be found with its most ambitious objective.

Nuclear Disarmament: Movement toward nuclear disarmament, as mentioned in this chapter, was a secondary concern in and around the NPT. The language in the treaty tethered the item both to the cessation of the nuclear arms race and to a treaty on general disarmament, without detailing a process or timeframe for these achievements. The mention of nuclear disarmament alone was already a concession by the nuclear weapon states as they sought widespread support for the treaty. Initial drafts from the United States and the Soviet Union did not mention nuclear disarmament beyond the preamble; the final language was a watered-down version of a proposal by Mexico that had specified a series of clearly defined objectives.[22] More than forty-five years later, formal institutionalization in the area remains limited, steps toward legalization are nonexistent, and efforts to define "effective measures" further have taken as many steps backward as forward. This is the situation despite a vastly altered global security environment, a treaty expiration that provided non–nuclear weapon states considerable leverage, and abolition campaigns that have permeated the mainstream.

The environment for disarmament changed drastically with the end of the Cold War. The 1990 entry into force of the Threshold Test Ban Treaty and the Peaceful Nuclear Explosions Treaty and the 1991 signing of the Strategic Arms Reduction Treaty (START I) perpetuated the cooperative atmosphere between the United States and the Soviet Union, while the UN took a number of steps to strengthen its disarmament machinery, including reforming the Disarmament Commission and refocusing the First Committee of the General Assembly. Political pressures led President Bill Clinton to extend a limited U.S. testing moratorium in 1993, paving the way for a negotiating mandate issued by the UN's Conference on Disarmament "for a universal and multilaterally and effectively verifiable comprehensive nuclear test ban treaty."[23] Against this backdrop, the 1995 NPT Review and Extension Conference proffered a golden opportunity to promulgate change in disarmament. The resulting "Principles and Objectives" document adopted by parties in fact listed three relevant items: (1) completion of Comprehensive Test Ban Treaty negotiations by 1996, (2) negotiations on a fissile material production ban, and (3) a nuclear weapon state–led campaign to reduce existing stockpiles.[24] However, there was a glaring absence of timelines or verification mechanisms with respect to the latter two goals.

The two decades since have not been bereft of movement in nuclear disarmament. The Comprehensive Test Ban Treaty was adopted by a sizable majority in the UN General Assembly and was opened for signatures in September 1996. In 2000, the final document of the NPT Review Conference adopted a series of practical steps that departed from the tenuous language of declarations past. The so-called 13 Steps called for concrete action ranging from a five-year negotiation process for the Fissile Material Cut-Off Treaty to the issuance of regular reports by the nuclear weapon states on disarmament implementation and to the bilateral strengthening of the Anti-Ballistic Missile Treaty.[25] In 2010, parties opted for an encompassing sixty-four-step Action Plan in an unprecedented "conclusions and recommendations" section of the outcome final document. Nuclear disarmament was positioned as the very first item on the agenda, with parties reaffirming the "continued validity of [2000's] practical steps," and including twenty-two concrete actions toward the full and effective implementation of nuclear disarmament.[26] The plan also invoked international humanitarian law for the first time as a rationale for disarmament.

Still, these incremental movements have not inspired lasting institutional impact. Nearly twenty years later, the Comprehensive Test Ban Treaty is yet to be ratified. Increasingly it appears as a hollow concession by the nuclear weapon states to ensure the NPT's indefinite extension, just as the mere mention of nuclear disarmament in the original helped to ensure its passage in 1970.[27] The 13 Steps proved a temporary reprieve: they disintegrated almost immediately, with the nuclear weapon states seeking to excise mention of them altogether at the failed 2005 Review Conference.[28] Similarly, the failed 2015 NPT Review Conference has put the 2010 Action Plan in jeopardy. Even before the 2015 conference was convened, non–nuclear weapon states complained about the perpetuation of nuclear-based security doctrines and modernization plans, arguing that nuclear weapon states were not adhering to the expressed principles of transparency, irreversibility, and verifiability.[29] The lack of accountability mechanisms underscored the plan's relative impotency.

It would be disingenuous to disregard the movement in disarmament over the lifespan of the global nuclear nonproliferation regime. At the very least, the issue has come to occupy a greater place in the centerpiece treaty. Still, this process has come at a glacial pace—and is characterized by reluctance if not outright resistance. There is minimal discussion about the particulars of enforcing the original text, the 13 Steps, or the 2010 Action Plan. Existing programs are squarely on the level of political commitment rather than binding legal obligation. In this manner, it is hard not to see disarmament in the NPT as an instrument strictly of necessity, with nuclear weapon states acquiescing to symbolic change only to preserve the political capital of the regime. After all, prior to 2000 and 2010, parties expressed their fear of successive failed conferences, perceiving such as disastrous for the regime's legitimacy. But when it has come time to enact more drastic policy change, institutional rigidity has returned to the forefront. The 2017 Treaty on the Prohibition of Nuclear Weapons emerged precisely because of the non–nuclear weapon states on this front. Yet, while its existence is a watershed in disarmament progress, it also presents a possible source of division in years to come.[30]

Peaceful Uses: The path-dependent impact of noncommittal language in the original treaty text on nuclear disarmament is replicated in the obligation concerning peaceful uses of nuclear energy. There has been minimal development of Article IV's vague notion of facilitating "the fullest possible exchange of equipment, materials and scientific and technological information."[31] There have been initiatives to uphold the promise of nuclear energy, including the IAEA Committee on Assurances of Supply (1980) and the UN Conference for the Promotion of International Cooperation in the Peaceful Uses of Nuclear Energy (1987), but those have produced little results. If anything, the establishment of suppliers' networks in the aftermath of India and the creation of nuclear safety structures in the aftermath of Chernobyl seem to infringe on the inalienable right, with nuclear weapon states pushed to "re-think the prevailing orthodoxy surrounding the potential benefits of . . . nuclear technologies."[32]

The notion of the "fullest possible exchange" has gained some shape in the post–Cold War era. The IAEA has considered several multilateral proposals for activity under the guidance of Mohamed ElBaradei and successor Yukiya Amano. It established the Peaceful Uses Initiative in 2010 as a means of funding relevant projects and supporting development goals with nuclear technologies, and has approved sites in Kazakhstan and Siberia to house reserves of low-enriched uranium. However, these modest actions by the IAEA would appear to fall well short of the obligation of states described in the text, especially nuclear weapon states. There has been concern that the establishment of international fuel banks actually constitutes a preventive action against individual countries developing enrichment and reprocessing technology.[33] Meanwhile, prominent civil nuclear cooperation agreements between the United States and India in 2005 and between China and Pakistan in 2010 seem to violate the exclusive nature of the inalienable right promised to NPT parties.[34] Those deals have contributed to the antagonism and dissatisfaction surrounding the global nuclear nonproliferation regime; still, the lack of clarity regarding the implementation of Article IV endures.

The Rigidity of the Regime

The Nuclear Non-Proliferation Treaty aimed primarily to hold the number of recognized nuclear weapon states steady at five. It targeted a select group of advanced industrial and industrializing states with research and production capabilities, checking interstate transfers of nuclear materials, technology, and know-how in order to prevent diversion. Reflective of its narrow focus, the IAEA designed a Small Quantities Protocol that exempted states with little or no nuclear material and no nuclear facilities from safeguards activities.[35] Still, stemming in part from the ambitious principles expressed in the treaty preamble, the broad substantive scope encompassed by its text, and drastic alterations to the surrounding geopolitical and security environment, there have been consistent efforts by groups to impose change to the proceedings of the treaty and regime ever since the NPT entered into force. The post–Cold War era especially has borne witness to such campaigns, with parties restructuring the review process in advocating a more proactive orientation. However, in examining its character, scope, and legalized form, the NPT has routinely demonstrated a low ceiling for enduring institutional change.

Even in the post–Cold War period, during which the nuclear landscape has been far more conducive to change across all jurisdictions, the status quo has stubbornly persisted. Changes in procedure—including the aforementioned modifications of the review process, regular consultations among the nuclear weapon states, and the issuance of regular reports on disarmament implementation—have not been accompanied by significant changes in substance. The Comprehensive Test Ban Treaty is no closer to ratification than it was two decades ago, while negotiations for a Fissile Material Cut-Off Treaty have stalled altogether, despite mandates from multiple NPT review conferences. Neither the 13 Steps nor the Action Plan have demonstrated any longevity: they too stand mainly as abstract ideals, as vague blueprints, devoid of enforcement and oversight mechanisms. Overall, the limits of the regime's innovation have been manifest across its various elements. This has not been for a lack of need.

BEYOND THE NUCLEAR NON-PROLIFERATION TREATY

The global nuclear nonproliferation regime has undoubtedly expanded over the course of the past five decades. Growth has come at differential paces and degrees among its various aspects, and its focus on horizontal proliferation via diversion remains, but the regime centered on the NPT can be said to regulate interstate nuclear transfers in a rigorous manner, while analyzing the whole of the civilian nuclear programs of states parties. Organizations (e.g., the IAEA), negotiating forums (Conference on Disarmament), consortiums (Nuclear Suppliers Group), regional bodies (nuclear-weapon-free zones), and more all represent parts of the structure. The widespread normative influence of the global nuclear nonproliferation regime is demonstrated by violators who opt to mask their actions and by nonparties who still adhere to behavioral expectations and norms as much as they can.

Still, the nuclear proliferation landscape has also expanded, in a manner and at a rate that outstrip the institutions in place. The reconfiguration of global order in the post–Cold War era has upended the nuclear agenda. Concerns about nonstate actors, terrorism, and security and safety constitute a fundamental redefinition of the nuclear space, providing alternative pathways to proliferation. The international community must now divide its attention between state actors and nonstate actors in order to address the varied threats in existence. Yet, the NPT is thoroughly incompatible with nonstate challenges and has become somewhat stagnant even with state challenges (due largely to politics associated with its three pillars). According to one harsh analysis, the treaty, "as currently interpreted and implemented, lacks the institutional rules, practices and powers to deal effectively with proliferation challenges."[36] The cyclical pattern of review conferences during the past twenty years and the corresponding uncertain status of the 13 Steps and the Action Plan further suggest that the possibility for innovation in the regime must come entirely outside the NPT regime.

Nuclear Security Concerns

Indeed, recent additions to global nuclear order have come not within the structure of the NPT and the existing global nuclear nonproliferation regime but with piecemeal arrangements. The possibility of nuclear terrorism was propelled to the top of the global security agenda in the aftermath of the attacks of September 11, when it was revealed that al-Qaeda had designs to acquire a nuclear weapon.[37] The notion of a terrorist group gaining access to nuclear materials or weapons came to dominate security planning. Nuclear security thus came to occupy a distinct place in global nuclear order. The IAEA created the Nuclear Security Fund in 2001 and symbolically moved the Office of Nuclear Security out from under the Safeguards Department the next year. The discovery of warheads and missiles on a North Korea ship bound for Yemen in 2002 and the uncovering of the A. Q. Khan network in 2004—with the so-called father of Pakistan's nuclear weapons program admitting he had sold weapons technology to a number of parties over the years—underscored the urgency of the issue. After all, those two incidences revealed the existence, reach, and complexity of the international nuclear black market, presenting the potential means for nonstate acquisition. This was a pathway to proliferation entirely outside the scope of the NPT.

Faced with the challenge, the international community moved to piece together an apparatus pivoting on issues of nuclear security. This was far from a cohesive regime. President George W. Bush established the Proliferation Security Initiative in 2003, with eleven developed countries committing to a series of interdiction principles that targeted state and nonstate actors alike. The United States also led the charge for 2004's Security Council Resolution 1540, which impressed WMD nonproliferation obligations—targeting nonstate actors—onto national governments. Meanwhile, states voted in 2005 to extend the scope of physical protection obligations in the Convention of the Physical Protection of Nuclear Materials to nuclear materials involved only in national transfers. The vulnerability of nuclear materials also inspired the 2008 launch of the World Institute for Nuclear Security and the convening of the biennial Nuclear Security Summit series beginning in 2010. That illicit trafficking, nuclear security, and nonstate threats in general have continued to warrant minimal attention within the NPT review process underscores both the scope of the proliferation issue and the limitations of the regime centered on that treaty. Yet nuclear security should not demarcate the boundaries of nonproliferation innovation.

The Role of Regional Action

The outcome final document at the 2000 NPT Review Conference delivered an unambivalent message to the last holdouts, declaring, "States not currently states parties may accede to the Treaty only as non-nuclear-weapon states."[38] There would be no exceptions, no third category of NPT states: Israel, India, and Pakistan would have to renounce their existing stockpiles and dismantle their nuclear programs prior to joining. Of course, the security context surrounding each case renders the scenario highly unlikely. And therein lies the problem. The global nuclear nonproliferation regime has been tasked with issues that are increasingly regional in nature. Safeguards implementation will not resume in North Korea unless security concerns are addressed on the peninsula. The Conference on Disarmament will not find the consensus required to move toward the Fissile Material Cut-Off Treaty unless South Asian relations improve. Only the involved parties in the Middle East—and not directives from the UN—will decide on the appropriate steps toward a WMD-free zone there. Nuclear order has become intimately linked to localized security environments, underscoring the need to supplement the NPT with regional action.

Given the institutional rigidity demonstrated by the global nuclear nonproliferation regime over the years, it is significant that the treaty itself allows the possibility of a regional reorientation (at a minimum, it does not detract from it). As noted in chapter 1, negotiations for the Treaty of Tlatelolco establishing a nuclear-weapon-free zone in Latin America and the Caribbean took place in and around the same timeframe as negotiations for the NPT. The very text of the NPT preserves the rights of states parties to take such regional action.[39] This echoed a main principle in the founding General Assembly Resolution 2028. There was thus an established understanding that diffused and local action would help provide the means to the treaty's overall goals. Within a decade of Tlatelolco entering into force, all five recognized nuclear weapon states had signed and ratified the additional protocols obligating them to keep that area free of nuclear weapons. The emergence of four other nuclear-weapon-free zones since reaffirms the wide belief that the NPT is most effective not as a stand-alone treaty but as one piece of an expansive regime.

Beyond Nuclear-Weapon-Free Zones

Despite their successes, however, nuclear-weapon-free zones are no panacea for global nuclear order. First, they have reached their saturation point in global coverage, as the critical regions left uncovered hardly seem ripe for treaty negotiations. The international community has shown little appetite for more subregional zones (after the one-state zone in Mongolia), rendering that possibility unlikely for the Middle East and Northeast Asia. Second, there remain questions concerning their independent impact, as none exist in a region with nuclear states or nuclear aspirants. It took decades and a new global order before Brazil and Argentina ratified Tlatelolco, while South Africa did not sign onto the Treaty of Pelindaba until after it relinquished its weapons programs. Third and most fundamental, the zones echo the substantive shortcomings of the existing global nuclear nonproliferation regime. They coalesce strictly around state behavior and have rejected proposals for standardized energy cooperation, regional fuel banks, and binding security assurances. For good and bad, nuclear-weapon-free zones remain tethered to the NPT.

Developments at the regional level will determine the future of nuclear nonproliferation. It is revealing that NPT review conferences have devoted more attention to nuclear-weapon-free zones over the years: not only noting the right of regions to draft and conclude such treaties but also recognizing specific efforts and proposals, detailing obstacles to progress, encouraging action in particular areas, and—with the 1995 Resolution on the Middle East—mandating concrete action. Yet, with longstanding languishing proposals in South Asia, Northeast Asia, Central and Eastern Europe, and the Middle East, it is clear that nuclear-weapon-free zones are not a one-size-fits-all solution, even at the regional level. Instead, a more robust global nuclear order requires policymakers to consider a wider spectrum of institutional origins, forms, and purposes at the regional level. They must identify the nuclear challenges specific to their context, both those that exist presently and those likely to emerge in the near future. They must consider the surrounding geopolitical landscape, accounting for the presence of extant security frameworks, not to mention the state of economic, social, and cultural relations. Only in this manner can they contribute to a realistic, lasting, and effective nuclear order tailored to regional needs and circumstances. The NPT recognized the added value of regional action. The next chapter explains why the "new regionalism" provides a timely opportunity for a more purposeful reorientation.

CHAPTER 3

Foundations for Regional Nuclear Order

The limitations of the global nuclear nonproliferation regime—and its centerpiece Nuclear Non-Proliferation Treaty (NPT)—suggest the need for supplementary action. As discussed, states have started turning elsewhere for solutions, pursuing a piecemeal approach in the area of nuclear security and engaging in a globalist effort through prohibition treaty negotiations to push disarmament forward. This book posits that enhanced cooperation concentrated at the regional level would be an effective means of combating nuclear challenges present and future; the history of nuclear-weapon-free zones suggests a predilection with such solutions. Still, the possibility for further reorientation requires a foundation for movement in that direction. Subsequent chapters assess the presence of these conditions in individual cases. Yet any such strengthening of regional nuclear orders would not enter the realm of possibility were it not for general trends taking place at the level of global geopolitics—specifically, those involving regionalism.

The current "new regionalism" that came as the Cold War waned has been characterized as prolonged, varied, and substantial, as this chapter explores in depth. Rather than being defined by the traditional economic use of the term, the new regionalism is often associated with a primarily political process of rising consciousness, integration, and policy coordination among groupings of states.[1] Scholars have even come to regard at least some of its symptoms as permanent features of the international order.[2] Still, regionalism is not an unprecedented phenomenon, and the movement is called new regionalism because there have been old regionalisms, with the previous movement emerging in the 1970s.[3] Indeed, while the impact of that regionalist movement was clearly constricted by the Cold War environment in which it was fostered, it also provides a rather instructive case for the endeavor undertaken in this book, as the ramifications for nuclear order were—if modest—readily apparent.

CHAPTER OVERVIEW

As this chapter explains, the regionalism of the 1970s is a far cry from the regionalism that emerged in the mid-1980s, the one that continues to this day. This book makes the argument for increased nuclear nonproliferation activity at the regional level; this chapter posits that current environmental conditions are far more conducive to the reconfiguration of the existing nuclear order than in periods past. It begins with a brief overview of the 1970s wave and the impact on the nuclear sphere. Next, the chapter delves into the structural overhaul that took place with the end of bipolarity, examining the character of the new regionalism. It takes note of the increasing presence and role played by regional arrangements across the political, economic, social, and cultural spheres. It then details the notion of security regionalism: examining the promise and limitations of security arrangements writ large, the forms and functions of existing entities, and perceptions of their place in global order. The chapter concludes by advancing an analytical framework that directly links that process of regionalism to the possibility for and likely shape of nuclear cooperation at the regional level.

A FIRST PUSH FOR REGIONAL NUCLEAR ORDER

1970s Regionalism

In 1960, British prime minister Harold Macmillan referred to the idea that "the wind of change is blowing through this [African] continent."[4] His speech not only acknowledged the rise of national consciousness in South Africa and beyond but was remarkable in its acceptance of the process. It proved a watershed moment in British foreign policy, one that paved the way for the decolonization to follow. Over the course of the next two decades, a considerable number of developing countries consolidated their statehood and autonomy, not just in Africa but across the world. However, the process was painful, rife with tension and outright conflict. Exacerbated by Cold War conditions, sustained conventional conflict raged across the African continent. Superpower intervention played no small part in costly battles in Southeast Asia and the Middle East as well.

The emergence of the third world during this period thus was accompanied by a sense of resentment: "anti-West, anti-Christian, anti-foreigner, anti-globalization, anti-American."[5] If the Global South had ready motive to drive the reconfiguration of global politics, it seemed to gain the opportunity and means to do so with the energy crisis and economic recession of the early 1970s. A number of regional institutions emerged in this period, including the Association of Southeast Asian Nations (ASEAN), the Caribbean Community (CARICOM), and the Economic Community of West African States (ECOWAS). Developing countries further coalesced in the Group of 77 (G-77) and its streamlined chapter, the Group of 24, with the latter gaining representation in multilateral venues such as the International Monetary Fund and the World Bank. The Non-Aligned Movement (NAM) too became a political force in this period.

The rise of regional consciousness in the 1970s manifested itself in the nuclear landscape. The fear that the aforementioned conventional wars could escalate due to the encompassing Cold War environment provided the impetus for a number of denuclearization efforts at the regional level. In 1974, Iran and Egypt cosponsored a resolution to establish a nuclear-weapon-free zone in the Middle East; Pakistan put the idea of a South Asian zone on the agenda after India's nuclear explosion that same year. In 1975, with the support of the South Pacific Forum, New Zealand introduced the same possibility for its geographic area. The UN General Assembly requested a comprehensive study on such arrangements, with the resulting report heralding them "as a potentially powerful instrument to supplement" the NPT.[6]

Nuclear Order as Battleground

The fact that the regionalism of the 1970s was embedded in North-South tension reverberated across the nuclear arena. The 1974 Indian test explosion proved to be a breaking point. For nuclear weapon states, it presented a worst-case scenario. Nuclear trade was in the process of expanding to East Asia, the Middle East, and South America, regions with some degree of political instability. There was a fear that the nascent NPT would soon be overrun by proliferators. As outlined in the previous chapter, nuclear supplier states reacted decisively: the Zangger Committee and the newly established Nuclear Suppliers Group adopted self-imposed restrictions in accordance with NPT safeguards. However, that these groups sought to effectively restrict access to nuclear technologies was not lost on non–nuclear weapon states, who perceived these as further infringements on their inalienable right to development for peaceful use.[7]

Spurred by increased political capital amid a global economy in turmoil, developing countries pushed back. They pushed hard in light of the "disarray and divisions among the major Western industrial nations . . . to take the offensive within the United Nations."[8] The membership of the International Atomic Energy Agency (IAEA)'s Board of Governors increased from twenty-five countries to thirty-four in 1973; it became further politicized subsequently.[9] With non–nuclear weapon states defending their right to access peaceful technologies, IAEA technical assistance grew. Interrelated, despite significant organizational growth during the timeframe, non–nuclear weapon states moved successfully to "restrict . . . the respective shares of developing countries in safeguards costs."[10]

It was in the realm of disarmament that the contentious regionalism of the 1970s was most manifest, building upon existing antagonisms between the two classes of states established by the NPT. Shortly after the treaty entered into force, there was already disagreement between the nuclear weapon states and the non–nuclear weapon states about whether the former were in compliance with their obligations. At the 1975 NPT Review Conference, a group of states led by Mexico characterized the activities undertaken by the nuclear weapon states as modestly beneficial only in "a political and psychological nature," while "as disarmament measures . . . [they] appeared to be of no account."[11] The G-77 stated sharply that disarmament "provisions have not been fulfilled and have largely remained dead letter"—the confrontational tone another testament to the group's increased political strength.[12]

Over the course of the decade, the developing world sought to shape the disarmament debate, fleshing out a more precise vision toward the end goal. The final document of the 1975 NPT Review Conference called for nuclear weapon states to reduce underground tests, conclude a test ban treaty, and limit strategic arms.[13] In 1978, the UN convened the first Special Session on Disarmament (SSOD): its final document established a clearly set, unified, and expansive agenda, with a program of action that called for negotiations to (1) cease the modernization of existing nuclear weapons systems, (2) cease the production of nuclear weapons and delivery systems, and (3) initiate a phased reduction of existing stockpiles.[14] The document also created a new disarmament machinery, with the representative Disarmament Commission and the negotiating Committee on Disarmament.

The Limited Effects of 1970s Regionalism

Yet, change to the global nuclear order in the 1970s had its limits, especially in disarmament. The G-77 failed to pass draft additional protocols that would have committed nuclear weapon states to concrete action in testing and arms reductions, and it faltered in securing the provision of binding security assurances within the context of nuclear-weapon-free zones. Meanwhile, the SSOD program of action lingered unfulfilled deep into the next decade. But for the first time, parties wrestled with the ambiguous language in the NPT, debated different means of disarmament implementation, and expressly acknowledged the issue as intertwined with nonproliferation and global security. In the process, they provided the roots of the modern antinuclear and disarmament movement. This pushback by the non–nuclear weapon states occurred partly due to their frustration with the actions of nuclear supplier states in the wake of India, but it also reflected a fundamental friction sparked by the regionalist wave of the period.

Overall, the regionalism of the 1970s was a messy movement, characterized by nascent statehood and sovereignty, lacking the cohesion and solidarity required for a successful challenge to the international order, and broadly pitting the Global South against the militarily, politically, and economically superior North. Even the newfound attention to nuclear disarmament could be attributed to the superpowers' own desire to lessen the potential for nuclear confrontation.[15] Notably, none of the proposals for specific nuclear-weapon-free zones (including in Northeast Asia, the Middle East, and South Asia, as explored in subsequent chapters), for regional fuel cycle centers, or for binding security assurances came to fruition, reflecting the limits of the regional consciousness and order that emerged during the period.

THE NEW REGIONALISM

While Cold War conditions limited the character and impact of the regionalism of the 1970s, the collapse of bipolarity provided a wholly different and far more nurturing context for the next regionalist wave. The roots of that new regionalism came in the mid-1980s, linked to conditions that resembled those that had propelled the previous movement. The 1979 Iranian Revolution provoked a second oil crisis that triggered a recession in the early 1980s, driving economic reform across a number of economies, in particular in the United States and UK. With the global economic structure changing—due to the decline of agriculture, the rise of the service industry, and the greater integration of the developing world—the more than one hundred members of the General Agreement on Tariffs and Trade saw the need for a new negotiation. The Uruguay Round kicked off with a 1986 declaration that expressed the desire to achieve further trade liberalization, establish trade-related investment measures, and phase out unilateral and bilateral protectionism. This movement toward greater trade openness would be a prolonged, painful process, with talks running until 1994. But the environment reinforced the ascendance of free market principles as the Cold War approached its end.

Economic Regionalism as Response

In fact, the struggles of the Uruguay Round helped too in fostering processes of economic regionalism. From 1990 to 1994, there were forty-one notifications of regional trade agreements, reflecting states creating "safety nets . . . as an insurance against the possible collapse of the Round."[16] The process was not only encouraged but was led by advanced industrial countries. Members of the European Economic Community linked their currencies under the European Monetary System in 1979 and then took steps toward greater economic and political integration through the 1980s. The United States—severely affected by the recession—jumped into regional liberalization (and protection) with the bilateral Canada-US Free Trade Agreement, the Enterprise for the Americas initiative, the North American Free Trade Agreement, and the Free Trade Area of the Americas; President Ronald Reagan set the tone when he called for a North American "economic constitution."[17] Even the Soviet Union under Mikhail Gorbachev sparked similar processes in its satellites in the late 1980s, with the intent of developing the Russian Far East. This regionalist wave transcended old East-West divides.

The advocacy of influential powers for economic regionalism was unprecedented, standing in stark contrast to the earlier Cold War period.[18] The growth of the multilateral trade system was represented in a number of trade arrangements, particularly in the emerging Asia Pacific. The creation of the 1989 Asia-Pacific Economic Cooperation (APEC) underscored the effort of those countries to create new markets outside Europe. The APEC experience also revealed burgeoning regional competition, as Malaysian prime minister Mathahir Mohamad proposed an East Asia Economic Group in 1990 that left out APEC members in North America and the Western Pacific.[19] Meanwhile, the ASEAN Free Trade Area formed in 1992, encompassing all manufactured and agricultural products. The South Asian Association for Regional Cooperation (SAARC), established in 1985, similarly entered into force a preferential trading arrangement in 1995.

In Africa, the 1980 Lagos Plan of Action established a blueprint for movement "towards African economic integration ... to create a continent-wide framework for the much needed economic co-operation for development based on collective self-reliance."[20] With ECOWAS in place, the countries of East and South Africa established a preferential trade area in 1981; it would be succeeded by the Common Market for Eastern and Southern Africa in 1993. Other campaigns toward African integration came with the treaty of the Economic Community of Central African States in 1983 and the founding of the Arab Maghreb Union in North Africa in 1989, though both were plagued by inactivity and conflict. Still, in tandem, these agreements ushered in coverage of the entire continent. Indeed, the 1991 Abuja Treaty outlined steps to unite the trade blocs into a true African Economic Community, updating the Lagos Plan.[21]

Latin America too was not immune to the new regionalist wave. Previous efforts on the continent had primarily centered on political affairs. The few economic initiatives that did exist, including the Central American Common Market and the Andean Group from the 1960s, still drew upon the import substitution model. But the struggles of those campaigns, combined with the events of the 1970s and 1980s, led states to undertake trade liberalization and economic regionalism as part of a broader-based process of structural reform in the service of development goals.[22] A number of Economic Complementary Agreements emerged under the umbrella of the Latin American Integration Association and paved the way for the establishment of the Mercosur customs union agreement in 1991. That various country groupings linked up with reciprocal trade agreements with the West—the United States, in particular—did not diminish from the nascent regional market but rather bolstered it by signaling the viability of the new bloc.

Beyond Economic Origins

The presence of free trade areas and preferential trading arrangements represents the phenomena most often studied through the lens of the new regionalism. But the wave that began in the 1980s came to extend beyond economic currents. Intertwined with the presence of these trading blocs was a corresponding reconfiguration of power, sparked by a bottom-up, identity-based political process: an "extended nationalism" especially relevant among developing countries.[23] The waning and collapse of the Cold War structure further advanced patterns of regionalism. Indeed, the accompanying retreat of the two global superpowers swiftly imbued the third world with unprecedented autonomy. Forces that had previously stalled, if not altogether suppressed, localized forms of conflict were abruptly removed from the picture. In this vacuum, with more acute political and security vulnerabilities, the promise of regional organizations came to the forefront.[24] Regionalism was indeed "launched on the back of crisis, human disasters, and widespread political and economic failure."[25]

Scholars also point to the importance of Western Europe as a model for regional order in the new global environment.[26] While the European Community was centered on economic integration, its development in the 1980s had spillover effects in the political realm. The 1986 Single European Act not only set the objective of establishing a single economic market but also codified 1970's European Political Cooperation, thus revitalizing the drive for foreign policy coordination; its formal recognition of the European Council underscored an appetite for legislative and institutional integrative processes. The success of economic measures, such as with the European Community gaining bargaining power through the Uruguay Round, drove the political campaign.[27] This culminated in the 1992 signing of the Maastricht Treaty, which presented what became the three-pillar legal structure of the European Union: (1) the European Communities pillar, with economic, social, and environmental focal points, (2) the Common Foreign and Security Policy pillar, and (3) the Justice and Home Affairs pillar.[28] The European Community's evolution into the European Union (EU) did not come easy; still, the process had a signaling effect for the rest of the world.

The new regionalism thus entailed an unprecedented thoroughness and multidimensionality. With neighbors sharing greater economic interdependence while facing common sources of nationalist and regionalist insecurity, the value of regional order became manifestly clear. Indeed, the most visible sign of the new regionalism was the presence of regional and subregional institutions that spanned the spectrum of type, form, and locale.[29] The reform-minded leadership of Mikhail Gorbachev and eventual collapse of the Soviet Union paved the way for the creation of the Commonwealth of Independent States, the Collective Security Treaty Organization, and the Central Asian Economic Union. Meanwhile, the ASEAN Regional Forum, the Shanghai Cooperation Organisation, and the refocused Organization of American States provided venues for wide-ranging cooperation in those respective locales. Especially emblematic of the new world order, the Southern Africa Development Community, the Economic Community of West African States Monitoring Group, the Economic and Monetary Community of Central Africa, and the African Union came to complement or supersede existing arrangements, but with expanded agendas and a focus on integration along socioeconomic, political, and even security lines.

Into Peace and Security

The increasing presence of regional organizations did not go unnoticed. As mentioned, regionalist trends were encouraged by the most powerful state in the system. For instance, the significance of the North American Free Trade Agreement under President Bill Clinton was not confined to the substance of the agreement but was linked to its status as "a confirmation of America's good-neighbor policy . . . and a commitment to the concept of 'open regionalism' toward the rest of the hemisphere and the world."[30] Whether as a response to developments in Europe or to its own threatened status, the United States pursued regional hegemony in the Americas and nurtured a growing interest in East Asia. President George H. W. Bush first referred to the notion of a "Pacific Community" in 1991.[31] Clinton then announced a "New Pacific Community" in 1993 that went beyond APEC, previously the primary subject of U.S. efforts toward Asia Pacific regionalism. His initiative recast longstanding bilateral security agreements in the region (with South Korea, Japan, Australia, the Philippines, and Thailand), setting forth security priorities that included combating WMD proliferation and pursing "new regional dialogues on the full range of our common security challenges."[32]

The push toward security regionalism enjoyed another key booster. In the aftermath of bipolarity, the United Nations faced unreasonable expectations, as it was called upon to address many of the localized conflicts previously mitigated by the superpower presence. As a response to the new world order, UN secretary-general Boutros Boutros-Ghali submitted to the Security Council in 1992 a report titled "An Agenda for Peace: Preventive Diplomacy, Peacemaking and Peacekeeping." It acknowledged the blurring of national boundaries and the accompanying rise of regional associations, referring to their work to "deepen cooperation and ease some of the contentious characteristics of sovereign and nationalistic rivalries."[33] Strikingly, the report called for a greater diffusion of responsibility by the UN, with regional actors to serve preventive diplomatic, peace-keeping, peacemaking, and postconflict peace-building functions. While it expressly did not present a formal blueprint for cooperation and maintained the primacy of the Security Council, it espoused the overall utility of regional organizations and noted their contributions would "not only lighten the burden of the Council but also contribute to a deeper sense of participation, consensus and democratization in international affairs."[34]

The Boutros-Ghali report set a tone for security regionalism that persisted.[35] The secretary-general went on to initiate a series of high-level meetings in 1993 with the leaders of eleven regional organizations to facilitate further coordination on peace and security issues; a total of seven such meetings would be held over the next thirteen years, through the stewardship of Kofi Annan.[36] Calls for decentralization intensified following a string of high-profile UN failures in Somalia, Bosnia, and Rwanda. A 1996 report from Boutros-Ghali, "An Agenda for Democratization," was again pronounced in its enthusiasm for wider cooperation. It cited regional groups as "a healthy complement to internationalism," as "increasingly important potential partners," and posited the idea that efforts toward regionalism "should be strengthened internationally through United Nations-sponsored agreements on horizontal, interregional connections in all areas of endeavor."[37] The UN's fervent support reflected the widespread acceptance of the new regionalist wave. Key parties explicitly embraced the value of regional arrangements in bolstering the international order, in "addressing the growing gap between demand and supply [of security]."[38]

SECURITY AND THE NEW REGIONALISM

Significantly, the very conception of security also shifted in the post–Cold War era. In an increasingly globalized world, national security concerns expanded from the confines of military statecraft to include issues such as human rights, environment protection, even economics, as well as other nonmilitary sectors with the potential to present existential challenges to the state.[39] The West promulgated their values through the third world, "demanding economic reform, good governance, democratization, and respect for human rights as a condition for their assistance programmes," in this manner shaping notions of peace and security.[40] The development of UN peacekeeping operations and humanitarian interventions solidified the primacy of human security on the new security agenda; the localized nature of such issues in turn rendered it a key arena for regional cooperation.

The more diverse notion of security under the new regionalism contributed in turn to a multiplicity of form in cooperation.[41] Boutros-Ghali's 1992 report recognized that regional entities might include "treaty based organizations, regional organizations for mutual security and defence, organizations for general regional development or for cooperation on a particular economic topic or function, and groups created to deal with a specific political, economic or social issue of current concern"—a trend also reflected in the scholarly literature, with newfound discussions of governance, complexes, communities, and orders.[42] Linking these entities was simply the presence of "agreed and shared definitions of problems that can be managed and perhaps resolved only by collaboration beyond the national (but below the global) level."[43] In terms of function, they echoed the function of global and other multilateral institutions, which "provide information, reduce transaction costs, make commitments more credible, establish focal points for coordination, and in general facilitate the operation of reciprocity."[44]

Still, the nature of security provides both inherent challenges to pursuits of cooperation and natural limitations on the resulting arrangements.[45] Due to considerations about sovereignty, relative gains, and potential for conflict, international security institutions empirically do not demonstrate the same strength, complexity, or depth as economic institutions.[46] The post–Cold War context in which new regional security institutions emerged or were reformulated, furthermore, resulted in pushback against bipolar politics and an emphasis on nonintervention and state sovereignty.[47] That these entities primarily consisted of mid- and lower-tier powers provides another check on their reach.[48] Perhaps as a result, existing security arrangements at the regional level have generally taken shape as dialogues and irregular forums rather than formal alliances and organizations, oftentimes eschewing traditional, military-based matters in favor of "softer" human issues.

A Place for Regional Nuclear Order

The limits of security regionalism would seem to portend an inauspicious fate for regional nuclear cooperation. After all, the aforementioned challenges presented by security issues are amplified with respect to nuclear weapons, which represent the most naked, direct manifestations of states' security dilemmas.[49] Cooperation entails states forgoing a measure of control in their pursuit of the ultimate weapon, infringing on their force capacity. Further, the exclusivity of the nuclear club and the increasing complexity of extended deterrence in the post–Cold War era would seem to enhance considerations of relative gains. Nuclear weapons have value beyond their very usage; they are "political objects of considerable importance . . . as international normative symbols of modernity and identity."[50] Finally, the specter of conflict is obvious, as betrayal from the other side in the nuclear arena can lead down a path that includes the possibility of existential threat.

Yet, the higher threshold for cooperation should not be overstated. As noted, security institutions emerge when there exist common perceptions of the problem. This has been the case with nuclear weapons stemming from the height of the Cold War, with their further spread universally seen as undesirable, the possibility condemned.[51] From that base principle, there emerged a global nuclear order based on mutually supportive systems of deterrence and abstinence.[52] Over time, these weapons were seen as utterly abhorrent, with the development of a taboo associated with their usage.[53] Meanwhile, the international community continued to bolster the regime in place to regulate state-to-state transfers of weapons-usable materials and equipment. Indeed, for all its shortcomings, the global nuclear nonproliferation regime stands as one of the most durable and widely adhered-to security arrangements at the international level, and its centerpiece NPT enjoys an indefinite lifespan, near-universal membership, and consistent support from policymakers, scholars, and civil society alike.

This book dives deeper into those common perceptions, weighing the possibility for enhanced nonproliferation cooperation at the regional level. It analyzes whether the foundations exist for stronger regional nuclear orders, and what form such orders would take across the particular cases. As the last chapter indicated, regional orders would not stand antithetical to the existing global regime, and their potential added value has been underlined by the NPT text itself. It is true that integrated and encompassing orders—in the vein of Deutsch's pluralistic security communities, or even North Atlantic Treaty Organization (NATO)-like nuclear-sharing alliances—are an unlikely outcome in most of the world.[54] Still, because of the complexity and multifaceted nature of the contemporary nuclear landscape, regional nuclear orders have the ability to take far different shapes than they did under bipolarity. For instance, the 2011 disaster at Fukushima-Daiichi demonstrates the potential of nuclear safety and emergency response as venues for cooperation in Northeast Asia, providing a parallel to the soft focus that has delineated security regionalism broadly in the post–Cold War era. In short, the viability of regional nuclear orders must be assessed in light of the new regionalism and, in particular, the new security regionalism.

Analytical Framework

This book employs an analytical framework comprising three layers: (1) commonalities in issue definition, (2) patterns of regionalism, and (3) existing nuclear cooperation. Assessments of these components across each empirical case will inform the conclusions regarding the main outcomes of interest: that is, the possibility of and likely pathway toward strengthened regional nuclear order.

The three components of the framework were selected because they represent determinant factors in when and how order emerges in a multilateral context (as manifested in cooperative arrangements or institutions). This borrows from the seminal work of Koremenos, Lipson, and Snidal, which draws upon rational-choice analysis in assuming "states use international institutions to further their own goals, and they design institutions accordingly."[55] If one extrapolates from this perspective, strengthened regional nuclear order requires *common* political will and commitment. In short, regional nuclear order will be designed if states perceive it in their interests to do so. This is more likely when convergence exists in how states in a region define their goals within the nuclear sphere ("issue definition") and in how they define and identify themselves ("regionalism"). Interrelated, the specific foundation for order will likely emerge in issue-areas where cooperative activity already exists ("nuclear cooperation").

Foundations for Regional Nuclear Order
1. Commonalities in Issue Definition
    a. Shared understanding of the nuclear threat
    b. Belief in need for solutions above the national level
2. Patterns of Regionalism
    a. Presence of institutions, especially in security
    b. Shared identity, values and interests
3. Existing Nuclear Cooperation
    a. Deep engagement with global nuclear order
    b. Bilateral, subregional, and multilateral nuclear cooperative activity

Overall then, this framework is meant to assess whether common political will and commitment in nonproliferation is likely to emerge at the regional level. Detailed discussion of the three components follows.

Commonalities in Issue Definition: To reiterate, security cooperation requires a common perception of the issue. Thus, the possibility for stronger regional nuclear order hinges on shared understandings, both in terms of the identification and definition of the problem, and the necessity for action above the national level. The global norm against the use of nuclear weapons can belie the complexity of the issue across and within regions. In Northeast Asia, for instance, the presence of the North Korean nuclear weapons program dominates the landscape. But while most states in that region perceive an unambiguous threat, the assessment is not necessarily one that China shares (at least, it does not override the threat posed to China by a collapse of the North Korean government). The absence of common urgency thus helps explain the lack of regional cooperation on the issue and, in particular, the longstanding pause in the Six-Party Talks. Were there more convergence in issue definition there, a strengthened order would be expected: for instance, more pronounced efforts to resurrect the talks or stricter implementation of UN sanctions against the Kim Jong-Un regime.

Myriad examples further illustrate the centrality of common issue definition to the emergence of order. In the Middle East, the fear that Iran will move toward weaponization strikes similar "hard" security chords for many states, as does the ambiguous status of Israel's program. Yet the Arab-Israeli divide has resulted in drastically different perceptions of those two issues across the region, preventing cohesive action (as explored in chapter 7). Meanwhile, developing regions such as Southeast Asia and Africa lack altogether a common definition of nonproliferation and disarmament concerns. Even with nuclear-weapon-free zones present, it is primarily through the lens of nascent energy programs that the nuclear threat comprises the focus of regional institutions—if it does at all. Activities in the field lag behind as a result.

Each chapter therefore works to identify the nuclear proliferation issues pertinent to the grouping of states under study. Subsequent chapters assess the degree to which consensus exists regarding these subjects, disaggregating among subgroupings where appropriate. Chapters then move to characterize state perceptions of multilateral—in particular regional and subregional—responsibility in those domains. For instance, while the states of Southeast Asia have been generally averse to taking additional safeguards action, perceiving such as a violation of their NPT rights to develop for peaceful usage, they appear more amenable to cooperation under the umbrella of nuclear security, given the entanglement of the issue to illicit trafficking and piracy. ASEAN, meanwhile, represents a forum in which those latter two issues—both major concerns in the area—have been discussed regularly. Overall, the purpose of this first component of the framework is to pinpoint the specific jurisdictions under which regional nuclear order may be desired and thus is most likely to emerge.

Patterns of Regionalism: The second component of the analytical framework specifically considers the shape and scope of the new regionalism in the case in question, examining institutions and shared identity. First, it peruses the existing regional institutional architecture, including formal organizations—the most commonly cited marker of the regionalist wave. While the framework takes into account political and economic arrangements, most of the attention will center on existing security mechanisms. The deep integration of the European Union across the board might represent one end of the spectrum, while the absence of any multilateral security institutions in Northeast Asia represents the other. Variation along this line provides insight not only into the predisposition of those regions to strengthened nuclear order but also into the shape such order is likely to take. For instance, future intensification of nonproliferation in Europe might usurp the formal and organizational nature of the EU, whereas Northeast Asia might witness a more painful process marked by informal arrangements and networks.

Yet this second component of the framework looks beyond formal structure too. It identifies the general degree to which states engage with one another on such sensitive topics, in this manner fleshing out the existing level of security regionalism.[56] This includes the character of information sharing, policy coordination, and other such dialogues and processes over the course of the post–Cold War era. These traits could determine the ceiling of regional nuclear cooperation—whether groupings of states can tackle "hard" issues, or whether they will be restricted to more technical cooperation in areas of nuclear safety and security and thus take more indirect and laborious means to nonproliferation and disarmament.

Assessments of patterns of regionalism also consider relevant behavioral trends. This includes patterns of economic interdependence, the presence of preferential trade arrangements, and the flows of intraregional imports and exports. In the political sphere, it encompasses the emergence of confidence-building mechanisms or systems of conflict management. Finally, this component of the framework highlights the presence of regional identity, culling broader histories, cultural commonalities, shared values and interests—with special attention to the degree to which ruling coalitions espouse liberalism and internationalism.[57] Unity among such nontraditional characteristics as cognitive and institutional factors contributes to an atmosphere in which general regional cooperation is likely, even in the security realm.[58] A holistic perspective of patterns of regionalism also draws upon that logic in assessing the implications for nuclear order.

Existing Nuclear Cooperation: The third and final component of the framework directly examines the degree to which a foundation for nuclear order exists at all levels and, in particular, whether a foundation for regional nuclear order is already in place. As discussed in these first chapters, a regional reorientation does not come counter to the values of the global nuclear nonproliferation regime. Quite the contrary, as it builds on the latter's values, norms, and principles. Thus, it is necessary to gauge the degree to which states in a region are already involved with that regime. This includes the presence and activity of states in multilateral nonproliferation, arms control, and disarmament agreements and forums such as IAEA safeguards and Additional Protocols, the Convention on the Physical Protection of Nuclear Material and its amendment, the Comprehensive Test Ban Treaty, and so forth. It also considers the level of engagement in emergent forums, such as UN Security Council Resolution 1540, the Proliferation Security Initiative, and the Nuclear Security Summits. Such measures reflect the willingness that states have had to act upon their shared understandings of the nuclear issue.

Next, the framework teases out the preferences of states to engage in regional solutions in the nuclear sphere. This includes more encompassing arrangements such as nuclear-weapon-free zones, nuclear safety networks, and regional atomic energy commissions, as well as subregional mechanisms and bilateral agreements. This aspect of the framework thus aims to qualitatively map out the character of nuclear order already in a given region. By assessing its proclivity toward other nuclear activities (self-regulation, ad hoc arrangements, limited-term political forums), and by considering existing regional mechanisms, the framework can extrapolate whether the elements are in place for a more permanent, ambitious, and broader nuclear order.

Regional nuclear order does not and will not take place in temporal or spatial vacuums. Every nuclear-weapon-free zone since the Treaty of Tlatelolco has drawn heavily from its predecessors, while the European Atomic Energy Community (Euratom) continues to present a historical model for comprehensive order in the nuclear energy sector. Meanwhile, Resolution 1540 has inspired a wave of nuclear security activity in the past decade across the globe, including at regional levels. In speaking of the ultimate shape of regional nuclear order, then, processes of diffusion, translation, and learning—as highlighted by scholars of institutional change—can play significant roles.[59] The global, interregional, and historical context thus represents central aspects of the character of existing nuclear cooperation captured here. Overall, this last component of the framework delves into the likelihood that existing cooperation—whatever its origins—can be "redirected to new goals, functions, or purposes."[60]

Altogether, the analytical framework seeks to provide a comprehensive overview of the regional nuclear landscape. To this end, it identifies the nuclear-related concerns specific to that region. It assesses whether the relevant states have come to a shared understanding regarding both the presence of those threats and the urgency to address them in a multilateral context. Next, it steps back to relate the character of geopolitical relations. It measures the strength of ties binding the region, honing in on the institutions and behaviors that reflect cooperation or even integration, especially in the security arena. Finally, interweaving those variables, the framework tackles existing nuclear cooperation directly, gauging the involvement of states in both national and international campaigns. In putting these variables together, this book lays out the possibility for a strengthened nuclear order in each region, while charting the likely shape and boundaries of that order given environmental conditions.

Overall, this book makes the case for a more regional-centric approach with which to complement the NPT. The previous chapter linked the stagnation of the global nuclear nonproliferation regime to its founding characteristics, making the case for a reorientation centered on enhanced regional activity. This chapter has posited that the nature of global order is conducive to such a change, as the region as a political unit has come to play a preeminent role in international affairs. The foundation for regional nuclear orders—in all their various potential forms—rests largely in the strength and durability of the new regionalism. The second half of the book presents individual empirical cases, examining the degree to which these conditions hold true across individual regions. It begins by affirming the linkage between regionalism and nuclear cooperation, with two instances of functioning, if imperfect, regional nuclear orders.

CHAPTER 4

Established Orders
Western Europe and Latin America

The central relationship drawn in this book between broader regionalism processes and nuclear cooperation is not novel. The very concept of nuclear-weapon-free zones presupposes linkage between those variables. Taking into account the principles of local initiation and voluntary participation associated with those entities, it is logical to expect the presence of both a common regional identity and a convergence in nuclear interests. The onset of the five nuclear-weapon-free zones present in the world would seem to stand as a testament to the primacy of regions and the development of regionalism, as well as the corresponding impact on nuclear issues. Discussion of regional nuclear orders in the existing literature in fact often begins and ends with the arrangements that encompass 114 states parties in the world, including the entirety of the Southern Hemisphere.

However, as discussed in the preceding chapters, neither regionalism nor regional nuclear orders exist as dichotomous variables. The presence of a nuclear-weapon-free zone is not necessarily an indicator of a robust regional nuclear order, especially given the limitations of those treaties in addressing post–Cold War nuclear challenges. Those arrangements should not be taken as the sole outcome of regional nuclear cooperation. Similarly, the new regionalism that defines the contemporary era has taken distinct shape across the world. Integration processes are far more advanced in certain geographical areas and across certain substantive jurisdictions. The general character of this regionalist wave, as established, is incomparable to previous waves. All told, it is precisely the nuances of the relationship between regionalism and nuclear cooperation that this book explores further. Only with a better understanding of that relationship can this book begin to surmise the potential for strengthened nuclear order in a given region, and to consider its likely form and function.

CHAPTER OVERVIEW

The case studies in this chapter set the stage by primarily looking back, utilizing historical analysis to establish and delve into the nature of the relationship between regionalism and nuclear order. To this end, the chapter examines critical moments that have defined the longstanding, mature, functioning regional nuclear orders in Western Europe and Latin America. The chapter deploys the analytical framework outlined in chapter 3, highlighting the presence of existing institutions, the nature of intraregional relations, and the emergence of common identity. It details these environmental conditions first for the periods in which each nuclear order emerged. Notably, one of the orders centered on a community, the other a nuclear-weapon-free zone—underscoring the possibility of variety. The case studies then evaluate specific moments in the evolution of the two extant orders since their creation, while weighing their robustness moving forward. The chapter conducts this analysis while keeping in mind their relationship with the global nuclear nonproliferation order, reflecting the broader "reorientation" thesis advanced by the book.

The first half of the chapter examines the case of Western Europe. The presence of two nuclear weapon states among its membership provides an instructive case for regional order in the crucial case studies to follow. The study begins with the European Atomic Energy Community (Euratom), established in 1957 alongside several other European communities in a unique post–World War II flurry. It hones in on the process that led to the creation of Euratom, including unsuccessful attempts to forge an even stronger order that would have encompassed military aspects. The chapter then considers how the nuclear issue has evolved outside the community, through the European Union. Euratom's unaltered state (prior to Brexit) belies the ups and downs of nuclear nonproliferation cooperation in Western Europe, one that has outstripped the civilian boundaries of its jurisdiction—reflecting both regional integration dynamics and global threats on the nuclear landscape.

The second half of this chapter focuses on Latin America. That region provides an intriguing point of comparison to Western Europe, hosting a similarly durable and arguably more robust nuclear order, centered on the 1967 Treaty of Tlatelolco and its accompanying Agency for the Prohibition of Nuclear Weapons in Latin America and the Caribbean (OPANAL). Again, the study deploys the analytical framework that allowed for the construction of these elements and then considers how cooled tensions between regional rivals led to the bolstering of the order through the 1991 bilateral Brazilian-Argentine Agency for Accounting and Control of Nuclear Materials (ABACC). Finally, it analyzes oft-discussed emerging threats to that order—including the impact of Brazil's planned development of nuclear-powered submarines amid an increasing assertiveness in its foreign policy. The chapter concludes by drawing lessons for the cases that follow.

WESTERN EUROPE

Post–World War II Integration and Its Limits

The process that culminated with the signing of the Euratom Treaty in 1957 serves as a convenient microcosm of the themes discussed throughout this book: the impact of regional dynamics, the limits of security cooperation, the influence of great powers, and the complexities of nuclear order. The post–World War II period created a perfect storm of conditions for European integration, combining common regional interest with a distinct collective identity. States were linked by their shattered economies and fragile global statuses, by fears of military domination by the Soviet Union, and by their deep ties with — and shared dependence on — the United States and its Marshall Plan. The promise of a United Europe was further reinforced by dynamics linked to the long conflict: there existed the potential for reconciliation between France and Germany, for safeguarding against the latter's shift eastward, and for removing any incentive for parties to engage in "fratricidal strife."[1] It was under these auspices that Belgium, France, West Germany, Italy, the Netherlands, and Luxembourg signed the 1951 Treaty of Paris, which established the European Coal and Steel Community, a supranational organization aimed at creating a common market; it was envisioned as the first phase in a process of comprehensive regional integration.

Around that time, discussions commenced for some form of military integration as well. This endeavor had the wholehearted support of the United States, as President Dwight Eisenhower was eager to lessen the American presence in Europe. The same six parties would sign the European Defence Community (EDC) Treaty in May 1952, which outlined the creation of a pan-European defense force, specifying its core philosophy as "supranational in character and comprising common institutions, common armed forces and a common budget."[2] Yet, initial enthusiasm for the project waned, and the treaty fell apart in 1954 when it failed to secure ratification from the French government. Several factors accounted for its collapse. First, the common threat that had inspired talks — the Iron Curtain — appeared decidedly less threatening with the end of the Korean War and the death of Joseph Stalin. Second, French military leaders perceived their participation in the EDC as a loss in relative terms; it would lower France's status to the level of two countries that had been on the losing side of the war.[3] Such concerns were exacerbated by the United Kingdom's lack of participation. Third, there were fears that the EDC would mark an irreversible infringement on French national sovereignty.[4] Thus, even during a period of remarkable momentum toward integration and federalism, the trend toward regionalism was in effect undermined by divergences in issue definition.

The Creation of Euratom

While a true security community proved elusive, it was in that context that the concept for Euratom emerged. The EDC Treaty sought to put into place a comprehensive regional nuclear order in Western Europe. A European Defense Commissariat was to oversee and govern military technologies across all stages, including production and trade as well as research and development. Its jurisdiction would have encompassed both conventional and nuclear activities. As such, the proposed federal European authority "would have regulated the entirety of the nuclear sector ... from uranium enrichment, to power plant construction, to the fabrication of nuclear warheads."[5] The description paints an image of a level of supranational control over national military nuclear programs that is almost unfathomable. That the six states were willing to accept that in the EDC Treaty text—even if it ultimately failed—reveals the extreme postwar circumstances under which European integration emerged. It also hints at the favorable environment in which regional nuclear order was eventually established in Western Europe.

Indeed, the failure of the EDC did not altogether take the nuclear issue off the table from the European integration project. On the contrary, some sort of nuclear cooperation came to be seen as vital to that process. This was during a period of universal optimism about the promise of nuclear energy, driven largely by the "Atoms for Peace" initiative named after a speech from President Eisenhower to the UN General Assembly in 1953. The campaign that followed had particular reverberations in Europe.[6] Energy security was a major issue for the region, which saw its reconstruction under threat from the 1956 Suez Crises—and the accompanying oil shortage and energy crisis. The nascent nuclear industry thus came to be seen as a clear energy alternative. A 1955 report from the Organisation for European Economic Co-operation heralded nuclear energy as an ideal source and called for regional cooperation to overcome the significant startup costs related to the building of nuclear infrastructure. With remarkable commonality in how states perceived the issue, "the political goal of furthering European integration through the device of a nuclear energy community thus proved attractive."[7]

The failure of the EDC Treaty thus did not mark a death knell for European integration. Yet, French opposition to the delegation of military activities to a supranational entity did lead diplomats to shift their attention to the civilian side of the nuclear issue. The 1957 Euratom Treaty featured significant centralization in this arena; its affiliated institutions were to coordinate and facilitate research, handle the classification and protection of information, control the distribution of patents and licenses, set standards for protection of public health, and establish joint enterprises.[8] Its Euratom Supplies Agency would both own and control all access to supplies, from source materials to special fissionable materials, while the Euratom Commission would engage in inspection and control. Underscoring the goal of a common market were the provisions that gave Euratom institutions total control over negotiations with third parties, with existing agreements from individual member states to be assumed by the community. The totality of the mandate was no accident. U.S. secretary of state John Foster Dulles had expressly stated that his government "could make available substantially greater resources and adopt an attitude of substantially greater liberality toward a real integrated community."[9] Bilateral agreements signed between the United States and individual Western European states specifically contained an allowance for the community.[10]

Non-Proliferation beyond Euratom

The Euratom Treaty was a unique project, aimed at governing an industry that essentially did not yet exist. That—combined with the depths of European regionalism—helps explain the totality of its jurisdiction. After all, there was a global regulatory vacuum at the time of the community's establishment, as the International Atomic Energy Agency (IAEA) came into existence the same year. Procedures and guidelines from the Euratom control system even came to serve as a model for the IAEA comprehensive safeguards system devised to implement the 1968 Nuclear Non-Proliferation Treaty (NPT).[11] Yet, precisely because of the sequencing of events and the process that resulted in a more muted regional nuclear order in Western Europe (at least, as compared to the vision set forth in the EDC Treaty), the very defining trait of Euratom—its focus on civilian nuclear energy programs—would prove restrictive. Indeed, while the Euratom Treaty has sat largely unchanged since it came into existence, the regional nuclear order in Western Europe has not been so quiet. The intensification of nuclear nonproliferation activities in the region corresponded to some degree with events at a global level. Still, it is clear that the nature of regional dynamics and regionalism processes during the period help explain the timing and character of change that followed.

As outlined in chapter 2, the shock of India's peaceful nuclear explosion in 1974, during a time of increasing nuclear trade, including to states in unstable regions, had major reverberations for global nuclear order. For Western Europe, it essentially forced the region to intertwine the civilian and military aspects of the nuclear issue that the Euratom Treaty had sought to disentangle, to tackle the possibility of diversion of fissile material for weapons use. France and West Germany as well as the UK all moved to take part in the newly formed Nuclear Suppliers Group; the enlargement of the group from 1976 to 1977 included three more members of the European Community. The U.S.-led International Nuclear Fuel Cycle Evaluation entailed a global reevaluation of the nuclear threat, thrusting the nuclear nonproliferation issue into the heart of the European agenda. This recalibration continued with the 1981 establishment of a nuclear working group in the context of the European Political Cooperation (EPC) process. The maturation of the working group evolved with the EPC. The working group met often over the course of the 1980s, issuing statements with greater frequency. It adopted joint directives on nuclear exports in 1984 and then helped to set up the nuclear embargo imposed by the European Council on South Africa in 1986. Notably, 1986 was also when the EPC was codified by the Single European Act, marking the first significant revisions to the 1957 Treaty of Rome and the beginning of the next phase of European integration. The EPC issued declarations on nuclear energy and nonproliferation issues subsequently, underlining an evolving conception of the boundaries of the nuclear issue.

It was not until the end of the Cold War, however, that there emerged a more aggressive Europe in the nuclear arena. This reflected the pace of regionalism in Europe and in particular the progressive impact of the Single European Act, which pushed movement toward a single market and referred specifically to the coordination of states' "positions more closely on the political and economic aspects of security."[12] Successful movement on this front led to the 1992 Treaty on the European Union (also called the Maastricht Treaty), which enabled progress in coordination of foreign security policy by an order of magnitude.[13] There was particular urgency with respect to European integration on the nuclear issue. After all, the waning and end of the Cold War had overhauled the global security environment. There was an air of uncertainty regarding the strategic role of nuclear weapons in the new order. At the same time, there was an unprecedented push for nuclear nonproliferation and disarmament action. This was true following significant bilateral reductions made by the United States and the Soviet Union to their respective stockpiles, and especially the case following the revelations of Iraq's clandestine nuclear weapons program in 1991. France's accession to the NPT in 1992 presented another impetus for the European Union to cohere its policies in those issue areas—at least to the extent possible.

The first half of the 1990s was, in fact, marked by European involvement on the nonproliferation front. Nuclear proliferation threats placed high on the list of its Common Foreign and Security Policy, falling under the jurisdiction of both the Committee on Non-Proliferation and the Committee on Nuclear Affairs within the European Council. It was on the initiative of the twelve original European Union members that the UN Security Council highlighted the threat posed by WMD to international peace and security in a 1992 common declaration; it also affirmed the responsibilities of the UN in arms control, nonproliferation, and disarmament.[14] The group presented an initiative on safeguards strengthening that year to the IAEA that became a foundation for Programme

93+2—the outcome of the reform effort in the aftermath of Iraq. During this period, European Union states also engaged in threat reduction activities in the former Soviet Union and joined the Korean Peninsula Energy Development Organization. Perhaps their strongest efforts came in the successful push for the indefinite extension of the NPT in 1995.

Post-Cold War Unity and Disunity

The vast majority of European Union activity even during this bustling period centered on nuclear nonproliferation, not disarmament, and primarily was projected outward beyond the region.[15] States would soon revert back to "joint declarations based on the lowest common denominator."[16] Ironically, it was the 1995 NPT Review and Extension Conference that exposed the fundamental divide among states in the region, underlining the difficulties of an encompassing regional nuclear order that includes nuclear weapon states and non-nuclear weapon states alike. While the treaty itself secured indefinite extension, the review of its activities underscored the gap between how the two groups prioritized and perceived its three pillars—of nonproliferation, disarmament, and development for peaceful use. The European Union's withdrawal from nonproliferation activity in the years to come revealed fractures in its common identity. Indeed, as two of the five recognized nuclear weapon states, France and the UK generally held back the EU's involvement on arms control and disarmament affairs, even as they espoused the importance of those issues in the abstract.[17] Any hope of strengthening regional nuclear order beyond the civilian sector encountered pushback. The fact that many European states were also party to the nuclear-sharing arrangement under the North American Treaty Organization reinforced the obstacles. That is, despite the advanced state of regionalism in Western Europe, divergences in issue definition and even existing nuclear cooperation prevented further action.

In the new century, however, the European Union has seen its role in nuclear nonproliferation reinvigorated. Concerns about nuclear terrorism in the aftermath of the September 11, 2001, terrorist attacks provided a threat that transcended the two-class divide, recalling India's 1974 test and the discoveries in Iraq in 1991. This came during a favorable period, as overall patterns of regionalism in Europe reflected significant maturity. Security regionalism under the Maastricht Treaty had expanded, with the development of the European Rapid Reaction Force, the creation of the Common Security and Defense Policy, and the approval of the interlinked Berlin Plus agreement that linked the European Union to NATO in crisis management operations. While issues of arms control and disarmament were underserved, the 2003 European Security Strategy and the related Strategy against Proliferation of WMD set "effective multilateralism" as the centerpiece of the region's nonproliferation policy.[18] The centrality of the

UK, France, and Germany in the construction of the Joint Comprehensive Plan of Action with Iran in July 2005 (discussed further in chapter 7) further reveals the impact of a united Western Europe when confronted with a common perceived proliferation threat.

Taking Stock

The European example reveals both the significance and the limitations of regionalism on the character of nuclear cooperation. The orders that emerged in civilian nuclear energy in the 1950s and in nuclear nonproliferation in the 1990s reflect the effects of complex dynamics at play. Despite favorable geopolitical circumstances linked directly to progress in the European integration process, there remains fundamental divergence among states in how they define the nuclear issue. This is largely because of the presence of the UK and France in the European Union—two nuclear weapon states that continue to prioritize possession. The greatest progress toward a strengthened regional nuclear order, and the successes thereof, have come with cross-cutting threats that bridge the divide across classes: a common market in the absence of global nuclear governance, a focus on nonstate threats against a regime vacuum, a hard push on a potential extra-regional threat drawn from their integrated economic base. The in-progress UK exit from the European Union and Euratom will certainly reduce the geographical reach of regional nuclear order in Western Europe. Yet by virtue of its retreat, and with France as the lone nuclear EU member, some of the previous antagonism that has prevented a more united front may dissipate, possibly opening the door for more fervent nonproliferation cooperation.

LATIN AMERICA AND THE CARIBBEAN

The Treaty of Tlatelolco

Discussions of nuclear-weapon-free zones—and regional nuclear orders—long preceded the NPT, emerging as early as 1956, when the Soviet Union proposed a limitation of armaments and a ban on atomic weapons across Central Europe at the Disarmament Commission.[19] As a nod to the possibility of such arrangements, the direct precursor to the NPT—1965's General Assembly Resolution 2028—called specifically for a treaty that would not "adversely affect the right of any group of States to conclude regional treaties in order to ensure the total absence of nuclear weapons in their respective territories"—a phrase replicated in its entirety in the NPT.[20] Underscoring the intertwined relationship between the NPT and these regional arrangements was the overlap in their content, as the treaty encompassing Latin America was "integrated with, and supportive of, the international nonproliferation regime."[21] The 1967 Treaty of Tlatelolco called upon contracting parties to conduct timely negotiations for safeguards agreements with the IAEA, while entrusting the agency with special inspections powers. As suggested by the moniker, weapons were the sole focus of this first regional agreement.

Already, the content of the treaty hinted at the united front presented by the states of the region—the surrounding context of which is explored in the next section. Parties agreed not only to prevent the "testing, use, manufacture, production or acquisition" but also the "receipt, storage, installation, deployment, and any form of possession of nuclear weapons, directly or indirectly, by the Parties themselves, by anyone on their behalf or in any other way."[22] That clause, aimed to deter the geographic spread of such weapons, extended beyond the demands later posited in the NPT. Underlining the extra-regional aspects of the treaty, the text included two additional protocols that obligated both colonizing powers and the nuclear weapon states to keep the area free from nuclear weapons. They provided legally binding negative security assurances, outlining the acknowledgment on the part of nuclear weapon states "not to use or threaten to use nuclear weapons against the Contracting Parties of the Treaty."[23] In addition, the treaty contained an intergovernmental verification mechanism, establishing OPANAL, replete with its own General Conference, Council, and Secretariat.

Early Regionalisms

That the first nuclear-weapon-free zone emerged in Latin America was no accident, reflecting the advanced level of regional order already present. This was partially a product of the successor state remnants of the Spanish empire seeking to "construct stable, amicable, and productive relations between themselves," resulting in the emergence of a "thick array of international institutional rules" as early as the 1930s.[24] The formalization of these rules blossomed over the course of the next few decades. The Treaty of Montevideo established the Latin American Free Trade Association in 1960, which promoted the liberalization of a list of sectors and expanded intra-regional manufactured trade in the short term.[25] The Central American Common Market, established by the 1961 General Treaty of Central American Economic Integration, had greater impact, as it required a common external tariff while liberalizing more than 90 percent of trade categories.[26] Even when such economic arrangements failed to elicit desired effects, states persisted, suggesting a strong common identity and shared values and interests. Smaller economies in the region established the Andean Pact in 1969, moving beyond trade liberalization to joint capital-intensive projects and regional economic planning as well.

Concrete campaigns in the political and security arenas did accompany the slow and sometimes painful process of economic integration. The American hegemonic presence in the hemisphere was a natural driving force, with the founding of the Organization of American States in 1948 the clearest manifestation of the effect. Unlike its predecessor Pan American Union, the organization's role in political and security matters was explicit. It was to promote peace and security "by means of mechanisms for peaceful conflict resolution, arms limitation and hemisphere-wide solidarity"; this included the use of force as a potential response to regional incursions.[27] The very first mention of a Latin America nuclear-weapon-free zone, in fact, came in the context of the Organization of American States, with Costa Rica proposing the idea at a council meeting in 1958.[28] Yet, if the U.S. fight against communism was the impetus to Latin America order, it was that same fight that later sparked those countries to turn inward in their quest to establish a security community that would counter the hegemonic presence of the global powers. This emerged through a norm of noninterference.[29] Still, despite this strong regionalist foundation, mobilization would likely not have taken place without a trigger event that solidified common perceptions of the nuclear issue.

A proposal to establish the Latin American zone first came in front of the UN General Assembly in September 1962.[30] But it was the onset of the Cuban Missile Crisis a month later that propelled the process forward. It was later revealed that the Soviets had deployed FKR nuclear cruise missiles near the U.S. naval base at Guantanamo Bay in Cuba, and, separately, that a Soviet nuclear submarine was prepared to fire when forced to surface by American destroyers near the quarantine line.[31] Even without the full extent of this knowledge at the time, however, the region fretted over being reduced to helplessness, a pawn to the superpower conflict, and the frontline of potential nuclear conflict. William Epstein, later involved in the drafting of the treaty, noted "the shock of looking into the abyss of nuclear annihilation was greatest in the western hemisphere."[32] The spectrum of concerns in Latin America suddenly included the possibility of other nuclear bases in the region, an arms race between industrialized rivals Brazil and Argentina, and fallout from atmospheric nuclear weapons tests; political momentum quickly gained steam. In 1963, sparked by a letter by Mexican president Aldolfo Lopez Mateos, five countries—Bolivia, Brazil, Chile, Ecuador, and Mexico—issued a Joint Declaration on the Denuclearization of Latin America, leading to an eleven-country draft resolution presented to the General Assembly in 1963.[33] The drafting of Tlatelolco followed.

Incorporating Argentina and Brazil

The emergence of a nuclear-weapon-free zone can be directly connected to the strength of Latin American regional identity, institutions, and integration processes as described; the Organization of American States even reviewed the provisions of the Treaty of Tlatelolco during the drafting process.[34] Similarly, the shortcomings of the nuclear order that followed can be attributed to the nuances of those same regional dynamics. Indeed, while Brazil and Argentina signed onto Tlatelolco, neither would complete the process of ratification until the 1990s. Military coups in those countries in 1964 and 1966, respectively, resulted in the imposition of hardline foreign policies. The revitalization of the rivalry in that period left each regime unwilling to dismiss the nuclear option altogether, or to forgo nuclear technologies—a prioritization of the threat posed by the other party over the more general concern of nuclear weapons. The two sides also came to perceive the terms of the Treaty of Tlatelolco as impressed on negotiators by the nuclear weapon states, particularly with the terms on the transport ban, the entry into force process, and the issue of peaceful nuclear explosions.[35] In short, this was a nuclear order they did not perceive as true to the region. Ultimately, Brazil offered only a conditional ratification of Tlatelolco, contingent on full ratification of both the treaty and the additional protocols; it amounted to a refusal as Argentina neglected to ratify at all.

Further robustness of Latin America's nuclear order—in whatever shape—thus hinged on improved relations between Argentina and Brazil, identified as "a conditioning factor for the whole region."[36] Ironically, it was in the seeds of discontent with the terms of the zone that nuclear rapprochement between those countries began. Resentment in the 1970s, including against the establishment of nuclear supplier networks, led the sides to issue a joint communiqué on the importance of nuclear policy cooperation. A process of technological exchange among their respective nuclear energy commissions followed, creating a foundation of nuclear cooperation. This and increased cooperation in other areas, including the management of water disputes in the Panama Canal, paved the way for a 1980 Agreement on Cooperation for the Development and Application of the Peaceful Uses of Nuclear Energy.[37] Improved relations overall between the states then took off under the civilian presidencies of Raul Alfonsin of Argentina and José Sarney of Brazil in the mid-1980s.[38] Economic and political coordination accelerated, resulting in agreements on a Program for Integration and Economic Cooperation, a Treaty on Integration, Cooperation, and Development, and a Joint Declaration on Nuclear Policy. That final item created a permanent cooperation committee in 1988, consisting of the nuclear commissions and enterprises of both countries.[39]

Increased transparency across the whole of the nuclear arena—from advanced notification on newly operational gas centrifuge facilities to technical protocols for assistance in case of accident or radiological emergencies to head-of-state visits to sensitive installations—marked a process of nuclear rapprochement that continued into the next decade. Under Presidents Carlos Menem and Fernando Collor, Argentina and Brazil, respectively, reduced the military influence from their nuclear programs, culminating in a 1990 joint declaration wherein the two sides agreed upon the establishment of a Common System of Accounting and Control (SCCC) for all nuclear activities and the ABACC to check its application.[40] The 1991 Guadalajara Treaty confirmed this and also renounced peaceful nuclear explosions definitively. The convergence of safety concerns filtered into other aspects of the nuclear issue. Concurrently, the two sides entered into negotiations for comprehensive safeguards agreements with the IAEA and for amendments aimed at updating the text of the Treaty of Tlatelolco. This centered on alterations to the verification and control system, reducing the intrusive character of special inspections, and increasing the role of the IAEA vis-à-vis OPANAL. The final result was the ratification of the treaty by Argentina, Brazil, and Chile in 1994.[41]

The strengthening of the nuclear order in Latin America in the early 1990s took place amid a changing world. The collapse of the Soviet Union and the end of the Cold War had clear reverberations for global politics. Yet, it would be disingenuous to attribute the events in Latin America to the subsequent international push for dismantling nuclear weapons and ending fissile material production.[42] Rather, Argentina and Brazil had made an "independent move . . . to contribute to international peace and security by committing themselves to using nuclear technology only for peaceful purposes."[43] They did so in the context of processes of democratization, economic liberalization, and civil-military cooperation.[44] Their nuclear rapprochement was also part of broader bilateralism and normalization processes; the impact of these improved relations and shared values on regional nuclear order became manifest. If the Treaty of Tlatelolco represented a burgeoning Latin America in the 1960s, inspired by the Cold War conflict that had left them pawns, then its amendment in the 1990s reflected the warming of relations and integration into the region by the two most powerful actors in the region.[45] NPT ratification came afterward, in 1994 (Argentina) and 1998 (Brazil), which underscores a process that flowed outward from the region rather than inward from global developments or pressures.

The Potential for Rifts

The emergence of the bilateral nuclear order between Brazil and Argentina derived partly from their nuanced—and somewhat defiant—view toward the global nuclear nonproliferation regime. Neither side still has signed onto the Additional Protocol; their reluctance to provide an expanded right of access to IAEA inspectors is compounded by their perception that the nuclear weapon states have not done enough in nuclear disarmament.[46] Brazil's nuclear activity is of particular worry to a regime that has witnessed noncompliance cases across a number of countries lacking Additional Protocols, including Iran and

North Korea.[47] There have been questions regarding centrifuges at Brazil's uranium enrichment facility in Resende, with the country continuing to reject full visual inspections and access from the IAEA.[48] Meanwhile, the president of the National Nuclear Energy Commission defends the country's reluctance to open its universities to safeguards and inspections.[49] Brazil's behavior remains in many ways under a microscope. After all, if bilateral nuclear cooperation provides an anchor to regional nuclear order in Latin America—as much as, if not more than, the global nuclear nonproliferation regime—then the greatest challenge to that order lies with a breach of that relationship.

In fact, Brazil's activity in recent years has raised concerns about the future of ABACC and the Treaty of Tlatelolco, the institutional cornerstones of Latin America nuclear order. The country invested $160 million into accelerating its nuclear-powered submarine program, which included development toward a full uranium enrichment process, construction of a naval reactor, and construction of the submarine itself.[50] This marked the use of a loophole provided by the NPT and IAEA, as nuclear materials for use in submarine programs are exempted from international safeguards standards.[51] Argentina too has expressed similar interest in a nuclear-powered submarine, though there is some question about the level of substantive progress it has attained.[52] Regardless, Brazil's program represents a source of anxiety for the international community. Given its status as one of a handful of countries with the capacity to participate across the entirety of the nuclear fuel cycle, including mining and producing uranium plus generating electrical power from nuclear plants, the use of fuel anywhere near the 20 percent highly enriched uranium threshold seems to provide Brazil easy breakout capability.[53]

The previously fraught, contested relationship between Brazil and Argentina might suggest some vulnerability of the existing Latin American order to renewed competition. Yet, despite external concerns about the submarine loophole, all indications are that a very different dynamic is taking place at the regional level, one with positive implications for the stability of the nuclear order in Latin America. Indeed, the 2004 establishment of the Union of South American Nations and the South American Defense Council suggests a further coalescing of regionalism patterns in a manner that outstrips the processes of the 1950s and 1960s. After all, security arrangements from that earlier period, including the Organization of American States and the Inter-American Treaty of Reciprocal Assistance, were "perceived as functional to the US national interest, rather than to the needs of a South American defence vision."[54] There is a clear shift in the contemporary era from a hemispheric-based security agenda that encompasses Latin America to one that is becoming exclusive to it.

The reason for the transition can be attributed both to overall improvements in the economic status of states across the region and to Brazil's ascension in the post–Cold War era. Of course, the establishment of a cohesive South American security agenda faces a myriad of issues, stemming from disputes on threat perceptions, economic policies, even ideologies.[55] Yet, these differences have thus far not proven backbreaking. Brazil's accepted status as the predominant power in Latin America has resulted in a natural ordering for states; its "consensual hegemony" is a foreign policy that reinforces order and constrains would-be challengers.[56] Strident emphases on national sovereignty and anti-imperialism that united the region and characterized the Treaty of Tlatelolco persist in the security arena, as manifest in Brazil's expressed support for Argentina's claims to the Falklands.[57] As a result, there are now few regional or subregional arrangements that the ascending power does not shape, from the cited Union of South American Nations and the South American Defense Council to the Community of Latin American and Caribbean States—all of which lack a U.S. or Canadian presence.[58] Meanwhile, would-be regional challengers lack the political, military, or economic force required to upend the increasingly institutionalized order.

Stability and Order

There is some fear that Brazil's transition into a global leadership role may increase the appeal of the nuclear weapons option. Such a move would deal a devastating, likely fatal, blow to both the bilateral nuclear cooperation enjoyed with Argentina and the broader regional order centered on the nuclear-weapon-free zone. Yet, there is little indication that this will happen. Brazil's immediate security environment is one almost bereft of high-level threats: the end of Hugo Chavez's reign in Venezuela in 2013 leaves the country with even fewer challengers to its regional hegemonic status. Meanwhile, Brazil's emphasis on consensual institutional arrangements—especially in the past two decades—has resulted in regional political, economic, and security integration processes that match its core values and interests. This remarkable regionalism in South America not only ensures Brazil's greater investment in protecting that order but also severely raises the costs of it violating that order—to which the Treaty of Tlatelolco, and norms of nuclear nonproliferation and disarmament, are centerpieces.

Latin America boasts one of the most robust regional nuclear orders in the world. The strength of that order seems unlikely to wither moving forward. Integration processes have only accelerated, providing a strong underpinning for continued nuclear cooperation among states. In addition, while the ABACC is no longer an arrangement between equal rivals, its institutionalization accounts for high levels of trust and reciprocity between Argentina and Brazil, establishing baselines for transparency and accountability. This is especially relevant as Brazil stands as the consensus representative and emerging power of the region and thus represents the biggest threat to upend the existing order. Yet, the nature of that country's ascension appears as another reason why the durability of Latin America's nuclear order is likely to hold. Even as it criticizes the NPT for its two-class system, even as it registers disapproval of the sanctions-heavy approach toward noncompliance cases, Brazil seeks to reform the international order—for instance, via the G4—rather than overhaul it. Even as "it stressed both peaceful development and autonomy from the north, [it sought a role in] fixing a problem important to the West": the Iranian nuclear program.[59] Unless Brazil perceives an existential nuclear threat, then, it seems unlikely that this stance will change. Without the change, the regional nuclear order in Latin America is more likely to strengthen than weaken.

CONCLUSION: ROBUST REGIONALISMS AND NUCLEAR ORDERS

At first glance, it appears rational to attribute the nuclear orders examined in this chapter entirely to the policy preferences of the predominant power in the particular region. France's rejection of the military integration proposed by the EDC Treaty altered the very course of the federalist movement in Western Europe; accordingly, its support for civilian nuclear integration drove the order established with the 1957 Euratom Treaty. That the United States and the Eisenhower administration played no small part in the process only underscores the realpolitik in play in a vulnerable postwar Europe. Later, it could be argued that French accession to the NPT allowed the European Union to engage actively in nuclear nonproliferation activities in the early 1990s. In Latin America, meanwhile, Brazil's commitment to both the ABACC and the Treaty of Tlatelolco appears as the stabilizing force underneath the robust nuclear order in Latin America. It was Brazil's altered foreign policy and corresponding rapprochement with Argentina beginning in the late 1980s, after all, that underpinned an evolved Latin American order. Contemporary concerns over the country's submarine program further reveal the limits of security institutions in the face of a determined power, especially involving a core security concern such as the nuclear issue.

There is no doubt that France and Brazil have had great influence in their respective regions. Yet, power-centric narratives fail to account fully for the timing and character of the regional nuclear orders examined in this chapter. It was no coincidence that Euratom came at the same time as the 1957 Treaty of Rome, which created the European Economic Community. The decade was one of an unparalleled integration movement. Postwar economic struggles and the emergence of Cold War dynamics drove the push for a united Europe, while energy security and competitive concerns propelled states to engage in a region-wide specialist market for nuclear power. The next phase in Europe's regional integration, marked by the Single European Act and Maastricht Treaty, would provide a similar foundation for its involvement in nuclear nonproliferation. Meanwhile, in Latin America, processes of economic and security regionalism had long been in place, inextricably linked to a regional identity forged in parts by a shared Spanish heritage in the postcolonial era and the American hegemonic influence. The Cuban Missile Crisis then provided the trigger event that created a nascent order centered on a nuclear-weapon-free zone. Decades later, rapprochement between Brazil and Argentina ushered in a second phase of regionalism, one more native, institutionalized, and impactful. That it has accompanied even more enhanced security order across South America portends well for its future.

There is pause in considering the applicability of these nuclear orders beyond the borders of Europe and Latin America. For starters, both came at a quite different world time, especially as it pertains to the nuclear landscape. The foundation for those two orders, encapsulated by the 1957 Euratom Treaty and the 1967 Treaty of Tlatelolco, in fact predate the centerpiece global instruments in those fields: the IAEA and the NPT, respectively. This sequencing set into motion a process of path dependence, with Euratom and OPANAL as the default institutions in which states in those regions cooperate on relevant nuclear issues. Another obstacle to generalizing is the fact that neither order should be considered perfect. The nuclear alliances in the European Union have limited cooperative efforts in nuclear nonproliferation and disarmament in particular, while the state-centric origins of the Latin American order belie the need for members to shift their focus to the next frontier: nonstate proliferation. Still, each case provides much insight for the rest of this volume. At a minimum, the two cases reveal the clear link between regionalism and nuclear cooperation, as the histories of their orders are intertwined with the histories of their economic, political, and security integrations. Europe and Latin America present ideal case studies of sorts, the levels of their regionalisms a barometer for the crucial cases examined in subsequent chapters. Northeast Asia, Southeast Asia, and the Middle East clearly do not demonstrate comparable trends in regionalism. But it is where that movement has occurred that may hold the answer to their nuclear futures.

CHAPTER 5

Northeast Asia

The lack of an inclusive multilateral order is one of the defining characteristics of Northeast Asia, the region in the world with the greatest number of nuclear-armed states present or directly engaged in its geopolitics. Scholars and analysts alike regularly dismiss the possibility of establishing an overarching security institution in the foreseeable future.[1] In relating their skepticism, they cite the role of historical grievances and ongoing territorial disputes, an interrelated lack of common identity, and the presence of regional and great power competition (including shifting dynamics in the balance of power). The dysfunction of the regional political environment has at times even overwhelmed steady progress toward economic regionalism. For instance, the flaring of tensions in 2012 between the triumvirate of China, Japan, and South Korea over interpretations of wartime history and territorial disputes halted a trilateral summit process for three years. A Jekyll and Hyde dynamic appears in place.

Absent inclusive institutions, regional security order in Northeast Asia has heretofore been dictated by longstanding bilateral alliances between the United States and Japan and between the United States and South Korea. The "hub-and-spoke" system has in recent years elicited nascent steps toward bilateral cooperation between Russia and China. Aside from these pairings, traces of formal organization are scant—with their origins largely outside the region. This includes the Association of Southeast Asian Nations (ASEAN) Regional Forum, the ASEAN Plus Three Meetings, and the ASEAN Defence Ministers Meeting-Plus: all of which have memberships and agendas dominated by Southeast Asian states. Other initiatives such as the Shangri-La Dialogue and the Shanghai Cooperation Organisation are similarly focused elsewhere, both geographically and substantively. Forums such as the Northeast Asia Cooperation Dialogue and the Council for Security Cooperation in the Asia Pacific feature delegates from the region, but in strictly private capacities. The general shape of security regionalism remains wanting.

CHAPTER OVERVIEW

There appears an inauspicious environment for a strengthened nuclear order in Northeast Asia. Inclusive regionalism processes are few, and a common identity is altogether absent. Yet, the nuclear issue has been a consistent focal point for cooperation in the region, with numerous past instances of institutionalization coming directly in response to developments in North Korea's nuclear program. In the 1990s, this included the Korean Peninsula Energy Development Organization and the Trilateral Coordination and Oversight Group. In the 2000s, this took the shape of the Six-Party Talks, which represented the first inclusive multilateral security institution exclusive to the region.[2] Later rounds of those talks even inspired concrete discussion of "a permanent peace regime," with a regional peace and security mechanism the subject of a working group established subsequently.[3] While both the Six-Party Talks and their associated working groups were shelved after Pyongyang withdrew from negotiations in 2009, the other parties have discussed the possibility of resumption ever since. Overall, the region seems to present a case in which fundamental commonalities in threat—and issue—definition offer a ray of hope in spite of less than conducive environmental conditions.

This chapter thus assesses the possibility of a stronger regional nuclear order in Northeast Asia. It details the shifting security dynamics in the region, identifies contending visions of the security landscape, and considers the degree to which these different visions can be reconciled. While a regional security order is not a necessary precondition for strengthened regional nuclear cooperation, the presence of the longstanding threat on the Korean peninsula on the top of both agendas ensures that the two will be inextricably linked. The bulk of the chapter then turns to existing (or proposed) cooperative arrangements in the nuclear arena. Identifying proliferation and proliferation-related issues relevant to the region, it systematically analyzes (1) the degree to which states participate in existing mechanisms and engage in cooperative activities, and (2) the possibility that existing arrangements can form the basis for a more encompassing nuclear order. It examines four venues in particular: the Six-Party Talks, the nuclear security framework, the nuclear safety regime, and a discussed nuclear-weapon-free zone. The chapter concludes with a vision of future nuclear cooperation in Northeast Asia.

A SECURITY ORDER FOR NORTHEAST ASIA

Neither fundamental conflicts nor recent tensions have suppressed all forms of regional cooperation in Northeast Asia, even in security. On the contrary, the region is "becoming increasingly defined by more universal and non-military norms of state behavior."[4] Fueled by growing economic interdependence, China, Japan, and South Korea in particular have connected through over fifty trilateral consultative mechanisms and a hundred cooperative projects.[5] The aforementioned pause in the trilateral summit did not affect meetings and initiatives at lower levels of government; it was in fact a meeting at the deputy foreign minister level that helped to break the deadlock in 2015. The symbolism of a bottom-up thawing of tensions should not be ignored. Even across the nuclear arena, there has been a parallel movement toward multilateralism, semi-regular discourse, even the language of community and policy coordination against regional threats. The possibility for further institutionalization hardly appears remote, and it is perhaps the volatility of the present that has worked to deepen commonalities in threat perceptions.

Future Uncertainties

Rapidly shifting dynamics in Northeast Asia suggest the untenable nature of the status quo. First, uncertainty surrounding the future of the U.S. commitment provides a significant source of instability. While much was made of Washington's pivot to Asia under President Barack Obama, domestic and global developments since have constrained the role of the United States in the Asia Pacific. The retreat looks likely to intensify under the presidency of Donald J. Trump. The Obama administration had already taken steps to empower local institutions, with particular outreach to ASEAN and the East Asia Summit. In turn, Japan and South Korea have adjusted their policies accordingly, hedging against the likelihood of a reduced U.S. role in Northeast Asia. In Japan, for instance, Prime Minister Shinzo Abe has aggressively sought a reinterpretation of Article 9 of his Constitution. His ruling Liberal Democratic Party pushed forth legislation in September 2015 that allowed the country's self-defense forces to defend its allies for the first time under a policy of "collective self-defense"; it became law in March 2016.[6] The country has also made greater strides toward multilateralism; its first-ever National Security Strategy in 2013 stressed the promotion and development of established security dialogues.[7] Overall, Abe's strategic partnerships aim at a "transition to a balanced multi-polar system in East Asia that is friendly to a measure of Japanese diplomatic leadership."[8]

South Korea too targeted a greater role for itself under former president Park Geun-hye, who set forth a comprehensive vision of regional security cooperation through a step-by-step approach that would accumulate trust in advance of a true regime and consultation body. While the future of the Northeast Asia Peace and Cooperation Initiative (NAPCI) is in limbo following Park's impeachment, her successor Moon Jae-in did not hesitate to declare similar intentions for a more assertive role in the region. This included a vision of Seoul leading efforts to resolve the North Korea crisis and to negotiate a solution between the United States and China over the Terminal High Altitude Area Defense (THAAD) anti-missile battery system (Moon even delayed further deployment of the system in June 2017, a concession to China at the expense of the United States).[9] It is revealing that both spokes of the hub-and-spoke system in Northeast Asia are expressly pursuing security orders that lessen their reliance upon the United States.

Second, the status quo in Northeast Asia is unlikely to hold because the hub-and-spoke system is incompatible with China's rising ambitions. Beijing's growing emphasis on norms of inclusion and multilateralism will invariably lead to a process of competitive institution building. Already, a revealing 2010 joint statement with Moscow explicitly stated the need for a new regional security and cooperation architecture.[10] This has crystallized since, with China taking on a leadership role in the Shanghai Cooperation Organisation (Eurasian based) and the BRICS grouping (Brazil, Russia, India, China, and South Africa). At the May 2014 Conference on Interaction and Confidence Building Measures, President Xi Jinping outlined an expansive vision for an "Asian security mansion"—drawing upon ASEAN and the League of Arab States as comparisons.[11] Beijing also decided to convene its Xiangshan Forum annually rather than biennially; underscoring the shift from what had been a Track-II effort were invitations to the South Korean, North Korean, and Japanese defense chiefs, among other high-level officials. Finally, as the chief mediator and facilitator of previous rounds of Six-Party Talks, China continues to serve as the biggest proponent of their resumption, with a foreign minister looking beyond the North Korean issue to suggest parties "enhance institution-building," so that the talks will "serve as a realistic and viable multilateral security mechanism safeguarding peace and stability in Northeast Asia."[12]

The future of security order in Northeast Asia appears very much up in the air. While ASEAN-led institutions have proven invaluable as multilateral venues for dialogue to date, bridging the U.S.-China divide, they have not shown promise of further development and are criticized for being ineffectual talk shops. As the next chapter discusses, their impact on a broader Asia Pacific order is limited by core principles of sovereignty and nonintervention. The lack of progress toward the realization of the ASEAN Political-Security Community reinforces the limits of its reach. In addition, Northeast Asian issues beyond the Korean peninsula have been short-changed in ASEAN forums, perhaps understandably given the overall membership composition and origins of those venues. The centrality of the Southeast Asian identity in the ASEAN Regional Forum, the ASEAN Plus Three Meetings, and the ASEAN Defence Ministers Meeting-Plus, for instance, combined with the vulnerability of a Southeast Asian–led order to the whims of neighboring powers, suggests these forums are inadequate in meeting the demands of Northeast Asia, especially given the shifting dynamics discussed.

Competing Visions?

On the surface, two strategic triangles underpin competing, and seemingly irreconcilable, visions of the security landscape in Northeast Asia.[13] First, there exists the American hub-and-spoke system, a U.S.-Japan-South Korea nexus that was reenergized under the Obama presidency. As discussed above, there has been some movement by Tokyo and Seoul linked to their concerns about U.S. withdrawal from the region, but no significant fissures have emerged. Any vulnerability in the triangle stemming from a U.S. shift, furthermore, can be partially negated by closer ties between the two Northeast Asian spokes. This reorientation has occurred in modest doses thus far, largely in response to the growing North Korean threat. All three sides signed a joint memorandum of understanding on information sharing and safeguarding regarding Pyongyang's nuclear and missile programs in 2014, for instance, while North Korea's fifth nuclear test in September 2016 sparked working-level discussions toward a bilateral General Security of Military Information Agreement between South Korea and Japan. Movement in the direction of a true triangle—versus two bilateral alliances—would be significant from the standpoint of regional order.

Second, there exists a China-Russia-North Korea link, dominated by the two global powers and marked primarily by their increasing bilateral ties. In 2014, Russian president Vladimir Putin enthusiastically characterized Sino-Russian relations as having "reached the highest level in all its centuries-long history," referring to unprecedented levels of trade, energy cooperation, and joint investment projects.[14] Fearing the expansion of the U.S. missile-defense system, the two neighbors have engaged in a joint missile-defense exercise of their computer command staff and have sought to intensify their security cooperation.[15] Meanwhile, the joint leadership of those countries in the Shanghai Cooperation Organization and the BRICS summits suggests an alternative vision of global order, with the Eurasian focus challenging traditional geographic groupings.

Yet, the image of these two competing triangles belies a more complex reality. The inevitability of U.S.-Chinese conflict is far from that, and despite Russia's heightened tensions with the West, economic considerations continue to keep the main components of the two nexuses within reach. The U.S. pivot to Asia included myriad efforts to engage China, with the two establishing the bilateral Strategic and Economic Dialogue in 2009, while convening the Consultation on People-to-People Exchange, the Joint Commission on Commerce and Trade, and the High-Level Dialogue on Cybercrime and Related Issues, among others. There now exist more than ninety institutionalized dialogues and consultation mechanisms between the two sides, who "may already be considered close allies in the economic sense."[16] Evan Medeiros, the former Asia chief on the U.S. National Security Council, underlined in 2016 that both the rising power and the established power desired to "work to make sure that rivalry didn't become inevitable."[17] Meanwhile, Russia's and China's campaigns—both joint and individual—to counterbalance American hegemony are similarly complicated by their ambitions: the former aims to develop Eastern Siberia and the Russian Far East; the latter seeks recognition as a global political force. Both sides have moved toward rapprochement and greater cooperation with Japan and South Korea, suggesting the taming effects of economic interests on the political and security agendas.

Expectations for Northeast Asian regional order should be kept modest: the modest patterns of security regionalism reflect differences in the strategic calculus of states, which feature a lack of commonality on definitions in a host of fundamental issues, including the North Korean threat, territorial and maritime claims, and the status of Taiwan. Still, even with a comprehensive security order out of the realm of possibility, all sides have reasons to seek strengthened cooperation. Both China and Russia desire diplomatic victories, as they seek to establish their global presences and bolster their economic circumstance. Russia's hosting of the 2012 Asia-Pacific Economic Cooperation summit was a revealing strategic move, and even its continued tensions with the West over Ukraine and Syria only reinforce for Putin the value of stable relations with the Northeast Asian troika. Meanwhile, as discussed, Japan and South Korea desire to increase their presence on the international stage, while the Trump administration appears amenable to their lessened dependence on the United States. The greater regional role sought by President Moon in South Korea is especially notable, given the country's unique position without a true rival, North Korea notwithstanding: it can lead without eliciting immediate protest or balancing action. That all sides—save North Korea—herald the value of the Six-Party Talks and endorse its resumption is revealing of some common desire for a more substantial order, one that could assuage at least some security concerns.

THE ROLE OF NUCLEAR ORDER

To date, steps toward further institutionalization of an order exclusive to Northeast Asia have been quite limited. For instance, the trilateral summit process between China, Japan, and South Korea—establishing the Trilateral Cooperation Secretariat in 2011—has coalesced around economic cooperation, disaster management, and social and cultural exchange. That even this non-security-based venue succumbed to the aforementioned tensions in 2012 reflects the fragility of diplomatic relations in the region.[18] It is telling that the two most thorough visions for security order in the region—South Korea's NAPCI and Mongolia's Ulaanbaatar Dialogue on Northeast Asia—come from two of the smaller presences in the region and foresee long-term processes that only culminate with security cooperation. Both focus instead on nontraditional security issues, stressing the importance of regularity in dialogue, of confidence-building measures, and of lessening mistrust through interaction. Still, the existence of these inclusive and comprehensive plans reflects continued progress, albeit slow, toward a more coherent regional security order. The nuclear issue stands at the heart of the process. The next section of this chapter pinpoints the major threats across the nuclear landscape, analyzing the degree of convergence in both issue definition and the prescription of regional solutions. It analyzes relevant forums in Northeast Asia for these issues, seeking insight as to their potential as a base for strengthened nuclear cooperation and, interconnected, a broader security order.

The Six-Party Talks

Beyond North Korea? Beyond the common thread of United Nations membership, the long dormant Six-Party Talks remain the only venue in which the entirety of the Northeast Asian region is engaged.[19] While North Korean foreign policy has long been shrouded by a degree of mystery, the threat of its nuclear program has provided a unifying security issue for the region, even instigating discussions about a broader security order. The first mention of a permanent peace regime on the Korean Peninsula came within the context of the Six-Party Talks in September 2005. Previous rounds of talks had been convened in immediate response to trigger events—for instance, with the escalation that followed Pyongyang's withdrawal from the Nuclear Non-Proliferation Treaty (NPT) in January 2003, and the visit by an unofficial U.S. delegation to the Yongbyon nuclear reactor that affirmed North Korea's capacity to produce plutonium in 2004. Both the Chairman's Statements from the April and June 2004 round of Six-Party Talks were narrowly focused to the crisis at hand.[20] In contrast, the September 2005 round featured a wider substantive focus. The resulting Joint Statement expressed its greater ambition through a commitment to "joint efforts for lasting peace and stability in Northeast Asia."[21] The document also referred to the parties' desire to promote economic cooperation and featured an agreement by both the United States and Japan to take steps to normalize their respective bilateral relations with North Korea.

While North Korea's nuclear program remained at the forefront of the agenda, the September 2005 Joint Statement established broader contours for subsequent rounds of talks. Steady negotiations resulted in a February 2007 document that specified initial steps toward denuclearization of the peninsula, including an action plan for phased implementation.[22] North Korea agreed to shut down and seal the Yongbyon facility in exchange for fifty thousand tons of heavy fuel oil aid. The sides outlined the next phase as well, with North Korea receiving economic, energy, and humanitarian assistance up to the equivalent of one million tons of heavy fuel oil should it declare and disable its entire nuclear program. Besides the particulars of the exchange, the action plan provided structure for longer-term regional goals, establishing working groups centered on five topics, including one for a Northeast Asia Peace and Security Mechanism (NEAPSM) that would meet in March 2007. Russia, which chaired the group, enthusiastically heralded it as a mechanism for "the creation of reliable political and legal guarantees of security in Northeast Asia."[23] The Joint Statement also outlined a ministerial-level meeting that would take place at an unspecified time in the future and would be convened strictly for the purpose of promoting regional security cooperation. Parties reaffirmed the need for the meeting in subsequent rounds of Six-Party Talks; meanwhile, the NEAPSM working group convened for a second time in August 2007.[24]

The July 2008 round of the Six-Party Talks primarily concerned the process of disabling facilities at the Yongbyon complex. Parties set forth a timeline for both this action and the corresponding provision for economic and energy assistance. In October 2008, the United States and North Korea reached agreement on verification measures, leading the United States to remove North Korea from their list of State Sponsors of Terrorism. However, North Korea prevented inspectors from accessing samples at Yongbyon the next month; this led to the failure of the sixth round of talks to produce a Joint Resolution. Notably, one success in those December 2008 talks was Russia's circulation and discussion of the "Guiding Principles of Peace and Security in Northeast Asia." The NEAPSM working group would meet for the third time in February 2009. However, following a failed satellite launch by Pyongyang in April 2009, and an immediate condemnation by the UN Security Council, North Korea formally withdrew from the Six-Party Talks process. The talks—along with the working groups—have been stagnant since.

The Difficulty of More: The NEAPSM working group established in the context of the Six-Party Talks remains the only instance of concrete movement toward a regional security order exclusive to Northeast Asia, while simultaneously being inclusive of all the countries therein. That the talks themselves ascended from an ad hoc arrangement dealing with the immediacy of the North Korean nuclear crisis into a forum that expressed ambitions about enduring peace and cooperation mechanisms reflects the political will for institutionalization at the time. Support for the process was widespread among the involved powers: China was the first to broach the possibility of transition out of the Six-Party Talks in 2005, U.S. secretary of state Condoleezza Rice played a pivotal role in the establishment of the five working groups, while Russia assumed the chairmanship of the NEAPSM working group. South Korean ambassador Sungnam Lim spoke for many when he expressed the hope that the group would "evolve into a more full-fledged body for promoting regional security dialogue and regional confidence-building measures."[25]

The working group provided the blueprint for redirecting the Six-Party Talks beyond the North Korean nuclear threat, a textbook example of institutional conversion.[26] Yet, the persistence of the threat and the pause in the talks since 2009 prevented any further shift in attention from the Korean peninsula to a permanent regional security order. The break is instructive. Even with a seventh round of talks, the fragility of the process since 2003 does not bode well for the construction of a more ambitious nuclear (or security) order. While the NEAPSM working group represents an unprecedented step for the region, it made modest gains at most, with parties focusing on its launching and operation across its three meetings in lieu of reaching consensus on guiding principles or substantive work.[27] In fact, any process of institutionalization that emerges from the context of the Six-Party Talks is fraught with complication. After all, progress hinges on North Korea's participation, an unlikely reality given the ruling regime's general hostility against multilateralism. It is revealing that no attempts were made to convene the working groups separate from the talks. With their fates tethered, the venue does not appear to offer enough stability.

The case to be made for deriving order through the Six-Party Talks centers on the following set of arguments. First, North Korea's nuclear program constitutes the greatest threat to the whole of Northeast Asia. Even China, which prefers the program to a collapsed regime in Pyongyang, is subject to the destabilizing effects of its ally's stockpile. Second, all sides remain in agreement that the talks present the only venue through which denuclearization of the peninsula can take place. More than a year after the talks were halted, Russia foreign minister Sergei Lavrov stated matter-of-factly that "it will be necessary to return to them as there is no other mechanism to settle the problem."[28] That reality has not changed. Notably, as leaders continue to call for the resumption of the talks, they have regularly invoked its broader goals as set forth in the September 2005 Joint Statement. A statement from China and Russia in May 2014 underlined not only the importance of the talks but the fact that an agreement was reached that would establish a permanent peace and security institution in Northeast Asia.[29] In short, referring to the analytical framework deployed in this book, the long pause of the Six-Party Talks has not withered away commonalities in how parties defined the issue at hand and assessed the need (even the venue) for action. Still, the centrality of North Korea's participation in the process is problematic and presents a possibly insurmountable obstacle. Its increased pace of ballistic and missile tests in 2016 and 2017 has enhanced its isolation, making this possibility less likely. If the country indeed represents the kind of common regional threat that can spark cooperative action, the construction of a permanent order may necessitate its omission from the process—a condition China is unlikely to accept. The intractability of the situation on the Korean peninsula thus suggests then that the best path forward must be multifaceted.

Nuclear Security Framework

A Burgeoning Structure: The vulnerability of nuclear materials and facilities appears as an especially relevant issue in a region that houses multiple nuclear-armed states and multiple nuclear energy programs. North Korea's involvement in the black market of weapons-usable materials and technologies provides another dimension to the issue. Yet the weaknesses of the larger nuclear security regime are all too evident in Northeast Asia. Global concerns about nuclear security were expressed as early as the 1970s, but the framing of the issue had clear limitations. For instance, the 1980 Convention of the Physical Protection of Nuclear Materials applied only to materials involved in international shipments, while the 1992 Cooperative Threat Reduction Program targeted only WMD stockpiles in the post-Soviet satellites. As suggested in chapter 2, the conversation was reframed only with the revelations of al-Qaeda's nuclear aspirations following the September 11 attacks. Recognizing the scope of the issue, the International Atomic Energy Agency (IAEA) created the Nuclear Security Fund in 2001 and the Office of Nuclear Security the following year. The urgent, dispersed, and untraditional nature of the threat was underlined with a 2002 incident involving a North Korean ship bound for Yemen with ballistic missile parts and the 2004 unveiling of the A. Q. Khan proliferation ring—which supplied the nuclear programs of Iran, Libya, and North Korea.[30]

By the time of the 2004 U.S. presidential election campaign, both George W. Bush and John Kerry referred to nuclear terrorism as the preeminent security threat to the country.[31] Yet, over a decade later, the response of the international community remains in flux, its piecemeal structure characterized by disparate, largely voluntary, and often-underdeveloped instruments. This lack of cohesive action is perhaps linked to the broadness of the issue, with nuclear security defined as "prevention and detection of, and response to, theft, sabotage, unauthorized access, illegal transfer or other malicious acts involving nuclear material, other radioactive substances or their associated facilities."[32] Exacerbating policy disorder is the lack of an IAEA mandate on the issue; its documents are nonbinding, meant merely for guidance. The United States has taken a lead role: establishing the 2003 Proliferation Security Initiative to interdict ships engaging in illegal transfers, ushering in 2004's UN Security Council Resolution 1540 to address the role of nonstate actors, founding the Global Threat Reduction Initiative to reduce vulnerable materials at civilian sites, and announcing alongside Russia the Global Initiative to Combat Nuclear Terrorism in 2006 to build capacity for prevention, detection, and response. In 2010, President Obama convened the Nuclear Security Summit to draw further attention to the issue.

Still, the reliance on national implementation helps to explain the shortcomings of the global nuclear security order. This is manifest across Northeast Asia, with North Korea striking in its lack of engagement with any of the aforementioned instruments. In addition, accusations of politicization are rampant in an issue area that lacks any global institution with a true mandate, in a region home to a number of geopolitical rivalries. China, for instance, opposes the U.S.-led Proliferation Security Initiative on the grounds that it violates the UN Convention on the Law of the Sea. Both the United States and the UN have also caught criticism over the expansive legislative aspects of Resolution 1540. But perhaps the greatest challenge to nuclear security order stems from the fallout of Russia's incursion into Ukraine in February 2014. Moscow's suspension from the Group of Eight struck a major blow to the Global Partnership Against the Spread of Weapons and Materials of Mass Destruction, and its withdrawal from the 2016 Nuclear Security Summit is foreboding for a process whose future is already tenuous under the Trump administration. In that announcement, Russian ambassador Sergey Kislyak pointedly pushed back on further cooperative efforts in nuclear security, focusing instead on the IAEA, "created by all of us to deal with these issues."[33] Indeed, Russia has suspended or halted a number of bilateral agreements with the United States on nuclear security issues, including the 1992 Cooperative Threat Reduction Program and a 2000 pact on the disposal of plutonium.

On the Agenda: There are a multitude of reasons why the countries of Northeast Asia should be attuned to the nuclear security issue, and why cooperation there could provide a foundation for strengthened regional nuclear order. Among the twenty-five countries possessing more than one kilogram of weapons-usable nuclear materials, Russia, China, and North Korea rank among the bottom third in terms of security provision.[34] North Korea is notable for its lack of information on laws and regulations; the ever-present possibility of regime collapse provides even more consternation about its control over its modest yet growing stockpile. Meanwhile, Russia was cited for the high quantities of materials housed, the dispersal of those materials among locales, and the levels of corruption among public officials. Smuggling remains a high priority risk in Russia and former Soviet facilities, with even nonweaponized materials a relevant proliferation threat in coming decades.[35] The heavy presence of nuclear energy in China, South Korea, and Japan further underscores the importance of tackling the security issue in the region.

Besides the relevance of the issue (suggesting the likelihood of commonality in perception), the relatively nascent and decentralized nature of the global nuclear security regime provides the opening for a greater regional presence. U.S. ambassador Bonnie Jenkins specifically referred to outreach at the regional level as critical to the Nuclear Security Summit process. At the 2014 Summit, South Korean president Park called for a "nuclear security dialogue process" among the countries of Northeast Asia to that end.[36] There has been advancement toward this goal at a technical level: China, Japan, and South Korea first met in 2012 and 2013 to discuss collaboration among their Centers of Excellence, established for technical training and for engaging in research and development. Movement toward a more formal Asian Regional Network could provide the impetus for more widespread information sharing and coordination. The possibility of a comparable advisory process also exists with respect to Resolution 1540, as South Korea hosted a regional workshop attended by twenty-nine countries on the resolution's implementation in October 2014.[37]

Significantly, the states of Northeast Asia have tremendous capacities in the field of nuclear security. Not only are the majority of states active participants in the aforementioned initiatives, but they have donated to the IAEA Nuclear Security Fund and the World Institute for Nuclear Security.[38] Further involvement can contribute to a regional atmosphere of collaboration, information sharing, and transparency. Yet, expectations should be tempered, as nuclear security is marked by a "lack of clear authority, resources and government structure."[39] The regional and subregional outreach of Resolution 1540, the Proliferation Security Initiative, and other efforts remain rudimentary, while the durability of the Security Summit process is very much in question. The instability in the current context—that is, the nascence of existing nuclear cooperation—thus prevents substantial progress toward a strengthened regional nuclear order centered on that subject. Still, collaboration between China, Japan, and South Korea continues to grow, offering the distinct possibility for a bottom-up process. The relevance of the issue ensures some degree of entanglement in the years to come, and technical collaboration at the regional level could, in fact, shape the future of the global nuclear security regime as well. From the perspective of Northeast Asia, however, expecting such cooperation to burgeon into a broader nuclear order appears far too ambitious at a time when the issue itself is not clearly defined.

Nuclear Safety Regime

Energy Expansion: In contrast to the nuclear security issue, there exists a long-standing international legal framework centered on the IAEA for nuclear safety considerations. The agency was mandated as the primary international body on the subject; it has long been responsible for establishing safety standards and assisting states in implementing those standards.[40] The Chernobyl accident of 1986 inspired a series of agreements in the domain, with the IAEA playing a pivotal role in each: this includes the Convention on Early Notification of a Nuclear Accident (1986), the Convention on Assistance in Case of a Nuclear Accident (1986), the Convention on Nuclear Safety (1994), and the Joint Convention on the Safety of Spent Fuel Management and on the Safety of Radioactive Waste Management (1997). The wide adherence to the global nuclear safety regime is reflected in Northeast Asia: all countries except for Mongolia and North Korea are party to each of the above agreements, and all but those two are part of the thirty-five-member IAEA Board of Governors.[41]

Additionally, there exist other multilateral venues through which the states of Northeast Asia cooperate exclusively on peaceful nuclear use. The 1972 IAEA Regional Cooperative Agreement for Asia and the Pacific aims to build technical capacity for applying nuclear science and technology in diverse areas, and now counts China, Japan, Mongolia, and South Korea among its twenty-one members; a Regional Office established in South Korea in 2002 furthered its institutionalization. Those same countries participate in the Japan-led Forum for Nuclear Cooperation in Asia created in 1999; the forum involves annual ministerial meetings, with projects on research reactor development and safety as well as infrastructure strengthening. Increased attention to nuclear safety in the post–September 11 landscape inspired the launch of the Asia-Pacific Safeguards Network in 2009, with national authorities and agencies from China, Japan, South Korea, the United States, and Russia, among others, meeting annually on various aspects of safeguards implementation.

China, Japan, and South Korea have taken lead roles in the nuclear safety landscape. The Northeast Asian troika house ninety-two nuclear reactors between them and have thirty-five more at varying stages of construction.[42] Members of their national nuclear safety infrastructures are all party to the Asian Nuclear Safety Network, established in 2002 as a platform for information sharing and networking. Since 2008, the three have also held annual Top Regulators' Meetings on nuclear safety, agreeing in December 2013 on a framework to exchange information on emergencies and accidents and to discuss safety plans regularly. This was directly linked to the 2011 accident at Fukushima-Daiichi— an event that propelled the safety issue to the forefront of the nuclear agenda. Notably, work among the regulators continued even when the trilateral summit process was on hiatus from 2012 to 2015. President Park even expressly called for the creation of a China, Japan, and South Korea–led nuclear safety group akin to the European Atomic Energy Community (Euratom). Overall, then, existing safety cooperation in Northeast Asia—measured both in terms of engagement with the global nuclear order and in levels of intraregional activity—is remarkably robust.

Euratom Northeast? The idea that Euratom could serve as a model for a Northeast Asian nuclear community has long been invoked by policymakers and analysts alike.[43] At first glance, the comparison seems ill-suited, as the confluence of circumstances that led to the former appears unique to the European experience. As discussed in chapter 4, Euratom emerged in a postwar period in which European integration was uniquely prioritized, with its founding coming at the same time as the European Economic Community. The Atomic Energy Community was a beneficiary of the overall infancy of the global nuclear industry as well. With the widespread belief that atomic energy would lessen European dependence on the Middle East, Euratom gained a mandate to both develop and manage a regionally integrated nuclear industry. Such strategic considerations were also key to securing American support for the endeavor.[44] Further, the regulatory vacuum at the time—with the IAEA in its infancy—allowed Euratom to gain executive authority over all aspects of the nuclear sector: establishing common safety standards, protecting against materials diversion, and providing supply assurances.

Any discussion of an Euratom-like entity in Northeast Asia therefore must account for the drastically different conditions in place. At the same time, it is not a stretch to envision the applicability of elements of the case.[45] Patterns of regionalism clearly do not compare to the European example, especially in terms of shared values and interests and common identity—and the contrast to the concrete effort made toward an ASEAN Nuclear Energy Community is revealing, given the disparity between the Northeast and Southeast Asian regionalisms (as detailed in chapter 6). However, there has been a steady process of institutionalization in Northeast Asia, apparent even through the nuclear venues discussed. The trilateral cooperation between China, Japan, and South Korea presents a logical core for a nuclear community and has indeed been identified as such.[46] Meanwhile, the established state of the nuclear industry and the presence of the NPT-IAEA safeguards system do not detract from the spectrum of concerns that remain unaddressed in the altered landscape; the accident at Fukushima-Daiichi represents a rallying point in that respect. The cited growth of the nuclear energy sector in Northeast Asia invites attention on issues of safety, waste management, and emergency response, among others—items that are indicative of IAEA regulatory shortcomings. Moreover, the myriad gaps in nuclear security may provide the parallel to the nuclear proliferation concerns that resulted in the generous delegation to Euratom's mandate.

The notion of nuclear safety cooperation as a gateway for a strengthened regional nuclear order is promising. Parties would have the luxury of sidestepping the Korean denuclearization issue in a manner inaccessible to the Six-Party Talks and could lean on the institutional foundation and resources provided by the global safety regime in a manner unmatched in nuclear security. The emergence of regional collaborative arrangements in the issue area since 2000—the presence of existing cooperation—reinforces the viability of the process. Yet, there remain obstacles. Fragile Northeast Asian relations must improve before a shift from forums and networks to treaties or organizations with executive authority in traditional security affairs is feasible. The global push for an encompassing safety-security nexus can also be a hindrance, by virtue of inherent contradictions (i.e., limits of transparency in nuclear security). The involvement of the three recognized nuclear weapon states and North Korea also threatens to complicate confidence-building processes, echoing the problematic dynamic that resulted from the French presence in Euratom. Overall, while the issue of nuclear safety represents an intriguing possibility for institution building, it may be limited in its impact on a more comprehensive regional nuclear order.

A Northeast Asia Nuclear-Weapon-Free Zone

A Proposal Overshadowed: It would be remiss to discuss the potential for strengthened regional nuclear order in Northeast Asia without touching on a nuclear-weapon-free zone, given the common goal among states of denuclearizing the Korean peninsula. The idea derives too from the success of existing arrangements. As noted in chapter 2, five zones cover the entirety of the Southern Hemisphere and Central Asia, totaling 114 states parties. Especially relevant for Northeast Asia is the possibility of a subregional zone, first acknowledged in the 1975 Comprehensive Study of the Question of Nuclear-Weapon-Free Zones in All Its Aspects. The report noted precisely that these obligations "may be assumed . . . also by smaller groups of States and even individual countries."[47] The special report also related the view that a "limited area" zone could be "later extended to other States that agree to join it.[48] Notably, Mongolia declared itself a single-state zone in 1992 because it was surrounded by nuclear-armed neighbors China and Russia; after years of petitioning, the zone entered into force in 2000.

Ironic in retrospect, the first proposals for a nuclear-weapon-free zone on the Korean peninsula were introduced by North Korea in the 1960s and the 1970s.[49] Supreme Leader Kim Il-Sung sought to secure the removal of U.S. tactical nuclear weapons from South Korea. With the backdrop of bipolarity, the proposal gained the vocal support of Soviet president Mikhail Gorbachev—but fell victim to superpower politics in the UN.[50] It was not until the end of the Cold War that the zone appeared as a distinct possibility. Relations on the peninsula thawed dramatically in the early 1990s, with South Korea establishing diplomatic ties with the Soviet Union and China, U.S. president George H. W. Bush removing nonstrategic nuclear weapons from bases in South Korea, and both North and South Korea gaining UN membership in 1991. These developments paved the way for the 1992 Joint Declaration of the Denuclearization of the Korean Peninsula between the two Koreas. The legally binding agreement prohibited the acquisition of enrichment and reprocessing facilities and committed both sides to joint inspections to that end. The pact also created a

Joint Nuclear Control Commission. However, implementation efforts failed to gain momentum and faded altogether in 1993 following IAEA revelations about North Korean noncompliance with its NPT safeguards agreement.

The 1992 Joint Declaration remains the only legally binding commitment North Korea has made to denuclearize. As a result, it has often been invoked since, including in both the 1994 Agreed Framework and the September 2005 Joint Statement. Yet, the idea of a de facto nuclear-weapon-free zone on the Korean peninsula, let alone in Northeast Asia, has receded as the Six-Party Talks became the preferred venue for discussion of the security dilemma on the peninsula. Much of the talk about the zone since then has been driven by nongovernmental organizations. However, one notable exception includes a 2013 report from the UN Secretary-General's Advisory Board on Disarmament Matters, which suggested that Secretary-General Ban Ki-moon "consider appropriate action for the establishment of a nuclear-weapon-free zone in North-East Asia."[51] Meanwhile, President Tsakhiagiin Elbegdorj of Mongolia remains one of the most outspoken proponents of the zone, offering to work informally in order to assess its viability and identifying his comprehensive Ulaanbaatar Dialogue process as a stepping stone to this end.[52] Several other officials—working under the banner of Parliamentarians for Nuclear Non-Proliferation and Disarmament and the Asia Pacific Leadership Network for Nuclear Non-Proliferation and Disarmament—have issued similar calls for action.[53]

An Unlikely Path: Nuclear-weapon-free zones are highly regarded for their contributions to regional nonproliferation activity, their standing as confidence-building measures, and their impact on global disarmament norms.[54] Previous zonal treaties have been revolutionary in some respects, formally incorporating test bans, safety standards, and environmental concerns before such norms became widespread. They established institutions to ensure compliance in select cases and contain protocols that secure legally binding assurances from the recognized nuclear weapon states (though most are yet to be ratified by those states). The incorporation of South Africa into the Treaty of Pelindaba even provides a blueprint for a zone in Northeast Asia that includes North Korea, as it details the role of the IAEA and the African Commission on Nuclear Energy in verifying the dismantlement and destruction of nuclear explosive devices and related facilities. By virtue of their legitimacy, history, structure, and principles, then, a nuclear-weapon-free zone could serve as the basis for a strengthened nuclear order in Northeast Asia.

The lack of official dialogue on the topic, however, casts a sobering light on the possibility. Not only should such zones be "established on the basis of arrangements freely arrived at among the States of the region concerned," but the "initiative ... should emanate exclusively" from those states.[55] Parties in Northeast Asia have simply not had the desire to pursue such an arrangement. While some officials, notably Hideo Hiraoka, the chairperson of the Parliamentarians for Nuclear Non-Proliferation and Disarmament, have expressed the desire to get mention of a zone into the final document of an NPT Review Conference, this has not yet translated to success.[56] Indeed, previous Review Conferences and Preparatory Committees have referred only to the denuclearization of the Korean peninsula, with the Six-Party Talks as the agreed-upon venue for that process. Even the specification of a Northeast Asia nuclear-weapon-free zone in such a manner might have limited impact. After all, as explored further in chapter 7, the full support of the UN secretary-general, a 1995 resolution, and consistent Review Conference pressure have not prevented stagnation on the proposed WMD-free zone in the Middle East. There exists simply no common belief that the zone represents the proper regional solution for the nuclear issue.

Substantive concerns further complicate any effort to establish a nuclear-weapon-free zone in Northeast Asia. None of the existing zones include any recognized nuclear powers; the duties and obligations ascribed to them have been heretofore confined to protocols outside the main text of the treaties. A Northeast Asia zone would have to include distinct responsibilities for China, Russia, the United States, and perhaps North Korea, thus recalling the two-class divide that has been problematic for the NPT. Even the bandied idea of a limited zone that includes only the Korean Peninsula and Japan entails its own obstacles. The standard language that prohibits "receipt, storage, installation, deployment and any form of possession" would have to be altered given the reality of the United States' extended nuclear deterrence. In addition, given the presence of the global powers in Northeast Asia and the strategic significance thereof, determining the physical boundaries of a subregional zone presents a massive challenge. One reason that the recognized nuclear weapon states have neglected to ratify other nuclear-weapon-free zones in full has to do with their concerns over the freedom of movement of ships and aircraft in international waters and airspace.[57] Overall, then, conditions in the region strip away many of the benefits of the arrangement.

CONCLUSION: A NUCLEAR-BASED SECURITY FRAMEWORK

There is no denying the difficulties of establishing a more concrete nuclear order in Northeast Asia. To begin, the staggered nature and current suspension of the Six-Party Talks demonstrates the singular impact of the North Korean regime on any institutional processes that encompass the nuclear issue. The country has long seen regionalism "exclusively through the prism of security, survival, and geopolitics."[58] The denuclearization of the peninsula appears both as a prerequisite for movement and a seeming impossibility. Even if parties excluded North

Korea, the regime's actions or destabilization could provoke South Korean and Japanese responses, directly threatening the viability of any cooperative arrangement. In addition, the prominence of the United States in any nuclear-based order provides another source of tension. Its inclusion could provoke a tepid response from China and Russia, both invested with imposing their own visions for regional order. The arrangement overall would be especially susceptible to great power politics, detracting from strictly regional concerns: consider the impact of the situation in Ukraine on Russian participation in the global nuclear security campaign.

Still, with the end of Barack Obama's pivot to Asia, and with China continuing to lay claim to its global status, there is an inevitability of upheaval in the security dynamics of Northeast Asia. The best hope for a strengthened security order might just emanate from a crisis event.[59] Indeed, financial crises played a catalytic impact in the development of Northeast Asian economic regionalism. Similarly, the standoff on the Korean peninsula, the 2011 accident at Fukushima-Daiichi, and the newfound focus on nuclear security matters have provided impetus for recent movement in nuclear institutionalization. Furthermore, states in the region engage one another on topics of nuclear security, safety, and energy, if in a scattershot manner. The expansive nature of the nuclear issue has allowed modest doses of transparency, information exchange, and confidence building across disparate arenas.

The difficulties of establishing a more robust nuclear order reflect fundamental difficulties in building security institutions in conditions that are far from ideal, a product of not only geopolitics but also sociocultural and historical elements. For instance, how parties define their borders (including maritime territory), how they perceive the status of Taiwan, even how they address World War II atrocities, have had an impact on notions of identity and interest, coloring individual perceptions and definitions of regional issues in Northeast Asia. Still, as has been evident in the economic arena, this does not preclude movement toward regionalism. The unique centrality of the nuclear issue in Northeast Asia further renders it a logical basis for strengthened regional cooperation. The North Korean program remains a persistent threat, while concerns about energy security and the related growth of nuclear energy ensure that issues of safety and security will only become more prominent items on the agenda. Overall, parties have shared definitions of problems across the landscape that can transcend their differences. Perhaps further exogenous shocks can build on the foundation in place—especially among China, Japan, and South Korea. In such a scenario, security institutionalization might take the form of a robust nuclear order, with the latter feeding back into the expansion of the former.

CHAPTER 6

Southeast Asia

The discussion of nuclear cooperation in Southeast Asia is inseparable from an account of its regional institutional architecture, in particular the overarching presence of the Association of Southeast Asian Nations (ASEAN). Indeed, it was within the context of an ASEAN Working Group that the Southeast Asia nuclear-weapon-free zone (SEANWFZ) was negotiated and drafted; it entered into force in 1997. ASEAN's profile has steadily increased in the post–Cold War era, with the creation of the ASEAN Regional Forum (ARF), ASEAN Plus Three (APT), the East Asia Summit, the ASEAN Defence Ministers' Meeting (ADMM), and the ADMM-Plus. That ASEAN's extended presence has been accompanied by a broader security agenda only underlines its centrality in a strengthened nuclear order.

Despite the ubiquity of ASEAN, there remains some debate as to the potential for and character of strengthened nuclear cooperation in Southeast Asia. There is little question that the association has made significant contributions to community building and to the creation of a cohesive regional identity.[1] Still, whether that can translate to a concrete security order is another question altogether, given constraints linked to ASEAN's membership composition and foundational principles. Calls for the ARF to enact "important changes to move beyond the image of a 'talkshop' or 'paper tiger'" reflect a common critique.[2] Further complicating the dynamics of the region is the fact that Southeast Asian order exists in the context—oftentimes the shadow—of Asia Pacific regionalism and remains subject to the machinations of neighboring powers China, Japan, and India.

CHAPTER OVERVIEW

It is with the backdrop of both shifting security dynamics and an evolving institutional architecture that Southeast Asia will confront emergent challenges across the nuclear landscape. The region has been linked to the trafficking of weapons-usable materials and technologies, with some countries pinpointed as "a central entrepôt for the A. Q. Khan black market nuclear network."[3] Concerns about its role in global proliferation are exacerbated by the increased presence of terrorist groups in the region in the twenty-first century. Interrelated issues of nuclear security and safety will also become directly relevant as Indonesia and Malaysia proceed with their plans for power plant construction (Vietnam's plans are in the air after it suspended development in November 2016). Meanwhile, China's active territorial claims on the South China Sea not only directly affect many of the states in the region but could render Southeast Asia an unwitting home to conflict between nuclear-armed powers. Finally, despite recent reforms, a number of states still cast a wary eye toward Myanmar and its potential nuclear ambitions—a consequence of its relationship with North Korea, poor record under past military rule, and stop-and-go progress in democratic reform.[4] Overall, the lack of nuclear-armed powers in the region obscures the inevitable centrality of the nuclear issue within it.

In light of the evolving nuclear challenge, whether the two-decade-old Bangkok Treaty provides the best foundation for strengthened nuclear order in Southeast Asia remains to be seen. As discussed in chapter 2, nuclear-weapon-free zones have significant limitations that echo those of the Nuclear Non-Proliferation Treaty (NPT). This is especially evident in a region in which the greatest challenges will likely center on nonstate actors. This chapter then engages in an analysis of the treaty and beyond. Drawing from the toolkit of institutional theory, it begins by assessing existing security institutions in Southeast Asia, drawing links between their development and broader patterns in regionalism. There is particular attention on the evolution of ASEAN in the post–Cold War period, as the chapter highlights the promise of the association as well as its myriad contradictions and obstacles—including competing East Asian and Asia Pacific regionalisms. In this context, it evaluates the place of nuclear issues in the existing order and the viability of the SEANWFZ in addressing identified challenges. The chapter concludes by sketching out a vision for the likely evolution of nuclear order in Southeast Asia—of broad-based cooperation in nuclear security, safety, and nonproliferation.

ASEAN AND SECURITY REGIONALISM

At the time ASEAN was inaugurated in 1967, the arrangement was decidedly subregional in nature. Indonesia, the Philippines, Malaysia, Singapore, and Thailand were linked by their noncommunist regimes and free-market orientations. Only with membership expansion in the 1990s did ASEAN—which by then included Brunei Darussalam as well—become inextricably linked to the whole of Southeast Asia, as Vietnam, Laos, Burma, and Cambodia all joined between 1995 and 1999.[5] This expansion period came as a product of a shifting strategic landscape. The resolution of the situation in Cambodia in particular led to the inclusion of broader regional political and security assessments in the ASEAN Ministerial Meetings.[6] During this time, the association sought to move away from its foundational purpose of "fostering regional autonomy and avoiding external intervention" to actively creating a unified society.[7] This marked a philosophical shift from the prescribed "continuation of cooperation [in security matters] on a non-ASEAN basis" outlined in the 1976 Bali Concord.[8]

The uncertain environment in the immediate post–Cold War era gave ASEAN a major push in its evolution. A number of external powers, notably the United States, Australia, and Canada, made calls for a regional security forum across the Asia Pacific. Fearing the possibility of marginalization, ASEAN member states moved quickly to seize the process.[9] A steady diet of security discussions across ministerial and postministerial conferences in the early 1990s culminated with the establishment of the ARF in 1994. Still, this was a modest endeavor, as the forum was to be inclusive, "informal, without an intervening bureaucracy, and built on personal and political relationships."[10] Far from cooperative security or a military pact, the ARF aimed only to build mutual confidence, foster dialogue and consultation, and emphasize areas of common interest rather than resolve controversial issues.[11] The expansion of ASEAN into security matters was a measured toe in the water, prioritizing norm development and practice, thus ensuring the continuity of its core principles.

The Bangkok Treaty

The withdrawal of global powers from the region also allowed the states of Southeast Asia to resume a goal long put on hold. The height of the Cold War had contributed to several false starts in the implementation of the 1971 Declaration of Zone of Peace, Freedom and Neutrality and its centerpiece nuclear-weapons-free zone. The aforementioned agenda expansion in ASEAN that began in the late 1980s finally opened the path for the adoption of an encompassing Programme for Action at the 1987 Third ASEAN Summit Meeting to this end.[12] The nuclear issue became a point of emphasis in the post–Cold War era as ASEAN contemplated extending its reach into security affairs. Indeed, the Chairman's Statement at the very first ARF meeting in 1994 listed nuclear nonproliferation measures as a subject necessitating further study.[13] Continued negotiations by an ASEAN working group resulted in the signing of the Bangkok Treaty in December 1995 and its entry into force in 1997.

As with the ARF, the Bangkok Treaty was a manifestation of the ASEAN way. This was evident even in the very boundaries of the applicable zone. The SEANWFZ was the first to include the continental shelves and exclusive economic zones of states parties, thus extending the areas outlined in the Latin America and South Pacific treaties, and representing a nod to the import of sovereignty and territorial integrity outlined in the 1976 Treaty of Amity and Cooperation.[14] The change appeared also to be a defiant response to China's claim to territories in the South China Sea, a particular point of contention for ASEAN states.[15] Another unique aspect of the treaty underlined the reach of the zone of applicability. For the first time, a nuclear-weapon-free zone recommended punitive action should the five legally recognized nuclear-armed states violate their obligations specified in their separate protocol.[16] This was a clear effort on part of the ASEAN states to exert their presence and stature through the treaty.

Most of the obligations in the Bangkok Treaty echoed its predecessors in Latin America and the South Pacific. Still, principles of sovereignty and noninterference that define the ASEAN way thoroughly permeated this early manifestation of regional nuclear order too. This was a process of translation—outlined in institutional theory, with larger cultural-cognitive principles filtered in a manner palatable to the local context.[17] The treaty's sole structural feature, the SEANWFZ Commission, would be composed of foreign ministers and meet in conjunction with the ASEAN Ministerial Meetings.[18] The treaty text emphasizes dialogue in lieu of formal enforcement mechanisms. In fact, states are largely afforded the opportunity only to gain more information: access to International Atomic Energy Agency (IAEA) assessments, requests for clarification about ambiguous situations, requests for fact-finding missions.[19] The dispute settlement process even includes as a last resort arbitration and consultation with the International Court of Justice.[20] The primacy of sovereignty reveals the clear impact of a set of norms that limited the means and manners of interactions—lessening formality and opportunities for confrontation—accepted under ASEAN auspices.[21]

ASEAN Vision 2020

The entry into force of the nuclear-weapon-free zone in Southeast Asia marked a pivotal step in the realization of the 1971 Declaration of Zone of Peace, Freedom and Neutrality. However, the 1997 Asian currency crisis dealt a major blow to ASEAN, undermining members' confidence in the arrangement and calling attention to shortcomings in a foundational issue area, economic development.[22] Leaders responded by articulating an ambitious plan toward formalization, advancing a more coherent and encompassing vision of community. The ASEAN Vision 2020 depicted a true concert, "outward looking, living in peace, stability and prosperity, bonded together in partnership in dynamic development and in a community of caring societies."[23] The 1998 Hanoi Plan of Action elaborated further, setting a six-year timeframe for action.[24] It sought to build regional peace and security via cooperation and technical assistance and even espoused strengthened integration. Much of its focus was on economic cooperation, though its specification of information technology infrastructure and environmental development hinted at a broader scope.

In accordance with its 2020 Vision, ASEAN member states put into place a number of instruments for crisis management. Still, many of these security measures lacked accompanying institutions or enforcement mechanisms, limiting their impact.[25] The 1997 Regional Haze Action Plan moved to improve national and regional firefighting and monitoring capabilities. Sparked by economic crisis, ASEAN Plus Three held informal meetings beginning that same year and officially formed in 1999; members sought to raise levels of intraregional trade and investment.[26] In 2001, ASEAN states adopted Rules of Procedure for dispute settlements. And following the September 11, 2001, terrorist attacks in the United States, ASEAN adopted a Declaration on Joint Action to Counter Terrorism, calling for greater coordination, intelligence exchange, and sharing of best practices. Several states signed the 2002 Agreement on Information Exchange and Establishment of Communication Procedures to combat transnational crime, as Malaysia also founded the Regional Counter-Terrorism Centre. Overall, there was a "strategic redefinition of the existing ASEAN institution . . . a case of institutional conversion."[27]

The ASEAN Vision 2020 truly crystallized in 2003. The drive for an ASEAN concert came to include the notion of a security community, replacing the aforementioned scattershot effort that largely featured ad hoc measures in disparate issue areas. In contrast, the Declaration of ASEAN Concord II (also known as the Bali Concord II) specified the goal of a community built upon three pillars: political and security cooperation, economic cooperation, and sociocultural cooperation. Security for the first time was expressly placed front and center, with a new "principle of comprehensive security" that took into account political, economic, and sociocultural elements.[28] The signing of the concord by the entirety of ASEAN lent formality and legitimacy to the new multidimensional nature of regionalism. The Vientiane Action Programme for 2004–2010—the successor to the Hanoi Plan of Action—honed ASEAN's focus on nontraditional security areas, listing five areas necessary for a true security community: (1) political development, (2) shaping and sharing of norms, (3) conflict prevention, (4) conflict resolution, and (5) postconflict peace building.[29] This period thus marked a fleshed-out and reoriented ASEAN.

Toward an ASEAN Security Community

If the Bali Concord II provided a new blueprint for regionalism for the states of Southeast Asia, what followed was an incremental layering atop it. The 2006 establishment of the ADMM represented a pivotal first step toward the realization of the ASEAN Security Community. Building upon the Vientiane Action Programme, the ADMM provided a regularized forum for defense officials to discuss transnational and nontraditional challenges. The prominence of these issues in the globalized world resulted in an expansive agenda, as the first ADMM discussed disaster prevention in the context of the avian flu, nonproliferation with attention to the Korean Peninsula, and issues of longstanding concern such as maritime security, terrorism, and human and drug trafficking.[30] At their second meeting, the defense ministers declared their intention to strengthen security cooperation through "cooperative activities such as seminars, workshops, training and exercises."[31] It was a decidedly practical and hands-on approach.

The establishment of the ADMM thus ushered in a process of security institutionalization. Concerns common among member states on proliferation, piracy, pandemics, and trafficking created an opening in which the newest regional forum inserted itself. ASEAN's leadership grew further amid a backdrop of intensified great power rivalry, with its role at the forefront accepted as the least objectionable outcome by involved parties. The notion of ASEAN centrality in a more inclusive Asia Pacific security order took shape with the 2005 establishment of the East Asia Summit, intended as the next step in the evolution of the ASEAN Plus Three into a holistic regional body.[32] Reiterating the lofty goals set forth in the Bali Concord II, the summit was to be "a forum for dialogue on broad strategic, political and economic issues of common interest and concern."[33]

The 2007 ASEAN Charter marked the further institutionalization of the association, with the formalization of rules, principles, and workings lending it a more coherent "legal personality. . . [and] formal decision-making capacity and contracting capacity in the international arena."[34] The charter strengthened the office of the secretary-general and the secretariat, while establishing a Committee of Permanent Representatives and Sectoral Ministerial Bodies for each of its three communities. The twelfth ASEAN Summit that produced the charter also moved up the timeline for establishment of the ASEAN Community to 2015.[35] The deepening imprint of ASEAN came amid a shifting security landscape, with territorial disputes in the South China Sea occurring with greater frequency.[36] ASEAN states responded by expanding the East Asia Summit to include the United States and Russia as means of balancing against China's aggressive posturing. In addition, the ADMM spawned an ADMM-Plus process, consisting of Experts' Working Groups to facilitate cooperation in maritime security, counterterrorism, humanitarian assistance and disaster management, peacekeeping operations, and military medicine.

The Limits of ASEAN

Despite the presence of so many security institutions coalesced around ASEAN, however, there remains debate about the efficacy of those entities and questions about whether they can evolve into something more comprehensive and permanent. That the memberships of the various forums often do not overlap—

with varying levels of inclusion of the greater Asia Pacific—has prevented the emergence of a more cohesive security community. This is an outcome of the piecemeal manner in which these institutions emerged. Indeed, some argue that ASEAN has acted primarily to preempt the imposition of great power-dominated structures, rather than in service of a coherent vision.[37] The dominance of the ASEAN way has also provided significant challenges. For example, the ARF contains an emphasis on information over legality and lacks any sort of enforcement mechanisms. In the same vein, the oft-criticized East Asia Summit is "reflective of the ambiguous nature of many existing East Asian linkages . . . [with] no painful commitments, no explicit rules, and no particular institutions."[38]

The primary obstacles to the realization of a true ASEAN Political-Security Community—and to stronger regional nuclear order—relate to the uneasy juxtaposition between its founding principles and its post–Cold War membership expansion. The inclusion of nondemocratic countries has at times affected ASEAN unity for the worse, rendering consensus decision making and dialogue mechanisms exercises in futility.[39] The mixture of regime types has also been a hindrance even beyond intraregional relations: Myanmar's status was seen as detrimental at the global level, undermining the democratic values and human rights espoused in the ASEAN Charter.[40] It remains to be seen whether the country's reform efforts from 2011 to 2015 will stick. Meanwhile, that ASEAN-led initiatives have been widely accepted by the international community can belie the reasons why this is the case. The group of small and middle powers lacks strong leadership, lacks international clout, and is seen as generally harmless. For some, then, ASEAN has constructed a regional order built upon the least common denominator.[41] The process of creating a political-security community is thus challenged by the inherent limitations of the association.

SOUTHEAST ASIAN REGIONALISMS

As the above overview and analysis demonstrates, ASEAN's domination of the political landscape in Southeast Asia is misleading in several ways. First, its construction of regional security order is significantly limited by its norms and core principles. Cooperation has primarily taken place in nontraditional areas, stressing dialogue and collegiality over legality and enforcement. Second, its involvement in leading or inspiring a number of venues suggests a more unified security vision than what actually exists. On the contrary, its security community remains an abstract ideal, and the diversification of venues reflects contending notions of what security regionalism in Southeast Asia would entail. Third, and interrelated, the well-delineated and coherent region hinted at by Vision 2020 again belies reality. Southeast Asia is too often entangled in competing images of regionalism and regional order, from that involving the entirety of the Asia Pacific to that specifying the East Asian subunit. It stands as a common battleground for great power politics, as suggested by the spectrum of security institutions. These have had negative influences on the region's notion of common identity. This chapter therefore turns next to the complex regionalisms that involve Southeast Asia.

Economic Regionalisms

A crisis in Cambodia in the 1980s provided a critical juncture that propelled political and security concerns to the forefront of the ASEAN agenda.[42] This shift severely challenged member states' commitment to the association's defining principles of restraint and noninterference, setting the tone for a debate that continues to this day. In the absence of a comparable seminal moment in the economic sphere, ASEAN member states kept to the status quo during that period, focusing primarily on development goals. Indeed, states gave preference to strengthening trade and investment ties with the outside world, with regional integration seen to "discriminate against more efficient non-regional producers and thus undermine the competitiveness of ASEAN economies in world markets."[43] Initiatives for economic cooperation in the 1970s and 1980s—including a 1977 preferential trade arrangement—failed to gain strength, with intra-ASEAN trade settling at around 16 percent of total ASEAN trade.[44] Any efforts to establish a trade bloc among states were further stalled by the opposition of the United States, the biggest importer of goods from East Asia.[45]

A push for economic regionalism did not emerge until the end of the Cold War. This came due to the shifting orientation of ASEAN economies, stunted progress in the Uruguay Round of the General Agreement on Tariffs and Trade talks (charted in chapter 3), and corresponding proliferation of preferential trade agreements and free trade areas elsewhere in the world (as discussed in chapter 3). The promise of the region now inspired a rush toward integration; that ASEAN did not have a head start resulted in a process notable for "not only its diversity and overlapping nature, but the fact that these [regionalism] projects delineate at least three distinct configurations of region."[46] An initial foray took shape with the 1989 establishment of the Asia-Pacific Economic Cooperation (APEC). While the Southeast Asian nations, fearful of Western dominance, initially expressed reservations regarding the arrangement, they ultimately joined, making a strategic decision to preserve access to the U.S. market under its umbrella. Notably however, they would later create an East Asia Economic Caucus within APEC.

If APEC represented a loose, "open" regionalism that prioritized general cooperation and the removal of barriers over subunit protectionism against external competitors, then the 1992 Framework Agreement on Enhancing ASEAN Economic Cooperation represented a more traditional—and exclusive—approach to economic regionalism. The agreement set forth a fifteen-year process for the establishment of the ASEAN Free Trade Area, centering on a Common Effective Preferential Tariff scheme that would progressively reduce tariffs on intra-ASEAN trade. It called for cooperation across a number of specific sectors, from industry to finance to food and agriculture.[47] The target tariff level of 0 to 5 percent was advanced from the original 2008 deadline to 2003 and then 2002; intraregional trade increased from about 19 percent before the agreement to 25 thereafter.[48] The rapid pace of success of the ASEAN Free Trade Area resulted in the ASEAN Economic Community, which targeted regionalized services and investments and a more integrated market.

Economic regionalism took on even greater expediency following the 1997–98 Asian Financial Crisis that originated in Thailand, which demonstrated the severe shortcomings of ASEAN resources and institutions in the face of global volatility. A third configuration of regionalism followed, marked by the strengthening of the East Asian grouping via the ASEAN Plus Three (with China, Japan, and South Korea). This marked a revitalization of a push for East Asian cooperation linked to the East Asia Economic Caucus, which had been undercut by the surrounding APEC environment.[49] What drove APT was Beijing's particular eagerness to access the Southeast Asian economies, with regular meetings among finance, economic, and labor ministers, among others. One outcome from the process was the Chiang Mai Initiative, a currency swap arrangement that would also provide a pool of foreign exchange reserves: the specific amount expanded from its original $78 billion to $240 billion in 2012 and eventually transformed from swap networks into a single agreement in 2009—becoming the Chiang Mai Initiative Multilateralization.[50]

Identity Crisis

The concurrent origins of distinct yet overlapping regionalisms involving Southeast Asia—one centering on ASEAN, one involving the larger East Asia region, and one including the whole of the Asia Pacific—are thus quite apparent in the economic sphere, a product of history and circumstance. ASEAN's considerable ambition toward a greater global role is tempered by the fact that its internal unity is often called into question.[51] As suggested earlier, this dates back to its post–Cold War expansion, which resulted in a grouping with increasing political, economic, and social diversity. That membership expansion came without clear common admission criteria (beyond geographical placement) underlines the ultimate contradiction of the association. After all, ASEAN is centered on principles of noninterference and sovereignty, emphases on dialogue and informality, and lack of discrimination on the basis of regime type, development level, and so forth. Its strength is thus simultaneously its weakness, with states reluctant to centralize further, enact any institutional hierarchy, or introduce core leadership—traits that might have monopolized regionalism around the ASEAN core. Instead, the ASEAN way not only fosters internal competition but also opened the door for the aforementioned competing regionalisms.

The origins of East Asian regionalism in fact long predated Beijing's advances in the aftermath of the Asian Financial Crisis. Japan and South Korea had made similar proposals for a common market in the 1970s and 1980s, though those were rejected by ASEAN members. Still, the lack of an economic process prior to the late 1990s should not obscure the camaraderie that existed among East Asian nations, one linked to their role "on the frontlines of the Cold War" as the Korean and Vietnam Wars raged.[52] Indeed, Japanese militarism from the 1930s and 1940s, subsequent economic and social upheavals during World War II, and respondent nationalism in the postwar years imparted upon the grouping of states a common sense of historical experience—and identity.[53] With the East Asian "miracle" involving Japan and the four tigers—Hong Kong, Taiwan, South Korea, and Singapore—entailing greater flows of aid and development to Southeast Asia, states there deepened their ties even without moves toward economic regionalism or political integration. The financial crisis thus solidified a long-dormant common regional identity. Not only were East Asian nations forced to act collaboratively in its aftermath, but they developed a common resentment over the lack of Western intervention on their behalf.[54]

Still, China's successful push for APT in the 1990s reflects not only a burgeoning East Asian identity but also global politics in play. The push and pull of Asia Pacific regionalism is a process that underscores the degree to which Southeast Asia remains subject to broader geopolitical machinations. Even Japan's acquiescence to the forum revealed the competitive aspect of regionalisms, as its leaders perceived they could not afford to be left on the sidelines. APT's enrichment into political and security issues over its existence has come to reflect a decidedly Chinese vision of unity that marginalizes the role of the United States.[55] In response, the United States and its allies have bolstered venues such as the APEC and the East Asia Summit, both of which allow a more open regionalism with prominent roles for the United States (while including Russia among their memberships as well). It is these dynamics, especially bare in the economic sphere, that also help explain the limited progress toward an exclusively Southeast Asian security order. These then are the complex dynamics in which Southeast Asian states are intertwined: the grouping's defiance and efforts to control its destiny manifested in ASEAN, the association's underlying principles and limited resources undermining its self-sufficiency, and its value as a growth sector attracting the presence of great powers.

THE NUCLEAR ISSUE

As posited, the development of institutional architecture in Southeast Asia reflects the presence of competing regionalisms, sparked by an ASEAN that is limited by design. The defining traits of the association also contribute to the fact that venues such as the ARF, the ADMM-Plus, and ASEAN itself remain works in progress even in an altered post–Cold War environment, largely centering on confidence building and joint exercises in nontraditional areas. Overall, "diplomats [continue to] struggle to discuss hard security issues."[56] Visions of a security community appear entirely aspirational, and progress toward the political and security pillar of the Bali Concord II lags far behind the others. Even as some officials declare that they have fully implemented the ASEAN Political-Security Community Blueprint for 2015, such roadmaps appear increasingly more as time markers than any true barometers of substantive progress; indeed, parties have shifted their attention to a blueprint for the next decade.[57]

The messiness of identity and regionalism processes in Southeast Asia has obvious ramifications for the nuclear issue. Competing regionalisms create potential divergence both in the manner in which nuclear threats are defined and in the means through which states seek to address them. For instance, an ASEAN that recedes into the background as the United States takes institutional helm of the Asia Pacific is likely to be held hostage by great power politics. Its nuclear agenda would be overrun by immediate concerns, in particular the North Korean nuclear weapons program and China's modernization plans. In contrast, an ASEAN that deepens ties with the Plus Three, for instance, through enhanced economic cooperation such as the proposed strengthening of existing free trade agreements, would drift toward a more distinctly East Asian order. The resulting order—composed of states all seeking to develop or expand civilian nuclear energy programs—would likely place greater emphasis on nuclear safety and security concerns.[58] Finally, an ASEAN that reimagines and redefines itself to maintain centrality would upend the existing landscape, accelerating nuclear energy development, perhaps even considering weapons programs should provocations in the South China Sea persist.

Nuclear proliferation is not an issue readily linked to Southeast Asia. For at least another half decade, the region will be wholly devoid of nuclear energy programs, let alone nuclear weapons programs. Still, the region is intimately connected to innumerable facets of the global nuclear threat, including trafficking, safety, and security. It stands near the frontlines of a number of rivalries featuring nuclear-armed states, including India, Pakistan, China, and the United States. By virtue of its geopolitics and economics, because of the perceived value of its location, standing, and potential, the future of the global nuclear nonproliferation regime will require greater involvement on the part of ASEAN member states. That security regionalism has been steadily creeping in is indicative of a process that will be echoed in the nuclear arena. Yet, the struggles of the former—with competing and sometimes overlapping definitions, visions, and priorities—seem to portend similar growing pains in the latter. The final section of this chapter examines in depth the future of a strengthened nuclear order in Southeast Asia. It begins with an assessment of the structure in place.

Revisiting Bangkok

The contributions of the Bangkok Treaty to a functioning nuclear order in Southeast Asia should not be ignored. Yet paradoxically, it is arguably the presence of the treaty that has stagnated further nuclear nonproliferation progress, distracting its states—and lulling them into a false sense of security—as the nuclear threat continues to evolve. Much of the dialogue in and around the nuclear-weapon-free zone in place has involved ASEAN seeking to persuade the five recognized nuclear weapon states to accede to their separate protocol. Yet, this appears as a futile mission: the United States and France remain staunchly opposed to the provision of legally binding negative security assurances, while the United States has also expressed concerns with the expanded geographic zone of application that includes continental shelves and exclusive economic zones.[59] Perhaps more problematic from the perspective of regional nuclear order is that the substantive content of the twenty-year-old treaty appears increasingly anachronistic.

Fundamentally, the SEANWFZ remains tethered to the Nuclear Non-Proliferation Treaty and the IAEA. As the Southeast Asian nations are all party to the NPT, with comprehensive safeguards agreements in place, the zone derives value largely symbolically, which makes the lack of support from the nuclear weapon states more striking. As detailed in chapter 2, the post–Cold War era has also exposed the limitations of the existing NPT regime. Yet, the SEANWFZ is problematic in manners unique even among nuclear-weapon-free zones. For starters, the text details a ban against nuclear weapons but lacks the "unassembled or partly assembled forms" clause present in the 1985 Treaty of Rarotonga.[60] The treaty does not expressly prohibit the manufacture of some nuclear-related components, nor research on weapons acquisition.[61] The lack of precision in the text thus provides clear loopholes even for states parties. In addition, the deference to state sovereignty weakens the zone's foundation. As discussed, the SEANWFZ lacks a permanent secretariat, while its attached commission does not function on its own. Questions about compliance would elicit only "fact-finding missions" from the IAEA, lacking the kind of force and authority that would be inherent in special inspections from an ASEAN committee, for instance.[62]

As suggested earlier in this chapter, the shortcomings of the SEANWFZ as a foundation for strengthened nuclear order are further exacerbated by the nature of threats in the region. The NPT-IAEA system is state oriented, with an emphasis on preventing diversion of nuclear materials from peaceful nuclear energy programs to weapons usage. The Bangkok Treaty is directed similarly. But while this proliferation pathway is one that will become relevant for the states developing energy programs (Indonesia and Malaysia), it represents just one possibility in the region. The involvement of nonstate actors is a consideration that Southeast Asian nations have to be acutely aware of, given the presence of terrorist groups, high levels of illicit trafficking, and the historical use of those channels by the A. Q. Khan network. That the nuclear-weapon-free zone was never designed for these alternative possibilities and devotes just scant attention to issues of nuclear safety suggest the need for complementary action in Southeast Asia moving forward.[63]

Regime Participation

Apart from the Bangkok Treaty, the overall level of nuclear cooperation exclusive to Southeast Asia is limited. States have demonstrated a preference for voluntary national implementation of existing international standards, an unideal stance given already modest levels of participation in multilateral regimes. For instance, while all Southeast Asian countries are party to the NPT, only five have entered Additional Protocols into force.[64] Especially alarming is the reluctance of states to engage the nascent nuclear security structure and to implement initiatives that target the proliferating role of nonstate actors. After all, this is an area where Southeast Asian involvement is critical for the whole of global nuclear order. Yet, Indonesia, Laos, Myanmar, and East Timor have abstained from the U.S.-led Proliferation Security Initiative; Brunei, Cambodia, Laos, Myanmar, and East Timor have been absent from the three Nuclear Security Summits convened. While all except East Timor have submitted national reports in accordance with UN Security Council Resolution 1540, just two—the Philippines and Singapore—have submitted updates past 2008.[65] Significantly, the submission of reports does not even indicate the presence or quality of enacted legislation.

The multifaceted nature of regionalism in Southeast Asia has fostered the emergence of other forms of nuclear cooperation, including in the areas of nuclear security and nonproliferation. A number of states participate in the Asia-Pacific Safeguards Network, the Forum for Nuclear Cooperation in Northeast Asia, and the Regional Radiological Security Partnership, for starters. The practical utility of these confidence-building measures should not be overlooked. At the same time, each of these arrangements are of an informal character, with no binding obligations or political commitments attached. It is precisely their emphasis on dialogue that attracts the small group of Southeast Asian states that participate. The disparate nature of these networks—including distinct memberships—further hinders the possibility of broadening their scope into a stronger regional nuclear order. Overall then, proliferation concerns are simply "not yet seen as pressing issues for the region."[66] Issues surrounding WMD remain ill-defined, secondary to developments in domestic politics and economics. This lack of perceived importance, and subsequently of a need for action above the level of the state, is especially harmful given the already understaffed secretariat and circumscribed agenda of ASEAN.

A Safety-Based Order

While progress in nuclear security and nonproliferation are lagging in Southeast Asia, the idea for establishing an atomic energy community in the vein of Euratom has come into fruition in the context of ASEAN Community discussions. First proposed in 2011 at the International Conference on Safety, Security, and Safeguards in Nuclear Energy in Bangkok, the ASEAN Network of Regulatory Bodies on Atomic Energy (ASEANTOM) held its first meeting in 2013. This was a uniquely Southeast Asian initiative. Notably, participants expressly cited that the main purpose of the network was not to support SEANWFZ.[67] Rather, citing the increased nuclear and radiation utilization across the region, the network aimed to enable the regular exchange of information and experience among members, while developing domestic capacities across the spectrum of the nuclear arena. In addition to presenting a standalone forum for regular meetings, that ASEANTOM included an action plan with twenty-two fields of activity rendered it the most significant form of regional nuclear cooperation within Southeast Asia since the Bangkok Treaty.[68]

ASEANTOM remains a "fledging operation," one viewed primarily as a complement to existing bilateral partnerships with the IAEA.[69] Still, one cannot understate the importance of continued technical and regulatory cooperation at the regional level, in a regularized forum. Southeast Asian nations have demonstrated a consistent willingness to engage safety-based cooperative mechanisms, especially in comparison to nonproliferation and security arrangements. That an exclusively Southeast Asian network came about thusly should not come as a surprise. In fact, it is precisely the nuclear safety issue that offers a realistic base for strengthened regional nuclear order. Taking into account ASEANTOM and other institutions such as the Asian Nuclear Safety Network, there exists clear agreement among states regarding the importance of energy and economic security in the region. After all, the current rate of development across the whole of the Asia Pacific has significant implications for energy consumption, while the lack of fossil fuel reserves renders the nuclear option vital.[70] As these countries look to engage the global market for nuclear trade, concerns about safety, security, and safeguards will manifest and become intertwined. After all, "in order to be seen as a responsible trading partner and party to technical cooperation," states will alter their behavior accordingly, conforming to international standards.[71]

Indeed, ASEANTOM provides a tantalizing glimpse of the potential for strengthened regional nuclear order in Southeast Asia. It was even designated as a sectoral body of the ASEAN Political-Security Community in December 2015, reflecting both the evolution of the definition of the nuclear issue in the region and the ambitious vision for the future of the body. While its activities have heretofore been largely technical and informal, the aforementioned action plan expresses a more ambitious agenda in the sharing of best practices, mutual exchange of information, domestic capacity building, and so forth. As the network itself develops capacity, it is not unreasonable to expect cooperation to take on more formalized shape. Meanwhile, global trends linking safety and security to nonproliferation could expand ASEANTOM's substantive agenda, especially with the impending context of nuclear energy programs in the region. That is a key moment that could provide the impetus for ASEANTOM to evolve beyond its technical and facilitating origins into a more centralized political forum. A Euratom-like mandate over the nuclear sector is extremely unlikely; yet, ASEAN member states will have incentive to maintain regional unity in negotiating agreements with third parties. It is this pathway—a manifestation of ASEAN's multitude of goals, including economic development, protection of sovereignty, and pushback against outside powers—that could necessitate a shift in ASEANTOM, propelling a more comprehensive regional nuclear order.

A safety-based nuclear order represents a feasible outcome in Southeast Asia precisely because it dovetails into the ASEAN way. The nuclear security structure in particular has been dominated by the West and especially by the United States, while the two-class system of the NPT has been a longstanding point of contention, even coloring the Bangkok Treaty. For ASEAN states, as well as the Non-Aligned Movement and the Global South, the existing global nuclear order often appears as an extension of Western power. Southeast Asian states, largely removed from immediate nuclear threats, rarely feel directly invested in border and export controls, for instance, perceiving these primarily as infringements on their sovereignty. In contrast, energy security affects developing economies more directly, as evidenced by the establishment of ASEANTOM within the confines of the ASEAN Community. As suggested, a safety-based order could eventually and organically envelop other nuclear threats, leading to the internalization of relevant norms and standards, then perhaps projecting outward into more formal implementation thereof.[72] Such a process could develop alongside the nuclear energy sector within Southeast Asia. It would also be received far better than any externally-imposed mechanisms.

CONCLUSION: ORDER THE ASEAN WAY

While there exists a nuclear-weapon-free zone in Southeast Asia, one would be hard-pressed to argue that the Bangkok Treaty as constituted can remain the vanguard of regional nuclear order. It was established amid a perfect storm of conditions: the resolution of the conflict in Cambodia, the corresponding expansion of ASEAN, the post–Cold War push for global nuclear disarmament. But the passive order, fundamentally dependent on ASEAN Ministerial Meetings, is ill-suited to address the spectrum of challenges that decorate the nuclear landscape. The treaty contains a number of loopholes, has failed to elicit support from the nuclear weapon states, and has little to say about the issues and actors most pertinent to its jurisdiction. The future of global nuclear nonproliferation requires more regional activity from the states of Southeast Asia. Not only is the area home to maritime transportation channels that have already proven critical for the nuclear black market, but its nascent nuclear energy programs will emerge in an environment marked by domestic instability and regional tension. The commitment to safety, security, and safeguards in Indonesia and Malaysia (and Vietnam, should it resume development) will have reverberations far beyond those countries.

At the same time, there is no discussion of regional nuclear order in Southeast Asia without accounting for the encompassing shadow cast by ASEAN. The association has dictated the character of almost every multilateral cooperative mechanism in the region to date; its members harbor a deep-seated distrust of alternative, non-ASEAN venues. Additionally, ASEAN has already set forth a coherent vision for a security community. Fundamental structural change thus appears unlikely. The economic realm provides an instructive case of the stability of these perpetually competing regionalisms, with incremental movement that never quite upends the status quo. Even a drastic transformation of the security environment—for instance, in the South China Sea—is unlikely to elicit institutional change given the relative power status of member states, the varied memberships, and the particular histories of the states involved. It is therefore within the ASEAN context that nuclear order in Southeast Asia has developed to date and will have to develop in the future.

Because nuclear nonproliferation and security concerns inherently challenge the ASEAN way, a strengthened regional nuclear order in Southeast Asia must come from alternative means. This chapter has posited that the process must come internally, via the issue of nuclear safety. Economic security already enjoys consensus at the top of both domestic and regional agendas, and the development of nuclear energy sources will be key to sustaining development rates. In turn, it is through the energy issue that ASEAN members have engaged and will engage international standards. Thus far, this has taken place chiefly with nuclear safety: the development of ASEANTOM was a watershed moment. But the interconnectedness of the nuclear issue will force Southeast Asian nations to further their regional cooperation. Nuclear energy is not only critical as a means to a stronger regional nuclear order in Southeast Asia but may provide the very foundation for a genuine ASEAN Political-Security Community—a possibility recognized by member states themselves.

CHAPTER 7

The Middle East

The geopolitics of the Middle East has experienced drastic change in these early stages of the twenty-first century. The American invasion and occupation of Iraq, the Arab Spring and subsequent Arab Winter, and civil wars in Syria and Yemen have contributed to the upending of regional order. To date, this has taken shape with the remarkable rise of Islamist movements and a corresponding marginalization of the influence of foreign countries, in particular the United States and other Western powers. Meanwhile, the Westphalian notion of sovereignty is being challenged by the rise of the jihadist group Islamic State and the caliphate it pursues. The full impact of these events for the region is yet to be determined. Still, it is abundantly clear that "the old paradigm of the Middle East has been shaken and, in many cases, has fallen down."[1]

Against the backdrop of political and security upheaval remains the ever-present specter of the nuclear threat. It is true that the 2015 Joint Comprehensive Plan of Action (JCPOA) negotiated by the P5+1 (the five permanent members of the United Nations Security Council—the United States, United Kingdom, Russia, France, and China—and Germany) with Iran marks one of the biggest diplomatic victories for the global regime centered on the Nuclear Non-Proliferation Treaty (NPT) in recent memory. Yet a number of states in the region and beyond continue to watch the implementation of the deal with wary eyes. Israel's nuclear program is another persistent concern, exacerbated by the ratcheting of tension across its affairs, manifested in its outspoken criticism of developments related to the Arab Spring and intensified conflict in the occupied Palestinian territories. Meanwhile, that the Islamic State has demonstrated a willingness to utilize chemical weapons and expressed a desire to acquire nuclear weapons could present the greatest immediate concern to the security landscape of the Middle East.

CHAPTER OVERVIEW

Despite the vast uncertainty engulfing the region, it would be remiss to presuppose a new Middle East unrelated to all that has come before, to impose a narrative of total geopolitical transformation absent any semblance of continuity. It is undeniable that the region has long resisted any sort of comprehensive economic or political institutions, let alone any sort of durable security order. Still, there exist traces of regionalism, or at least subregionalisms. One prominent example is the Gulf Cooperation Council, with member states in recent years even pushing for a "Gulf Union" as a means to counteract the Shi'ite Muslim influence in the region.[2] In addition, recent years have seen the rise of the Quartet Cooperation Council featuring Turkey, Syria, Jordan, and Lebanon. Mostly, regional dynamics remain dominated by the presence of the Arab League, and "Arabness forms the hegemonic discourse that shapes the international relations of the Middle East."[3]

The first part of this chapter parses processes of subregionalism that contribute to the order present in the Middle East. It considers in particular the degree to which "Arabness" and general identity politics that dominate the region have permeated political and economic relations, as well as the manner in which multilateral entities such as the Arab League have engaged the subnational ethnic and sectarian factionalism, including in the aftermath of the Arab Spring. Next, it examines the impact of those limited regionalisms in the nuclear sphere. After all, it was largely the push of Egypt—on behalf of the League of Arab States—that elevated the proposed WMD-free zone in the Middle East to its place nearly atop the nuclear agenda. What is the shape of existing nuclear cooperation in the Middle East? Is there a place in the nuclear sphere for subregional order, and if so, what form might it take? The final part of this chapter considers in depth the potential impact of the 2015 JCPOA and the overall Iranian situation on strengthened regional nuclear order moving forward.

STUNTED REGIONALISMS

With the onset of the Arab Spring, a number of scholars and analysts have posited the possibility of a brighter future for regional cooperation and institutionalization in the Middle East.[4] In doing so, they attribute the absence of regional order to the stable authoritarian regimes that long dominated the geopolitical landscape. Such inward-looking ruling coalitions were defined by their aversion to the global structure, often building their legitimacy upon a narrative of self-reliance and extreme nationalism.[5] Almost without exception, these regimes were staunch supporters of national sovereignty. Consequently, political coordination took place primarily in the context of personal and informal relations centered on individual leaders. Many governments are characterized by weak and underdeveloped institutional structures as a result.[6] Furthering these challenges to regional political and security order was the presence of foreign powers, as their bilateral alliances with regional states headed off any internally exclusive movement. Accordingly, the shift in these conditions thus presents opportunity for change.

The Economic Challenge

While authoritarianism provides a face to internal intransigence against Middle East regionalism, the foundation of that resistance is linked to the basic economic structure undergirding the region. It may be the case that even political change is a necessary but insufficient condition for strengthened regional order. Indeed, the dispersal of oil created a vast wealth gap between the oil haves and the oil have-nots, contributing to "their disparate and nonintegrated macroeconomic policies" and "a disproportionate dependence on foreign markets for exports" for the first category of states.[7] Oil also contributed to the rentier economic structure of many Middle East economies. The rise of natural resource-dependent revenues has often come alone, with limited productivity and general competitiveness in other sectors such as manufacturing or industry. From 2008 to 2010, manufactured goods and other sectors accounted for only 24 percent of all exports from the region, and only 21 percent of those total exports could be considered medium or high technology.[8] It is the uniformity of these rentier economies—and the absence of complementarity—that contributes directly to stagnation in economic regionalism.

Despite substantial growth in diversification and exports over the last decade, economic integration within the Middle East remains low, as does the region's level of integration with the global economy. Efforts to institutionalize intra-regional economic relationships have not borne fruit. For instance, the Arab Economic Summits have taken little action to achieve a stated desire for an Arab Common Market. Similarly, the 1998 Pan Arab Free Trade Area (also the Great Arab Free Trade Area) aimed to remove formal trade barriers among its then-fourteen members (eighteen as of 2017) but has facilitated negligible activity despite reaching full trade liberalization of goods in 2005, with inner-Arab trade up only to 10 percent in 2010 from 9 percent in 1997.[9] Arrangements among the Arab Maghreb Union, the Gulf Cooperation Council (GCC), and the Agadir Agreement have witnessed similarly glacial movement. Intra-regional trade overall has stayed constant at 6 percent, in stark contrast to levels in the European Union (66 percent), the Association of Southeast Asian Nations (25 percent), and South America's Mercosur (15 percent).[10] With oil and gas excluded, the Middle East's share of the total world export of goods has only reached 1.8 percent, while its total services trade has remained between 2 and 3 percent.[11]

Emergence of Subregionalisms

Pan-Arabism: Despite their shortcomings, the emergence of the aforementioned economic arrangements in the post–Cold War era does reflect the presence of integration processes—however light—among subgroupings of states in the Middle East (and North Africa). This is significant as "the success or the failure of sub-regional processes may be a conditioning factor for processes of regional cooperation or integration."[12] From the lens of this project, such processes may provide an intrinsic foundation for strengthened regional nuclear order as well. The most encompassing of these entities, the League of Arab States, is critical given the fundamental division between Arab and non-Arab states in the region and the considerable size of the former group. As Arab countries share language and history, as well as cultural and religious values, their common identity would appear to provide the Middle East a natural base for integration.[13] Notably, however, the promise of the Arab League in this respect is obscured by its focus on encouraging bilateral relations and alliance building among its members, with little comparable attention on multilateralism.

In fact, the League of Arab States is an entity that rests not on integration but on the notion of "mutually independent, sovereign states."[14] That league decisions require unanimity in decision making provides a barrier not only to greater cooperation but simple institutional growth, defanging it further. Scholars suggest that the prism of sovereignty has contributed to its presence as "a forum of collective legitimation" rather than a true regional organization, with Arab nationalism existing strictly within the framework of statehood—and being subservient to it.[15] Even as governments invoke the ideal of the greater Arab nation, their foreign policies suggest a selfish appropriation of the Arab League. Naturally, every country has developed a different conceptualization of what Arab interest entails. Only in fairly innocuous areas of educational and cultural cooperation has the league been successful in fostering multilateral relations. In economic, political, or military arenas, this has not been the case, as integration by its very nature represents a threat to individual regimes. The emergence of subregionalisms in the Middle East reflects the presence of interstate rivalries and dynamics otherwise messily blanketed by the league.

Gulf Cooperation Council: The most successful subregional arrangement in the Middle East has been the GCC. Its establishment underscored an emerging Gulf identity linked to the fracture of broader pan-Arabism following the Six-Day War and the Camp David Accords of the late 1970s and the assassination of Egyptian president Anwar Sadat in 1981. In contrast to the Arab League, GCC members—Bahrain, Kuwait, Oman, Qatar, Saudi Arabia, and the United Arab Emirates—held commonalities in their compositions far beyond Arab identity. This included their regime types, economic structures, and security environments; in addition, the Saudi Arabia hegemon served as a stabilizing presence.[16] These traits were conducive to progress toward the "coordination, integration, and co-operation" espoused in its charter.[17] The document also set forth an organizational structure, featuring a supreme council composed of annual meetings between the six heads of states (the body also constitutes the dispute settlement commission and contains a consultative commission), a ministerial council convened every three months, and a general secretariat for executive implementation.

The circumstances surrounding the GCC's establishment offer promise—albeit limited—for the possibility of security order in the subregion. After all, common threat perceptions centered on Iran and Iraq pushed ruling elites to jointly enhance their internal security; this took the form of shared operational procedures, training, and military curricula.[18] Still, despite informal discussions, no regional military force emerged—an absence that became glaring as the Iran-Iraq War raged through the 1980s. The oil-centric nature of the respective GCC economies precluded meaningful cooperation on that front as well. Modest trends have been the norm, for instance, with the Gulf Organization for Industrial Consulting, which conducts market research on industrial coordination, and the Monetary Council, established to launch the process toward a still-elusive single currency. Parties have made integrative moves in other fields, with the ease of labor mobility for GCC citizens and regulatory mandates across a number of domains provided by the GCC Standardization Organization. While the council has not sparked deep subregional integration overall, and internal strife colors further progress in that direction, it represents the most significant strand of subregional order in the Middle East.[19]

Arab Maghreb Union and Others: The development of the GCC played no small role in the establishment of the Arab Maghreb Union in 1989. The five North African states—Mauritania, Morocco, Algeria, Tunisia, and Libya—implemented a similar organizational structure that included a presidency council (with attached consultative council), a council of foreign ministers, a court, and a general secretariat. The Arab Maghreb Union's founding treaty targeted four domains for common policies: international affairs, defense, economics, and cultural affairs.[20] But these goals have proven elusive, with progress crippled by the 1994 border closure between Algeria and Morocco. Comprising 77 percent of the subregional population and housing a gross domestic product three times the size of the other members combined, the two countries have essentially held the council hostage.[21] Even the 1994 declaration of a regional free trade zone has not improved intratrade levels beyond 3 percent, a product of "political differences and rivalries, protectionist commercial policies, ineffectiveness of bilateral trade agreements . . . and the [competitive] supply structure of these countries."[22] Cooperation in energy and security matters has similarly failed to spark more than dialogue. As long as Algeria-Morocco relations remain tense, the Arab Maghreb Union will continue to languish.[23]

Other subregional efforts in the Middle East have failed even to match this low bar. This includes the aforementioned Pan Arab Free Trade Area and the Agadir Agreement. Member states of the Economic Cooperation Organisation (founded in 1985 by Iran, Pakistan, and Turkey) have devoted a narrow spotlight to the transport and communications sectors, its Free Trade Agreement (2003) and Trade Promotion Organizations (2009) seeking eventually to create a single market for goods and services. Finally, the 2010 Quartet Cooperation Council represents the most recent subregional initiative, centering on Turkish foreign policy with Syria, Jordan, and Lebanon. Echoing the GCC model, with Turkey a natural fit in the Saudi Arabia role, the parties sought to set up a free trade zone, while encouraging integrative activity in energy, transport, tourism, and the economy. While there have been modest strides—for instance, with a transport ministers' meeting targeting border visa exceptions and the Levant Business Forum engaging the private sphere, the process has been thrown astray by subsequent events across the region.

Dawn of a New Regionalism?

As mentioned, the full consequences of the Arab Spring and subsequent Arab Winter are yet to be determined. Events since 2010 have already demonstrated a profound impact on the regional and subregional arrangements above. In February 2011, the Council of the Arab League suspended Libya's right to participate in its bodies and meetings due to the humanitarian circumstances in that country. A month later, the league issued a resolution calling for UN Security Council action in the form of a no-fly zone. While Arab League states continued to explicitly reject foreign intervention, these actions represented a softening of the noninterference principles long attached to the group.[24] The Syrian example marked an even more radical shift.[25] In a November 2011 resolution, members committed to providing protection for Syrian civilians, including contacting pertinent human rights organizations if necessary.[26] They took action against one of their own by imposing sanctions, calling upon Arab countries to withdraw their ambassadors, and convening opposition forces against the Syrian government. The resolution even suspended the participation of the Syrian government in the league despite a lack of unanimity in the vote.[27] The significance of these events should be not overplayed; after all, the league has acted inconsistently as the Arab Spring unfolded, with double standards apparent on human rights issues, and the less-than-optimal outcomes in the region could be a deterrent for interference in the future. That Saudi Arabia and Qatar spearheaded the action in Syria only reinforces the image of the league as advancing self-interests. A collective sense of purpose or vision remain lacking.[28]

At the same time, the actions of the Arab League provide precedent for it to carve out a more active role moving forward, or for its flexible orientation at a minimum. Arab nationalism has witnessed a clear resurgence in the face of the Islamic State threat. Instability explains moves toward greater unity on the part of the GCC as well, further fueled by concerns about the reliability of the West. Saudi Arabia in particular has been an outspoken voice for cooperation. Parties came together in December 2013 to create a joint military command and police force—a supplement to the Peninsula Shield Force created in 1984 and representing the implementation of a rarely invoked collective security treaty introduced in 1994. Even as the GCC agreed to suppress interference in the domestic affairs of other parties, it also outlined a substantial level of coordination in security, border regulation, and extradition obligations, the final item once a major point of contention for Kuwait. If the economic influence of the six countries ensures the council's presence moving forward, then the persistence of common security concerns could elevate it into a hub for a more expansive political and security order (echoing the process that accompanied the Iran-Iraq conflict of the 1980s). Even prior to the Arab Spring, in fact, the nuclear issue has served as a consistent source of concern—and potential rallying point—for the GCC.

A MIDDLE EAST ZONE

While patterns of regionalism in the Middle East are demonstrably modest, the process has still managed to pervade nuclear politics. This is especially the case with the longstanding push for a nuclear-weapon-free zone. The Middle East proposal was introduced in the UN General Assembly through a resolution cosponsored by Iran and Egypt; it was adopted by consensus in the General Assembly beginning in 1980. There were several reasons for the primarily symbolic move. First, states feared that the conventional wars of the period—many regional in nature and tinged with Cold War tensions—could escalate. This drove an emphasis on regional denuclearization efforts.[29] Second, states perceived nuclear-weapon-free zones as a viable option to improving the nuclear landscape as well as overall security conditions. Even if follow-through action was beyond reach, the perceived power of the gesture was significant.[30] The October 1975 special report requested by the UN General Assembly reinforced the point that these arrangements constituted key supplementary actions to the NPT.[31] Third, the proposal reflected the specific ambitions harbored by the Iranian and Egyptian regimes toward more prominent leadership roles in the region. Indeed, the nuclear-weapon-free zone process would gradually usurp the tension between Arab and non-Arab nations.

Resolution on the Middle East

The winding down of the Cold War had immediate ramifications for progress toward the Middle East nuclear-weapon-free zone. The International Atomic Energy Agency (IAEA) contributed to the process; this was an era of steady growth for the organization. The IAEA General Conference requested a technical study on different modalities of safeguards application in the Middle East, and the resulting 1989 report explicitly suggested the geographical scope of the zone (with Libya, Syria, Iran, and Yemen as its boundaries).[32] The director general then consulted with those states about the viability of safeguards application to relevant facilities. A 1991 IAEA resolution called for states in the region to apply full-scope safeguards as an initial step toward the realization of the zone.[33] It was during this time that the Egyptian president reframed the proposal as a WMD-free zone, following evidence of the existence of chemical and biological weapons in the region.[34] By the time UN Security Council Resolution 687 made demands of the Iraqi government relating to its WMD program following the first Persian Gulf War, the list of actions it outlined was cited as "steps towards the goal of establishing in the Middle East a zone free from weapons of mass destruction"—not just nuclear weapons.[35]

The revitalization of the Israeli-Palestinian peace process with the 1991 Madrid Conference provided an opportunity for the nuclear issue to emerge onto the regional agenda. Besides the bilateral track between Israel and its neighbors as well as with the Palestinian state, there were multilateral negotiations following Madrid that targeted broader regional issues. This resulted in the establishment of a working group of Arms Control and Regional Security (ACRS). Six ACRS plenary sessions were held between May 1992 and December 1994, all chaired by the United States and Russia.[36] Inspired by existing agreements in other regions, discussions centered on potential confidence-building measures in the areas of declaratory measures, communications, maritime agreements, military information exchange, and conflict prevention. The continuing dialogue led Qatar and Tunisia to host the fifth and sixth plenaries, respectively. The ACRS also contributed to the establishment of regional security centers and a regional communications network. However, the process fell by the wayside as peace talks stalled in 1995. The fundamental area of disagreement then, as now, centered on the timing of nuclear disarmament relative to regional security, with Arab states pushing for Israel to disarm, submit its facilities to safeguards, and join the NPT prior to any other action.

Still, given favorable environmental conditions, nuclear order in the Middle East then did not appear as elusive as it does two decades later. The discoveries in Iraq underscored the value of a WMD-free zone to the international community, pushing parties to accelerate that process.[37] Meanwhile, the impending expiration of the NPT in 1995 provided non-nuclear weapon states—Arab League members and Egypt especially—leverage to push their agenda forward. The Review and Extension Conference arrived at a pivotal post–Cold War moment that witnessed significant advancements in the nuclear nonproliferation and disarmament agenda, with the focus on nuclear-weapon-free zones at new heights. Parties noted that such arrangements, "especially in regions of tension, such as the Middle East . . . should be encouraged as a matter of priority."[38] The document that extended the NPT indefinitely noted that the establishment of regional zones prior to the 2000 Review Conference "would be welcome": the first elaboration of a timeframe, however soft, for such action.[39] Most notable was the "Resolution on the Middle East" that specifically called on parties to establish a WMD-free zone prohibiting delivery systems too and urged NPT nonparties in the region to accede to the treaty and accept full-scope IAEA safeguards.

Still, that UN member states felt compelled to adopt a resolution for the endeavor hints both at the weakness of Middle East regionalism and at the complexities surrounding the would-be WMD-free zone. It could be argued that widespread concerns with the Israeli stockpile provided a rallying point for Middle East states in the nuclear arena.[40] Yet convergence on definitions of that issue was far from clear-cut, which fed into (1) overriding political dynamics stemming from the Arab and non-Arab divide, (2) the lack of consensus on proper solutions given Israel's nonparty status in the NPT, and, interrelated, (3) the clash of philosophies regarding the Middle East peace process and the place of the zone therein. The Main Committee II report at the 1995 NPT Review and Extension Conference revealed the heated debate. With bracketed language indicating unresolved issues, it suggested that "current circumstances [[are/could be] conducive to the [early/progress toward] establishment . . . [should Israel adhere to Treaty and place all its nuclear activities under IAEA safeguards] . . .]."[41] Despite political momentum, then, the possibility for a WMD-free zone remained remote, especially given the general unwillingness of NPT parties to endorse subregional maneuvers. It could be argued that the UN resolution even neared infringement on the core principles of local initiation and voluntary participation attributed to nuclear-weapon-free zones, as outlined in 1975.

Revitalized and Ended?

For the Arab states, however, the 1995 resolution at the NPT Review and Extension Conference set high expectations. It suggested a more hands-on approach on the part of the international community, as the specific and extensive text stood in contrast to the lines on regional activity in previous outcome documents. Progress toward the zone resurfaced as an issue at the 2000 NPT Review Conference, with the final document not only reaffirming the ultimate goal but now calling for states to report by the 2005 conference "on the steps that they had taken to promote the achievement of such a zone."[42] This was again symbolic of a trend, as parties also assigned one of the newly established subsidiary bodies to examine regional issues broadly. In 2003, the UN General Assembly adopted a resolution that reiterated the importance of the zone and again pushed for an update on the implementation of the 1995 Resolution on the Middle East.[43] While the failed 2005 NPT Review Conference blunted the institutional momentum for the process, pressure—especially from the Egyptians—mounted.

The 2010 Review Conference of the NPT marked a revitalization of the 1995 resolution. Partly because of the pressure stemming from the failure of 2005, the result was concrete progress toward the WMD-free zone in the Middle East. Again, the final document reinforced the overall value of nuclear-weapon-free zones, referencing efforts in Southeast Asia to strengthen the Bangkok Treaty, recognizing the need for environmental rehabilitation in the context of the Treaty of Semipalatinsk, and commending the results of the first-ever Conference of States Parties and Signatories to Treaties That Establish Nuclear-Weapon-Free Zones.[44] The centrality of regional zones was made explicit. This was especially true with respect to the Middle East, as parties endorsed a series of practical steps aimed at jumpstarting the 1995 resolution. This included the convening of a conference on the issue by 2012, tasked "with a mandate to support [its] implementation."[45] Although no deadline was expressed for a treaty to establish the zone itself, the level of detail provided—on the role of the secretary-general and others, the appointment of a host country and facilitator—marked a pivotal step.

Momentum, however, dissipated as the 2012 deadline came and went. Finnish diplomat and facilitator Jaakko Laajava made some strides, in particular organizing a series of five consultative sessions with Middle East parties beginning in 2013 (though Iran reportedly participated in only one of those meetings) and gaining broad agreement on the conference agenda and its potential modalities. However, the future of Israel's nuclear status remained unresolved, with the United States unwilling to confront its regional ally, despite it being the "core request of . . . the League of Arab States, notably Egypt."[46] The Arab League's dissatisfaction manifested at the 2015 NPT Review Conference, which failed to produce a consensus outcome document largely because of the subject. According to the head of the UK's delegation, "this issue and this issue alone was the stumbling block."[47] As part of a last-minute plan drafted by the Russians (cosponsors of the 1995 resolution), some sought to impose a March 2016 deadline for the Middle East conference. But the United States decried the "arbitrary deadline," while Canada demanded that any negotiations on the issue include

Israel.[48] In the wake of the unsatisfactory outcome that followed, the 1995 resolution and 2010 Action Plan have lost significant luster. The Arab League has even called for a new conference process to emanate from the UN secretary-general, to be bolstered by working groups that would outline geographic demarcation and verification and implementation measures.[49] As the 2020 NPT Review Conference nears, it remains to be seen whether the Middle East zone will garner the same level of attention.

IRAN AND THE WMD LANDSCAPE

As reflected in the long and heretofore unsuccessful campaign for a WMD-free zone, the Israeli nuclear stockpile has consistently proven to be a major obstacle to the furthering of a Middle East nuclear order. There exists a fundamental gap in how parties define the most effective solution: with the Arab states first seeking the denuclearization of the Middle East prior to any further steps toward peace and security, and the Israelis discussing the zone only in the context of (or in the aftermath of) a comprehensive peace agreement that normalizes regional relations. In line with their respective preferences, Egypt and the Arab states have expressed little to no interest in general confidence- and security-building measures, citing perceived military asymmetries intimately linked to the Israeli nuclear program.[50] Yet, the Arab League's firm line can belie the nuances of the security dilemma in the region. That some scholars call for a missile-free zone in parallel with a WMD-free zone suggests a need to consider variables beyond the Israeli stockpile.[51] Fears about Iran's nuclear ambitions stand at the top of that list of "other" pertinent issues.

Iran and Proliferation Sanctions

Indeed, some suggest that Arab League states would place the threat from Iran even atop that of Israel as the most prominent security issue on the regional agenda.[52] Questions surrounding the Iranian nuclear program constitute a "strategic nightmare" for the Jewish state too, and given Tehran's conventional capabilities, the nuclear program represents potentially "the most formidable challenge" to Israel's nuclear deterrence.[53] It is striking that Israeli prime minister Benjamin Netanyahu voiced his adamant opposition to the JCPOA between Iran and the P5+1 long before the agreement was concluded in July 2015, precisely because the plan would not put a permanent end to the country's uranium enrichment activities.[54] The fact that it left the door ajar at all was sufficient cause for Israeli rejection. While many Arab states expressed high hopes for the deal, there was a notable level of apprehension among Gulf states too. Their concerns were intertwined with the impact of sanctions relief on Iran's regional role, with the fear that the country could more rapidly pursue a goal of regional hegemony even without a nuclear weapons program.[55] That there have been consistent voices within Iran against the nuclear deal reaffirms the JCPOA's fragility, especially in light of the decade-long noncompliance saga that preceded the agreement, as well as President Donald J. Trump's frequent and strident opposition to the agreement.

For some outsiders, there is concern that Iran will simply break the terms of the JCPOA. This is a belief that requires putting the agreement—and its impact on nuclear order in the Middle East—in context. After all, the nuclear issue vis-à-vis Iran is entangled in strained relations with the United States, which implemented unilateral sanctions following the 1979 embassy takeover and hostage crisis in Tehran. These measures were expanded through the next decade because of Iran's support for terrorism, narcotics trafficking, and money laundering. WMD proliferation concerns came onto the U.S. agenda in the 1990s; Germany, China, and Argentina, among others, enacted targeted trade restrictions directed at Iran's nuclear sector.[56] But the trajectory of tensions between Iran and the West, and the placement of the nuclear program as the defining component of that relationship, trace to revelations in 2003 of previously undeclared nuclear facilities. An IAEA investigation confirmed the country "failed to meet its obligations . . . [on] reporting of nuclear material."[57] By 2005, the United States escalated with asset freezes and banking restrictions directed at nuclear-related entities and individuals. In December 2006, UN Security Council Resolution 1737 put into place sanctions targeting enrichment activity and the development of delivery systems, establishing the multilateral sanctions regime in earnest.[58]

Skeptics of the JCPOA—including those in the Arab world—likely recall the instances of Iranian intransigence that greeted previous diplomatic efforts in the nuclear sphere.[59] Iran's renewal of enrichment activities that defied its November 2004 Paris Agreement with Britain, France, and Germany led to the IAEA resolution and Board of Governors' referral that resulted in Resolution 1737. Subsequent Iranian resistance heightened tensions, stalled multiple negotiation phases, and induced the growth of the UN sanctions regime. Iran's refusal to fully verify development and suspend enrichment activities drove a Security Council ban of arms exports and related materials in March 2007 and a travel ban with a call for bank monitoring and cargo inspection in 2008.[60] Following the revelation of a secret enrichment site in September 2009, a fourth round of UN sanctions in June 2010 formalized an embargo on weapons systems, banned ballistic missile–related activity, and expanded financial sanctions.[61] The European Union incrementally imposed its own series of sanctions across the trade, finance, energy, and transport sectors, culminating in a broad oil embargo and severe financial restrictions in 2012, including the removal of banks from the global SWIFT (Society for Worldwide Interbank Financial Telecommunication) system. Meanwhile, the United States solidified its targeted financial strategy with actions against the Central Bank of Iran.

It is difficult to definitively assess the impact of sanctions on the Iranian nuclear program. A U.S. National Intelligence Estimate in 2008 suggested that a "combination of threats of intensified international scrutiny and pressures, along with opportunities for Iran to achieve security, prestige, and goals for regional influence in other ways . . . [might] prompt Tehran to extend the current halt to its nuclear program."[62] Still, that report wrongly found that Iran had terminated its weapons program as early as 2003, an estimate revised to 2009 upon the discovery of further evidence of continued research and development.[63] The actions of the international community did contribute to an adversarial negotiating atmosphere, with the process stalled until the election of Hassan Rouhani to the presidency of Iran in 2013. Still, it is revealing that the Joint Plan of Action in November 2013—which preceded the JCPOA—took place in a P5+1 context. The venue demonstrates the centrality of the European Union sanctions regime, as well as the influence of Germany as Iran's largest trading partner in the Union.[64] Sanctions thus appeared to have made a "substantial contribution" to diplomatic progress.[65] Yet, the charted ebbs and flows of diplomatic efforts in Iran complicate efforts to project the impact of the JCPOA on the future of nuclear order in the Middle East.

The Significance of Iran

Iranian foreign policy stands as one of the key determinants in the possibility for strengthened regional order, including in the nuclear sphere, in the Middle East. With the ousting and subsequent execution of Saddam Hussein, costly conflicts in Iraq and Afghanistan, and ongoing fallout from Arab Spring elections, Iran has emerged as the major state-based threat to the status quo. Indeed, a number of challenges to existing order are "posed by, associated with, or potentially exploitable by" Tehran.[66] The country's military strength is a particular concern in light of the political alliances forged by the Iranian Revolutionary Guard Corps with groups holding grievances against the United States and Israel—many containing paramilitary capabilities, including Hamas in Palestine, Hezbollah in Lebanon and in Iraqi Kurdistan. Indeed, for those who opposed the JCPOA's termination of Security Council sanctions, the European Union's oil embargo, and U.S. oil sales and trade restrictions, the concern is that Tehran's hard *and* soft power in the region would spread with its reintroduction into the global economy.[67]

In light of a receding American presence in the Middle East, as important as Iranian activity are the perceptions of such activity. It is a promising sign for the future of regional order that Arab leaders have supported the JCPOA even as they voice their skepticism. Saudi king Salman has switched from the Israeli hard stance, while Egyptian foreign minister Sameh Shoukry referred specifically to the increased viability of a WMD-free zone in the Middle East as a result of the agreement.[68] For all the deal's imperfections (with provisions set to expire in ten to fifteen years, restrictions to the "anywhere, anytime" inspections hoped for, eventual reentry into the global arms trade, and so forth), it clearly hinders Iran's ability to enrich uranium, reduces its existing stockpile, limits its research and development work, reimplements the Additional Protocol, and contains snapback provisions of UN sanctions should the country not hold up its end of the bargain. Indeed, Israeli chief of the general staff Lieutenant General Gadi Eizenkot cited the "many opportunities" the JCPOA presented, suggesting it represented "real change . . . [and] a strategic turning point."[69] This followed the remarkable Israeli Defense Forces Strategy issued in August 2015, which had scant mention of the Iranian nuclear threat and rendered it "currently not sufficiently relevant to be included in the IDF's strategy for the next five years . . . the threat can be shelved for a decade or two."[70] Even with Netanyahu's consistent public and vocal denouncements, there have emerged some key dissenting voices in Israel.

The symbolic power of the deal also cannot be overstated, especially in the context of relations between Iran and the West. Not only are there ramifications for the NPT regime, but the continued commitment of both sides to the implementation of the JCPOA can alter the paradigm of Middle East politics. After all, the NPT has long presented a manifestation of Western imperialism for the Iranians; the perfect overlap between the five recognized nuclear weapon states and the P5 of the Security Council is a reminder that the treaty exists as a status quo instrument. Indeed, the aggressive and oftentimes confrontational stance adopted by Mahmoud Ahmadinejad during his presidency against the UN and IAEA was calculated, with opposition reformists painted as weak and susceptible to Western influence.[71] Even when Ahmadinejad expressed his amenability to the September 2009 uranium-for-fuel exchange proposal from the P5+1, he rejected it precisely because *any* interest was seen as "weak-kneed accommodation" by both the reformist and pragmatic conservative camps.[72] That Rouhani was able to sign the JCPOA not only reveals much about the altered domestic environment but also suggests the country is seeking to buy back into the existing nuclear order. The imposition of the Additional Protocol is especially significant in that regard, as Iran had previously only abided by those measures voluntarily, without formal adoption. It suggests a reorientation of the country's foreign policy—one reaffirmed with Rouhani's landslide reelection in May 2017—that could do much to assuage Arab and Israeli concerns and wither away hard-line stances.[73]

Since Implementation Day

Even a cynical reading of an implemented JCPOA—one that links the removal of sanctions to the country's inevitable rise as regional hegemon—might not preclude the possibility for strengthened nuclear order in the Middle East. As discussed, Iran played an NPT dissenter as it remained a treaty party. It has emerged as a poster boy for non-nuclear weapon states, consistently arguing that nuclear weapon states have not upheld the original bargain—in facilitating development for peaceful usage or taking steps toward achieving nuclear disarmament. It is no accident that Ahmadinejad convened an international conference in Tehran on disarmament and nonproliferation in 2010 the week after the first Nuclear Security Summit, its expressed purpose to hold the P5 accountable to their NPT obligations. The JCPOA is significant for non-Western states, then, as it provides a logical diplomatic solution: "recognition of Iran's nuclear rights in exchange for greater transparency in its nuclear activities."[74] Russia's moves to enhance its civilian nuclear cooperation with Iran beyond the Bushehr Nuclear Power Plant in the aftermath of the JCPOA affirm this recognition. In this manner, Iran's return to the existing global nuclear order provides a boon to the legitimacy of that order. This creates a foundation of existing nuclear cooperation that could set the stage for strengthened nuclear order in the future. In addition, easing some of the tensions with the West may allow stronger intraregional relations as well.

There have been a number of positive signs in the aftermath of the JCPOA, including the reopening of the British embassy in Tehran in August 2015, almost four years after it closed. While Iran's participation in the Vienna peace talks for Syria in October 2015 provided more fodder for those who fear its regional ascension, it also demonstrates its integration back into the international community. Nuclear cooperation deals with Russia and Hungary reflect the ongoing process. Perhaps most attention grabbing was the U.S.-Iran prisoner exchange involving eleven individuals just hours prior to the announcement of Implementation Day in January 2016. Normalization of relations remains far from the horizon. Tensions with the United States continue, fueled in particular by the ballistic missile tests conducted by the Iranian Revolutionary Guard Corps in March 2016. Yet even in this situation, there is a bit of a silver lining. Despite the United States accusing Iran of violating Security Council Resolution 2231 (which endorsed the JCPOA), the United States ultimately sanctioned Iranian firms unilaterally for their involvement; neither side has sought to revisit the deal. This has been the case to date under the Trump administration, which decided in May 2017 to uphold JCPOA-related sanctions relief even as the United States undertakes a comprehensive review of its policy on Iran.[75] The compartmentalization of the nuclear issue on both sides—from campaign rhetoric, regional and global power politics, and even ballistic missile activity—could be a hugely positive step for regional nuclear order in the Middle East.

CONCLUSION: HINTS OF A FOUNDATION

The prolonged inability to move on a conference that enjoys a clear mandate, eager conveners, and ostensibly widespread support (or pressure) demonstrates the futility of a Middle East WMD-free zone process in the existing regional environment. Philosophical disagreements about process, let alone substance, have to date overridden the presence of the 1995 Resolution on the Middle East and the persistent directives from the UN. But arguably this reflects only the incompatibility of the particular solution at this juncture. The core principles expressed by the 1975 Comprehensive Study of the Question of Nuclear-Weapon-Free Zones in All Its Aspects is prescient, as it stressed the importance of regional initiation and voluntary participation. Egypt (and the Arab League to a lesser extent) remains the lone loud champion for an arrangement that requires the participation of Israel and Iran and, given the longstanding nature of political and economic order in the Middle East, the active support of the United States and others. It lacks those. As a result, insufficient commonalities exist in issue definition. The zone understandably remains a study in frustration, an abstract that appears no closer to reality now than when it was hoisted atop the NPT agenda in 1995.

This chapter, however, has found cause elsewhere for some long-term optimism for the emergence of nuclear order in the Middle East. The current state of upheaval in the region has provided an impetus for enhanced patterns of regionalism, a prerequisite for deeper nuclear cooperation. This has been the case with the Arab League to some degree, though the unique circumstances of its involvement in Libya and Syria call into question the sustainability of this trend. At a subregional level however, the GCC appears a more promising candidate for closer ties. Its institutionalization provides a foundation upon which parties have fostered coordination on key political and security issues. Even group tensions—with relations with Qatar disrupted in 2014 and again in 2017 over its purported support of extremists—indicate an increasingly assertive GCC shaping its core values and interests. The lack of economic integration among states will undoubtedly prove a challenge in uniting agendas further. However, GCC states do hold shared perceptions of several key security issues: the receding role of the West, the threat posed by the Islamic State, and the emergence of Iran as regional hegemon. These will intensify, with Saudi Arabia likely to become emboldened by U.S. foreign policy under the Trump administration.[76] The presence of a joint military command and police force represents a significant move toward a more permanent security order that could be the foundation for nuclear cooperation.

Still, no GCC state is likely to push for a nuclear-weapon-free zone or a stronger nuclear order without fundamental changes in the security landscape of the Middle East. Again, as suggested by this chapter, however, the threat perceptions that account for regional stalemate also demonstrate a potential for change, with the full implementation of the 2015 JCPOA key to this evolution. Continued follow-through of the deal would dramatically reduce the threat Tehran poses to the region and beyond. Former U.S. secretary of state John Kerry acknowledged that "the crisis was the potential of a nuclear weapon"; the removal of that possibility thus has major reverberations.[77] As this chapter has argued, strong Israeli rhetoric can obscure the fact that even their threat perception has already changed. True, Iran's gradual integration into the global economy might allow it to fuel the flames of conflict in the Middle East in other ways, as currently in Syria and Yemen, especially as it ascends into regional hegemonic status in the face of a waning U.S. presence. Yet, if both Iran and the West can continue to disaggregate the nuclear issue from their complicated political relations, then the former's integration into the global nuclear order may accelerate.

In such circumstances, and taking into account the fragility of the JCPOA, it is not impossible to envision a pathway to nonmilitarized order in the Middle East. In addition, the June 2017 terrorist attacks by the Islamic State (ISIS) against Iran may inadvertently accelerate patterns of security regionalism by providing a common enemy for states; the fact that ISIS has expressed nuclear ambitions may impress upon them the need to come to agree on a distinctively Middle East solution. As noted, discussions of regional nuclear order have long been dominated by the consideration of a single divisive issue—Israel—and a single divisive solution—the WMD-free zone. The presence of ISIS could provide a much-needed alternative that inspires a shared understanding of another dimension of the nuclear issue. In such circumstances, a GCC-founded, Arab-led process for strengthened regional nuclear cooperation that includes Iran is not entirely out of the realm of possibility. The threat of nonstate actors combined with the growth of nuclear energy (especially post-JCPOA) could drive more cohesive efforts in nonproliferation and security: perhaps through the context of UN Security Council Resolution 1540 or the bottom-up technical cooperation in the vein of Northeast Asia. Only with a more stable order and a stronger base of nuclear cooperation—likely originating among the Arab states, given patterns of regionalism and subregionalism—will the Middle East be equipped to tackle the Israeli issue.

CHAPTER 8

Elusive Orders
Africa and South Asia

The crucial case studies examined—Northeast Asia, Southeast Asia, and the Middle East—house some of the most immediate concerns across the nuclear landscape. They contain prominent safeguards noncompliance cases, stand at the frontline of rivalries between nuclear-armed powers, and represent the locales for vast numbers of power plant facilities now and in the future. As argued in the preceding chapters, however, each case contains some semblance of movement that could eventually serve as the foundation for strengthened regional nuclear order. The economic triumvirate of China, Japan, and South Korea has sparked substantial technical safety and security cooperation. The barebones ASEANTOM suggests the emergence of regularized dialogue on nuclear issues in a manner that adheres to the principles of its foundational association. In the Middle East, a properly implemented Joint Comprehensive Plan of Action with Iran—alongside convergence against the Islamic State—could upend long-held perceptions of threat and spur further subregional activities. Each of these trends holds long-term promise.

At the same time, these cases also have the benefit of clear and convergent definitions of proliferation and disarmament issues at one level or another. Consensus certainly does not exist on all topics across the spectrum. Chinese concerns about the North Korean nuclear program remains secondary to their fears of a collapsed regime in Pyongyang. The whole of Southeast Asia has not quite registered nuclear proliferation high on the agenda despite its standing as a hub for illicit trafficking. The Middle East is still marked by splintered perceptions about the Israeli stockpile and the Iranian nuclear program. Yet, while the lack of consensus on such topics helps to explain why stronger regional nuclear order is fledging (or lacking) in each instance, there is overarching agreement about the relevance of the nuclear weapons issue. This also held true with historical examples in Western Europe and Latin America, as examined in chapter 4. As laid out in the analytical framework, irrespective of regionalism processes, any movement toward nuclear order requires shared understandings regarding (1) the identification and definition of the issue and (2) the necessity for action above the national level.

CHAPTER OVERVIEW

In some instances, however, those shared understandings of the nuclear issue are elusive. This final empirical chapter engages in a compact overview of two such regions: Africa and South Asia. It revisits the primary link drawn in this book between the possibility for and shape of strengthened nuclear order and broader regional trends (political, economic, security, and otherwise). Filtering analysis through the components of the analytical framework detailed in chapter 3, the chapter illustrates that the complexities of those broader dynamics can at times suppress any convergence in fundamental threat perceptions, preventing any modicum of political will on nuclear cooperation. As these elements represent requisite foundational elements of any nuclear order, let alone a robust one, the possibility for regional-level action to complement the existing regime centered on the Nuclear Non-Proliferation Treaty (NPT) thus requires far more groundwork than in other cases.

The first half of the chapter examines the case of Africa. The Treaty of Pelindaba established a nuclear-weapon-free zone in the region, as well as the accompanying African Commission on Nuclear Energy (AFCONE). Still, proliferation threats remain low priority on a continent beset by basic security and stability concerns. The case study begins with an analysis of how the existing nuclear order came to be created, tracing the emergence and eventual dismantlement of South Africa's nuclear weapons program. It then considers patterns of regionalisms on the continent; this includes the emergence of security regionalism in a post–Cold War environment centered on processes of conflict resolution and peacebuilding. With the lack of immediate nuclear threat (despite concerns about nonstate proliferation), South Africa being the only state housing even a nuclear power plant, and the presence of the zone and AFCONE dampening any sense of urgency, the study makes the case that strengthened nuclear order in Africa will have to come in the context of development goals.

The second half of the chapter turns to South Asia, in what can be considered a stubborn case of regional disorder. Despite the existence of the South Asian Association for Regional Cooperation (SAARC), it makes the case that India—as the dominant power—has preferred to engage its immediate neighbors bilaterally over leading any multilateral endeavors. This has contributed to scant progress in efforts at regional economic integration. The case study next turns to the security landscape, dominated by the deterrence-based order between nuclear-armed rivals India and Pakistan. There remains a substantial gap between their respective threat perceptions, as evidenced in the alarming lack of bilateral cooperative initiatives in arms control. Indeed, the environment appears more hostile than even Cold War conditions between the United

States and the Soviet Union. The case study ends by pinpointing other factors—political instability in Pakistan, U.S. and Chinese involvement—that further complicate the nuclear landscape in South Asia, perpetuating the divergence of definitions on the issue. The chapter then concludes by suggesting global consequences for the continued elusive nuclear orders in Africa and South Asia—underscoring the necessity for regional-level action.

AFRICA

Prelude in South Africa

Events in Africa reveal the permeating effects of the Cold War, with a deep interplay between global developments, regional politics, and domestic concerns—and ramifications for national nuclear policy and regional nuclear order. The Treaty of Pelindaba—entered into force in 2009—would not have been possible had South Africa not voluntarily dismantled its nuclear weapons program beginning in 1989. It was precisely this process that allowed the UN General Assembly, at the behest of the Organisation of African Unity (OAU), to convene in 1990 a group of experts "to examine the modalities and elements for the preparation and implementation of a convention or treaty on the denuclearization of Africa."[1] Guided by the 1964 Declaration on the Denuclearization of Africa, this group gauged the global drive for disarmament, trends in regional security arrangements, and different means of incorporating South Africa.[2] That venue brought about a proposal for an African nuclear-weapon-free zone, which in turn led the UN secretary-general to expand the group's mandate to include the drafting of a treaty or convention with a 1993 deadline.[3] A long process of negotiations culminated in the adoption of the Pelindaba text by the OAU Assembly of Heads of State in June 1995; the treaty opened for signatures in 1996.

The history of South Africa's nuclear weapons program—including its decision to dismantle—is intimately linked to its security environment under Cold War and immediate post–Cold War conditions. Pretoria's original decision to develop a nuclear weapons capability came in response to myriad external threats faced by the ruling National Party in the 1960s and 1970s. The country's apartheid policies contributed to its generally unstable political and military surroundings, which were exacerbated by the tug and pull of bipolarity. Cuba's buildup in Angola, Portugal's withdrawal from its colonies, and the corresponding threat of Soviet Union expansionism to the continent pushed South Africa to seek nuclear weapons development specifically "should the country's territorial integrity be threatened."[4] While U.S. support—in the form of intelligence sharing and military training—helped to prop up the National Party, paranoia about Washington's potential withdrawal provided another justification for the continued development of the program.[5]

U.S. policy toward South Africa ultimately changed when the Soviet Union began its reforms under the direction of Mikhail Gorbachev in the mid-1980s. One key change was Moscow's withdrawing of financial and tactical support from the opposition African National Congress, once perceived by key figures in the American Embassy and the Central Intelligence Agency as a communist movement and terrorist organization.[6] This altered the nature of politics in South Africa. President F. W. de Klerk moved to ameliorate relations across the domestic landscape, unbanning opposition groups including the African National Congress and beginning negotiations to end apartheid. The ruling National Party's grip over the country loosened too, with many closely associated with the nuclear program falling from power.[7] At the same time, and interrelated, South Africa's immediate external security situation was undergoing seismic shifts. Namibia's independence in 1990 marked the end of a conflict that had long dominated the sub-Saharan landscape, resulting in the withdrawal of Cuban troops and the cessation of regional military involvement from the two superpowers. With the Soviet threat abated in this manner, a nuclear deterrent suddenly appeared unnecessary to the internationalizing de Klerk.[8]

Regionalism Processes

As mentioned, the OAU had expressed its desire for a treaty to ensure the denuclearization of the African continent as early as 1964. Still, despite the endorsement and later pressure from the UN General Assembly, there was negligible movement toward a nuclear-weapon-free zone until South Africa acceded to the NPT in 1991.[9] There were a number of reasons for this. First, and perhaps most obvious, there could be no zone without the involvement of the one state in the region that had the technical capability to produce nuclear weapons (and, as later revealed, that was already in the process of developing its program). Second, African states lost their primary impetus for the zone when France ceased its nuclear testing in the Sahara after 1966. With the global nuclear nonproliferation regime put into place during the period, shared understandings concerning the threat of nuclear testing and the urgency of regional action subsided. In the absence of immediate concerns about French testing, the OAU reverted to core principles, which hinged not on security issues but on establishing a broader African unity, with the protection of sovereignty and territorial integrity at its core. This marginalized the nuclear issue; no cooperative efforts emerged even in the fields of nuclear science and technology until 1990.[10]

Overall, the OAU was emblematic of the conservative nature of Africa's regional cooperation, which aimed "to promote the security and interests of rulers, rather than ... increasing the size of economic markets, ensuring the rights of citizens, or overcoming capricious national boundaries."[11] Even efforts to those latter ends protected domestic imperatives at the expense of regional integration, in some instances to the point of their demise. Until the twenty-first century, African regionalism was characterized primarily by first the OAU and then the Lagos Plan of Action of 1980, which sought the development of an African Economic Community through a series of subregional structures, including the Economic Community of West African States, the Market for Eastern and Southern Africa, and the Economic Community of Central African States, and several substantively targeted arrangements such as the Inter-Governmental Authority for Drought and Development and the South African Development Community. Yet, the sum of these disparate parts was negligible, and lack of progress had become abundantly clear by the turn of the twenty-first century.[12] It was only in the post–Cold War era that African leaders looked beyond the OAU in the security arena, an implicit acknowledgment of the arrangement's shortcomings.[13] In addition, migration linked to conflict, rising economic disparity, emergent transnational crime—drug trafficking in particular—and the HIV/AIDS pandemic demanded a regionalism that far outstripped what had come before. The African Union, modeled after the European Union, launched in 2002 as a result.

The development of regional security order through the African Union played a role in the eventual entry into force of the Treaty of Pelindaba in 2009. Already, the addition of "nonindifference" to the principle of "noninterference" marked a symbolic transformation from the OAU. Further, the African Union established institutional mechanisms for purposes of security order. This included the 2002 creation of the Peace and Security Council aimed at tackling peacebuilding and postconflict reconstruction; the council was to "promote peace, security, and stability" and "develop a common defense policy for the [African Union]."[14] Two years later, the Union established four other elements of the African Peace and Security Architecture, including the Panel of the Wise, the Continental Early Warning System, the African Standby Force, and the Peace Fund; members later adopted a Non-Aggression and Common Defence Pact. In the subsequent decades, the African Union has—despite limited resources—sought to play a role in a number of regional conflicts—for instance, dispatching a peacekeeping mission to Burundi in 2003 and engaging in diplomatic negotiations during the post-election crisis in Zimbabwe in 2008. In another departure from the OAU, the African Union has not hesitated to suspend members in the aftermath of military overthrows—certainly a victory of nonindifference over noninterference.[15] This marked a clear expansion and greater assertiveness of the regional security order.

Order beyond Pelindaba

Still, while patterns of security regionalism in Africa appear as a promising foundation, there has been no corresponding push for a strengthened regional nuclear order. As the cessation of French testing had done in the 1960s, South Africa's nuclear disarmament in the early 1990s removed the immediate threat proffered to the continent, effectively displacing the nuclear issue from the agenda. This helps explain the long wait before the Treaty of Pelindaba entered into force, as there was little practical reason for states to push for ratification.[16] The primary value of the zone today lies largely in its symbolism, as a means with which to further legitimize the utility of nuclear-weapon-free zones as a concept. As stated about the NPT, given concerns about reputation, investment costs, and systemic stability, compliance with the nuclear-weapon-free zone in Africa appears as a given. After all, the vast majority of states parties do not have the capacity to consider nuclear energy programs. The only two nuclear power plants on the continent are housed in South Africa, which has plans to develop six to eight more by 2030. Within that timeframe, Nigeria and Kenya too hope to begin construction and eventual operation of their first plants. Yet this is a long way away, reflected in the relative inactivity of the laudable Forum for Nuclear Regulatory Bodies in Africa created in 2009.

The traditional pathway of diversion from peaceful uses therefore does not represent the greatest nuclear proliferation threat on the continent. The presence of the NPT-IAEA safeguards and the nuclear-weapon-free zone present major practical, legal, and normative obstacles for would-be proliferators that have no energy program in place. Further, AFCONE provides a safety structure intimately linked to the IAEA and will oversee the birth of the aforementioned programs.[17] It is no surprise then that the nuclear issue has not been on the forefront of the agenda of the African Union. However, the multidimensional nonstate threat will eventually demand regional attention beyond the zone in place. This includes the specter of nuclear terrorism, especially as offshoots of both Islamic State and al-Qaeda operate in North Africa; both groups have been linked with attempts to acquire or use nuclear weapons or weapons-usable materials. And this especially involves the porous borders and weak infrastructure of African states, particularly after the unraveling of the A. Q. Khan network in 2004 laid bare the vulnerabilities of the global supply chain. The fact that these actors have "functioned through transit hubs, front companies . . . and creative off-shoring of manufacturing" and bypassed existing controls focuses attention on the weakest link in that chain.[18] With the persistence of conflict, and the shortcomings of security order at the national and regional levels, Africa's struggles to control illicit flows will have ramifications both for the continent and the entirety of global nuclear order.

Of Extra-Regional Origins

Meager resources and competing national priorities offer daunting challenges to any campaign aimed at strengthening regional nuclear order in Africa. The poor participation of states in existing nuclear nonproliferation measures is indicative of this fundamental issue. For instance, the World Customs Organization research unit dismissed African programs aimed at extending export control culture into industry as efforts "focused on revenue collection rather than national security."[19] Fewer than half of the fifty-four states on the continent have entered into force the International Convention for the Suppression of Acts of Nuclear Terrorism; just twelve have ratified the amendment to the Convention on the Physical Protection of Nuclear Materials.[20] The region boasts one of the lowest rates of implementation of UN Security Council Resolution 1540, as only seventeen states have submitted or updated their national reports since 2008 (again, this does not include analysis of the character or quality of required legislation).[21] That nuclear power is a pipe dream for the vast majority of states continues to undermine any sense of urgency or commitment to nonproliferation in particular and the nuclear issue at large.

A stronger regional nuclear order in Africa therefore will require conditions that appear as an inverse of the expectations set forth in the rest of this book. The nuclear issue clearly does not register in Africa—the South African historical experience aside—and there is minimal common perception for the need for solutions above the national level. Neither of these will change without external intervention. The international community must prioritize Africa as a frontline against proliferation and bring those states deeper into the fold of existing global nuclear order if regional order is to emerge. The broad mandate and unique legislative aspect of Resolution 1540 could provide a means to that end. Workshops related to Resolution 1540 have already been convened in Africa on nuclear security policies, information management, and export controls—at times with the involvement of the African Union and the UN Regional Centre for Peace and Disarmament in Africa. Yet these efforts are scattered, taking place sporadically with participant turnover and little institutional memory. The 2016 comprehensive review of Resolution 1540 in fact recognized the continuing need "to develop approaches for cooperation with relevant international, regional and subregional organizations that fully take account of the specificities of each region."[22] Such a concerted effort—by the 1540 Committee, by Western states, and by other key voices in nonproliferation—is especially necessary as it pertains to Africa.

At the same time, while external developments could propel African engagement with global nuclear order, hopes for a sharper definition of the issue within the continent require a more innovative approach. A strengthened nuclear order will have to emerge in the context of other goals, given competing national priorities. Stakeholders must impose a framework in which "security and development communities, North and South, and donors and recipients can operationalize joint and sustainable activities."[23] If an emphasis on post–Cold War stability (domestically and regionally) helped to expand notions of peace and security as manifested in the African Union, then a similar focus that includes development is the likely key to its next evolution. Political stability requires secure borders, and economic growth demands an environment conducive to investment. With proliferation and disarmament abstract notions to the overwhelming majority of African states, export controls, safety and security cultures, and antiterrorism measures must be pursued through alternative means. Indeed, increased activity in the context of the African Regional Cooperative Agreement for Research, Development and Training Related to Nuclear Science and Technology could spark economic growth that has the byproduct of strengthening nonproliferation order. Only with a more stable foundation in place can states eventually build beyond the nuclear-weapon-free zone, imbue AFCONE with purpose, and further Africa's nascent nuclear order.

SOUTH ASIA

Regional Disorder

As with the case of Africa, regionalism processes have not been completely lacking in South Asia. The area is represented by the SAARC, founded in 1985 expressly for the purposes of fostering economic development and strengthening cooperation.[24] As with the OAU, however, SAARC's emphasis on principles of sovereignty, territorial integrity, and noninterference has constrained the propagation of any sense of integration. Decisions across the whole of SAARC are made by consensus, with contentious issues excluded from deliberations altogether.[25] The association has thus struggled to elicit interdependence even in the core economic aspect of its agenda. Despite modest gains in exports and investment inflows, South Asia remains "the least integrated region in the world"—with intra-regional trade holding just 2 percent of the regional gross domestic product, in comparison to a 30 percent rate for East Asia.[26] Experts attribute this to the lack of trade congruence among countries, as well as the interrelated lack of demand for each other's exports.[27] While garments provide one sector in which countries have integrated themselves into the global supply chain, this has been the exception; furthermore, that textiles dominate the economies of the region provides an impediment to diversification, removing incentives for integration.[28]

Concentrated efforts to execute against the economic goals set by the SAARC enjoyed mixed results. It took more than a decade after its establishment before discussions even commenced for a regional trade agreement, reflecting the looseness of the association. Only with the backdrop of the new, post–Cold War wave of regionalism did parties move to negotiate and implement a South Asian Preferential Trading Area aimed to reduce regional trade barriers. Yet, even as the resulting 1995 arrangement sparked some improvement, the overall pace and extent of policy reforms lagged—partially attributed by some to the lack of external aid.[29] A subsequent Free Trade Agreement was discussed as early as 1996, though security circumstances discussed later in this section delayed its establishment until 2004. Again, levels of intra-regional trade stayed constant. There remains "a cautious approach . . . to achieve the ultimate objective of free trade."[30] Instead, SAARC states have opted to engage in bilateral free trade agreements for the purpose of gaining preferential access. The emergence of India as a global economic power complicated regional integration efforts in this manner, as its bilateral transactions suppress more well-rounded intra-regional activity. Five years after the Free Trade Agreement, trade with India comprised nearly two-thirds of South Asian trade for Pakistan (with that number a tiny proportion of total trade), and more than 90 percent of regional trade for Bangladesh, Nepal, and Sri Lanka.[31]

Patterns of economic regionalism—slowed by severely imbalanced power dynamics and India's increased engagement with East Asia—still far outpace those in the security arena.[32] While the SAARC secured what appeared to be an early success with the 1987 Regional Convention on the Suppression of Terrorism, India and Pakistan could not agree on a common definition of "terrorist act," stripping the document of its power. Follow-up action, including the establishment of a SAARC Terrorist Offenses Monitoring Desk, has been plagued by a lack of information-sharing and transparency on all sides. A post–September 11 Additional Protocol to the Convention sits unimplemented, with inaction linked by some to the text in the SAARC charter that sought to avoid any contentious issues.[33] Other security components of the SAARC reveal similar shortcomings, with the Drug Offences Monitoring Desk struggling with its modest mandate, discussions of a regional police institution languishing, and the Convention on Mutual Assistance in Criminal Matters not fully ratified. The SAARC framework is simply insufficient for security cooperation, and no other arrangement presents a remotely realistic forum for such matters; security regionalism "is regarded to be nearly impossible by many observers."[34] Exacerbating the weakness in institutionalized regionalism is a lack of common sociocultural identity that is rooted in historical tension and rivalry.

India and Pakistan

SAARC's struggles to promote further collaboration on the issues of drug trafficking and organized crime can be largely attributed to the lack of an extradition treaty between India and Pakistan. The longstanding rivalry has dominated the regional landscape, rendering difficult—if not impossible—security regionalism processes across South Asia. Conflict has taken place on and off since each side gained independence in 1947. The intervention of external powers during the Cold War perpetuated the rivalry, as Pakistan enjoyed military and economic support from the United States, among others, and engaged in extra-regional arrangements—the 1954 Southeast Asian Treaty Organization and 1955 Central Treaty Organization—with the aim of securing assistance against India.[35] In response, the Soviet Union provided substantial support to India during a period in which the latter was embroiled in a 1959 border dispute with China, sparking the Sino-Indian War. Decades later, the 1979 Soviet invasion of Afghanistan would further bolster Pakistan's geopolitical significance in the eyes of the U.S. The global superpowers inflamed an already heated situation. In fact, India's security concerns centering on China and Pakistan accelerated the development of its nuclear capabilities in the 1980s.[36] And while Pakistan became more vulnerable with the end of the Cold War, and its value marginalized following the withdrawal of Soviet forces from Afghanistan, the Kashmir dispute with India continued to drive its nuclear ambitions.[37]

By 1990, the two sides had already settled into a deterrence-based order. Despite the lack of information surrounding the nuclear programs in each state, Pakistani leaders did not mind "openly discussing" the role of nuclear deterrence in preventing conventional conflicts with its neighbor.[38] Some have suggested that the knowledge of the other side's atomic capabilities was precisely why each moderated its behavior during a 1990 crisis in Kashmir.[39] In that instance, there appeared a number of conditions conducive to full-on war, including an uncertain international environment, weak domestic leadership, and tit-for-tat military confrontation. Yet, the scenario never played out, and the crisis winded down as both sides withdrew their troops.[40] Under Prime Ministers Benazir Bhutto and Rajiv Gandhi, the two sides even drafted a non-nuclear aggression agreement that forbade an attack—either direct or through assistance from a foreign power—on nuclear installations and facilities in case of war; the agreement entered in force in 1991, and the two sides have exchanged lists of sites every year since.[41] But any hopes that the agreement would expand into more bilateral nuclear cooperation would soon fade, as the tenor of bilateral relations was irrevocably altered after 1998.

The dual nuclear tests in 1998 by India and Pakistan put both nuclear weapons programs into the global spotlight, bringing what had been an implicit nuclear deterrence order out into the open. India followed its tests with a bit of political maneuvering, as its unsolicited declarations of a no-first-use policy and categorical nonuse against non–nuclear weapon states suggested an attempt to cast itself as a responsible nuclear power. However, the bilateral crises that have followed have only fed into the image of the two as rogues, with "no change in the general pattern of amity and enmity . . . [and a] cycle of apparently warming diplomacy and return to confrontation."[42] There can be a clear distinction drawn even between the South Asian deterrence-based order versus that between the United States and the Soviet Union during the Cold War. Pakistan has adopted an asymmetric escalation posture that has increased low-intensity conflict and created more confrontations. It is a strategy that enhances the risk of nuclear use, intentional or inadvertent.[43] The nuclear order in South Asia is one that exists in the loosest sense of the word.[44] While the sides have agreed on a couple of confidence-building measures, including the Lahore Agreement, in which each pledges to inform the other in the event of an accident relating to nuclear weapons, and another that involves prenotification should either side engage in ballistic missile flight tests, the buildup continues unabated.

Beyond Regional Disorder

The deterrence-based order that exists in South Asia is almost entirely antithetical to global nuclear nonproliferation efforts, one that actively threatens aspects of global nuclear and security order. The 1998 nuclear test explosions immediately undermined the NPT by rendering its definition of "nuclear weapon state" anachronistic.[45] Without the veil of ambiguity as in Israel, India and Pakistan emerged unequivocally as a new class of nuclear weapon state, with their arsenals entirely outside the existing governance structure. At the 2000 NPT Review Conference, parties upheld the definition of nuclear weapon states, declaring that "States not currently States parties may accede to the Treaty only as non-nuclear-weapon states."[46] The move to compartmentalize India, Pakistan, Israel, and later North Korea meant sidelining four states with nuclear arsenals from the regime. Furthermore, in the aftermath of the 1998 tests, the united front presented by the permanent five members of the UN Security Council withered in the face of domestic opposition and commercial interests, leading to little lasting consequence for either India or Pakistan.[47] It marked another blow for global nuclear order.

The political instability that marks South Asia, along with its susceptibility to regional crisis, has further adverse consequences. This was made manifestly clear with the uncovering of the Khan network. A. Q. Khan, head of the Pakistani nuclear program, admitted in January 2004 that he had sold weapons technology and information to regimes including Iran, Libya, and North Korea via an intricate proliferation ring. While Pakistan took major steps to dismantle the network from its end and to address its nuclear safety and security complexes, the environment in which Khan flourished remains vulnerable.[48] Pakistan was cited in the latest Nuclear Security Index for its problematic control and accounting procedures, cybersecurity infrastructure, and physical protection of sites and transport.[49] This is underlined by the fragility of its domestic political landscape, which suffers from corruption, ineffective governance, and the presence of opposition groups that may be interested in illicitly acquiring materials.[50] Even efforts to integrate India and Pakistan into the global nuclear order have had unintended consequences. A 2005 U.S.-India civil nuclear cooperation agreement that led to New Delhi being granted a trade exemption from the Nuclear Suppliers Group drew major criticism from compliant non-nuclear weapon states under the NPT. China's decision to provide nuclear reactors to Pakistan in 2010, an agreement cloaked in secrecy, drew similar consternation.[51] The India-Pakistan rivalry has therefore negatively impacted nonproliferation order directly and indirectly.

A strengthened nuclear order in South Asia seems almost entirely out of the realm of possibility. Relations between the two nuclear powers in the region perpetuate a cycle of confrontation; the meager confidence-building measures in the nuclear arena serve less as promises of collaboration and more as lowest common denominators to avoid accidental nuclear war. In light of the widening economic and political power gap between India and Pakistan, meanwhile, the latter seems locked into its asymmetric posture—conferring more value to its stockpile as a result. Both sides have inflexible individual security (and nuclear) perspectives. Hopes for a shift away from deterrence-based order is further squelched by the anemic patterns of South Asian regionalism. India's participation would be key to any such endeavor because it is the dominant power. Instead, it has preferred a global approach, enhancing its engagement with ASEAN and BRICS, for instance. Within South Asia, it has pursued bilateral relations. The impact on SAARC—the formal organization with the mandate to encourage regional integration—has been stark. As in the case of Africa, what might be necessary is a "paradigm shift from traditional to nontraditional security . . . from national security to human security priorities."[52] Yet as history demonstrates, the India-Pakistan rivalry—and the persistent territorial conflict over Kashmir—has undermined any sense of common identity, of shared values and interests, that could otherwise contribute to that shift.

Back from the Brink

Still, even without changes to patterns of regionalism or to issue and threat definition, India and Pakistan do have the ability to raise existing levels of nuclear cooperation a modicum. The Cold War détente between the United States and the Soviet Union provides a model of two diametrically opposed powers that still acted to avoid the threat of nuclear war. As charted in this case study, India and Pakistan have done this in the past. They came to terms on a non-nuclear aggression agreement that entered into force in 1991. And, shortly prior to the Kashmir War in 1999, the two sides signed the Lahore Declaration, which not only included notification on ballistic missile tests and nuclear accidents but more generally encompassed "bilateral consultations on security concepts, and nuclear doctrines, with a view to developing measures for confidence building in the nuclear and conventional fields, aimed at avoidance of conflict."[53] Deterrence-based order may have rendered nuclear stockpiles essential to both sides, but beliefs in the utility of the doctrine rest also upon an expectation of predictability. The intensification of measures such as those envisioned in the Lahore Agreement would preserve that expectation.

A similar boon to nuclear cooperation without the necessity of overhauling deterrence could also be achieved through the elimination of nuclear weapons and weapons-related systems that upend stability. While this would be a far more ambitious maneuver, U.S.-Soviet relations again provide a precedent, including with the 1987 Intermediate-Range Nuclear Forces Treaty that oversaw the elimination of intermediate-range and shorter-range missiles. In the case of South Asia, Pakistan's first-ever test of a nuclear-capable cruise missile in January 2017 draws attention to one possible target, given concerns about the particular susceptibility of that class of weapons to "the risks of miscalculation, misperception, rapid escalation, and arms racing."[54] The question of what is feasible at a bilateral level ultimately depends on the domestic currents in each country. Yet it is clear that in South Asia, the future of nuclear order will depend almost entirely on the relations between its two nuclear powers. As the security dilemma appears unlikely to change, goals of nonproliferation and disarmament are a moot point. Rather, the two sides must raise existing levels of nuclear cooperation by addressing a longstanding and common, if basic, concern: the prevention of accidental nuclear war. Perhaps this can eventually feed into a stronger safety focus.

CONCLUSION: REGIONAL POWERS IN CONTEXT

At first glance, the narratives of the elusive nuclear orders in Africa and South Asia seem primarily intertwined with the predominant power in each case. South Africa's weapons program during the Cold War put a pause on nuclear-weapon-free zone progress in Africa; its subsequent dismantlement of its program then propelled the process toward the Treaty of Pelindaba. India served as a conduit of Cold War conflict between the United States and the Soviet Union; the subsequent deterrence-based order became entrenched with the development of its—and Pakistan's—nuclear weapons programs. Neither characterization is necessarily inaccurate. Yet, the troubled state of nonproliferation and disarmament in the two cases can be attributed to factors almost entirely detached from such power-based explanations. In both Africa and South Asia, regional nuclear cooperation remains sorely lacking because there exist no shared understandings about the importance of the issue. The building blocks required for order have been lost amid other domestic concerns.

The lack of fundamental commonalities in the nuclear issue can be attributed to the lack of regionalisms and the stubborn divergence of values, interests, and identities—even despite the presence of regional organizations in both cases. After all, both the OAU and the SAARC emphasized sovereignty and non-interference; their efforts at economic integration were tepid at best, with states largely failing to adhere to the prescriptions of their respective arrangements. Perhaps a stronger African identity would have prevented the dissipation of enthusiasm for a nuclear-weapon-free zone after France stopped testing in 1966, or would have kept nuclear concerns higher on the agenda after the Treaty of Pelindaba was drafted. It remains to be seen whether the security regionalism under the African Union can overcome the low levels of nuclear cooperation in the region—marked both in terms of its weak engagement with global nuclear order and the lack of activity within the nascent AFCONE. Meanwhile, perhaps a stronger South Asian identity could have prevented the economic free-for-all that has reinforced the bilateral strategy pursued by India, pushing the emerging power to engage outside rather than take initiative with its neighbors. Nuclear policies cannot be taken in isolation; they exist in the context of and are informed by broader regional dynamics.

Especially concerning about the elusive regional nuclear orders chronicled in this chapter is their impact on global nuclear order, relevant as the character of nuclear proliferation itself shifts. The global supply chain will only be as strong as its weakest link. In Africa, states must embed proper safety and security cultures into their nascent nuclear energy commission, their burgeoning peace and security architecture, even their development structure. Proper implementation will require the guidance, support, and resources of external powers and organizations. In South Asia, the Cold War détente between the United States and Soviet Union provides a model for the contemporary standoff between India and Pakistan. There must be more confidence-building measures, more channels of communication, and modest safety and security standards—in the vein of agreements that barred attacks on nuclear installations and required notification of nuclear accidents. Such steps against full-on catastrophe provide a measure of nuclear cooperation and order that would not affect the deterrent capabilities of either country but could represent a foundation for action should relations between the two ever improve.

That the scant nuclear cooperation that does exist in Africa and South Asia takes such drastically different forms reflects the unique dynamics of each environment. That the patterns of regionalism are so varied underscores the different pathways to nonproliferation that are possible or realistic. The concluding chapter revisits these points in the context of the present and future of the global nuclear nonproliferation regime and of the need for strengthened regional nuclear order.

CHAPTER 9

The Future of Nonproliferation

The global nuclear order is facing its most vulnerable moment in decades. Former U.S. defense secretary William Perry in January 2016 made the argument that "the probability of a nuclear calamity is higher today" than during the height of the Cold War.[1] This is attributed particularly to deteriorated relations between the United States and Russia, who together account for 93 percent of the nearly fifteen thousand nuclear weapons in the world and house an overwhelming majority of the global stockpiles of highly enriched uranium and separated plutonium.[2] Tensions between Russia and the West have been heightened since the former's annexation of Crimea in February 2014 and were exacerbated by flare-ups linked to their involvement in the Syrian Civil War. This has resulted in greater brinksmanship between both sides. For instance, Russia deployed nuclear-capable Iskander missiles into its westernmost region of Kaliningrad in October 2016, in what appeared as a direct response to the U.S. expansion of its European Reassurance Initiative and the deployment of NATO battalions to the Baltic states and Poland in preceding months. Such buildups increase the possibility of miscalculation, misperception, and escalation that could lead to nuclear use.

The current nuclear landscape is rife with challenges. North Korea has made significant progress in its nuclear capabilities, conducting three nuclear tests and dozens of ballistic missile tests since 2016. Evidence suggests that Pyongyang will soon be able to produce enough weapons material for six nuclear weapons a year.[3] Its weapons development has had major reverberations across the whole of East Asia, further destabilizing the region. For instance, the United States' announced plan to deploy a Terminal High Altitude Area Defense (THAAD) anti-missile battery in South Korea drew the ire of China, which has tested new weapons in response while enhancing its defense cooperation with Russia. Elsewhere, border skirmishes along the Indo-Pakistani border have increased the volatility of that rivalry, which could be inflamed if India gained membership in the Nuclear Suppliers Group.[4] Widespread modernization plans, conflict in the South China Sea, and cyber-attack possibilities are other reasons why the doomsday clock sits at two minutes to midnight—the potential for global catastrophe the greatest in six decades.[5]

As alarming as the spectrum of challenges that decorate the nuclear landscape is the current standing of the NPT regime—the institution at the heart of global efforts to tackle the nuclear threat. The process of negotiations for the 2017 Treaty on the Prohibition of Nuclear Weapons relates the frustrations felt by non-nuclear weapon states regarding lack of disarmament progress; their grievances also account for the failed outcome at the 2015 NPT Review Conference. But it is the expansion of the proliferation landscape that has most directly highlighted the limitations—the blind spots—of the NPT and its surrounding regime, suggesting the value of and need for supplementary action. This is especially the case with the threat of nonstate actors, laid bare first with the revelations of the nuclear ambitions of al-Qaeda (and now the Islamic State) and the unraveling of the A. Q. Khan network. The involvement of states such as North Korea in the nuclear black market provides another challenge outside the scope of the NPT. Meanwhile, even in detecting diversion, the treaty remains limited by the fact that the Additional Protocol remains an entirely voluntary action, that there remain inconsistent renderings of noncompliance rulings and consequences. The fact that nonproliferation is now intertwined in North-South debates and linked to progress in disarmament and development for peaceful use underscores the need for innovation in nuclear governance.

Adding to the sense of urgency in nonproliferation order is the fallout emanating from troubled relations between Russia and the West. Russia's expulsion from the Group of Eight has slowed work within the Global Partnership Against the Spread of Weapons and Materials of Mass Destruction, aimed to enhance WMD security and destroy existing stockpiles and materials. Its withdrawal from the U.S.-led Nuclear Security Summit series in November 2014 defanged the 2016 summit and limits the impact of that venue moving forward. These are especially damaging actions given lingering concerns about nuclear security in Russia, given the already piecemeal nature of the existing nuclear security structure. In addition, Moscow has curtailed bilateral cooperation with the United States in a number of agreements, including the Cooperative Threat Reduction Program and the Plutonium Management and Disposition Agreement. One U.S. official lamented the collapse of two other bilateral research and development pacts, noting that "at least during the Cold War, we had pretty good scientific exchanges."[6] That both sides have accused each other of violations of the Intermediate-Range Nuclear Forces Treaty underscores the abysmal state of bilateral relations. As the two states form the foundation for arms control and disarmament activity, the global nuclear order suffers accordingly.

WAYS AHEAD

Despite—or perhaps because of—the aforementioned challenges, there exists a unique opportunity in the current period to remake the global nuclear order. The start of the 2020 NPT Review Conference cycle allows states parties an opportunity to move away from the bitter disappointment of 2015. Similarly, the recent conclusion of the comprehensive review of UN Security Council Resolution 1540 opens the door for states to recalibrate for the remainder of its ten-year mandate. The 2017 Treaty on the Prohibition of Nuclear Weapons could provide new momentum toward the delegitimizing of nuclear weapons, while a 2018 follow-up conference to the biennial Nuclear Security Summit series will allow states to reevaluate their approach in that field. Nuclear safety too continues to be reevaluated in the aftermath of the 2011 Fukushima Daiichi disaster and in light of the development and expansion of energy programs across the world.

Global nuclear order thus stands at a crossroads. Yet, the opportunity for change should not be confused with the inevitability thereof. History has demonstrated time and again the power of the status quo in the field and has highlighted the rarity of innovation and transformation. It is not difficult to imagine a 2020 NPT Review Conference that produces a substantive outcome document based on the lowest common denominator, reaffirming the 2010 Action Plan without providing accountability mechanisms—again kicking that can down the road. The 1540 Committee may continue to focus on reporting requirements rather than substantive evaluation of the legislation the resolution requires domestic governments to impose. The presence of a prohibition treaty might be a Pyrrhic victory that alienates nuclear weapon states from the disarmament movement altogether, furthering a divide that threatens advances in nonproliferation.

Clearly, political will remains a necessary condition to the remaking of global nuclear order. Following that, there appears a variety of approaches in the undertaking of any such effort. These can be classified into four paradigms: globalism, multilateralism, nationalism, and regionalism. The next section explores each of these approaches. It examines the potential policies associated with each and outlines inherent challenges and shortcomings.

Globalism

The NPT regime as constituted appears as a manifestation of a globalist approach to nuclear order. The size of its membership and vastness of its jurisdiction reflect an underlying philosophy that stresses the need for an encompassing institution to match the scope and interconnectedness of the nuclear challenge. From this perspective, the remaking of global nuclear order requires first and foremost a strengthening of the existing order (in contrast, the actions prescribed under the other paradigms would amount more to a supplementing of that order). In particular, great emphasis should be placed on tightening the NPT itself. Potential courses of action include setting clear definitions for what constitutes noncompliance, inserting punitive consequences for treaty withdrawal, and making mandatory the Additional Protocol. Future review conferences that produce outcomes such as the 13 Practical Steps or the 2010 Action Plan must include proper review and accountability mechanisms as well as timetables. There would also be a priority on integrating treaty nonparties India, Pakistan, Israel, and North Korea into the regime, perhaps through the creation of a third class of state within the text.

Of course, the current state of the nuclear nonproliferation regime is a testament to the difficulties of perpetuating a globalist approach. As suggested, the intertwined nature of the three pillars in the NPT has too often entangled the treaty in North-South politics, stagnating order on multiple fronts. Discussion of tightening definitions of treaty noncompliance, for instance, is near impossible due to the two-class system and the more abstract obligations relating to nuclear weapon states in disarmament and facilitating peaceful use. The divide between nuclear weapon states and non-nuclear weapon states has grown so wide as to appear irreconcilable in select instances—thus negotiations for a prohibition treaty in which none of the nine nuclear weapon states were present. Such acrimony reflects the fact that the proliferation issue specifically—and the nuclear issue more broadly—takes drastically different shapes across the world, undercutting the level of convergence in perspectives required for a successful globalist approach. Indeed, the sensitivity of security issues, combined with the Westphalian nature of sovereignty, places ceilings on the reach of a globalist-inspired nuclear order.

Multilateralism

Since the entry into force of the NPT in 1970, states have sought to supplement it through focused multilateral campaigns.[7] This includes the creation of the Zangger Committee and the Nuclear Suppliers Group in the mid-1970s, each featuring voluntary self-regulatory measures undertaken by states to ensure an adherence to International Atomic Energy Agency (IAEA) safeguards agreements. They include the Cooperative Threat Reduction Program and the Global Partnership in the post–Cold War period, measures to decommission and destroy existing stockpiles. Most recently, they include the U.S.-led Proliferation Security Initiative and the Nuclear Security Summit series, actions taken in response to the nonstate threat. The gift basket diplomacy of the final forum provides another model for strengthening global nuclear order through multilateral means, with the potential application of the high-level political approach in fissile materials reduction, nuclear waste management, and enhanced physical protection standards, for starters.

Still, any reliance on multilateral forums—whether in the shape of enduring structures or ad hoc arrangements—will engender myriad challenges. To begin with, these entities tend to be susceptible to political influence. The uneasy triangles of influence and competing institutionalisms discussed in chapter 5 with respect to Northeast Asia illustrate this competitive multilateralism in action. Critics of the Proliferation Security Initiative, for instance, question both its legality—vis-à-vis the UN Convention on the Law of the Sea—and its focus; the frequent targeting of North Korea and Iran seems to reinforce the image of the initiative as a blunt American instrument.[8] Further, a nuclear order composed of such "coalitions of the willing" may appear as less legitimate: consider the impact of India's exemption, and potential membership, in the Nuclear Suppliers Group, which not only has threatened the legitimacy of the group but undermined global nuclear order more broadly. Finally, by their very nature, multilateral forums will be less inclusive. This was the case with the Nuclear Security Summit series. Given the evolution of nuclear proliferation pathways and the wide-ranging impact of nonstate actors, the engagement of a limited number of states in strengthening nuclear order will leave rampant gaps across the global supply chain.

Nationalism

The nature of the Westphalian system and the primacy of sovereignty ensure that national action is and remains the conduit of global nuclear order. The NPT regime, for instance, rests on the implementation of safeguards agreements between individual states and the IAEA. The multilateral campaigns discussed above also include any number of political commitments, self-regulatory activities, and capacity building and investment enacted by domestic governments. The 2004 adoption of UN Security Council Resolution 1540 provided a blueprint for how the international community can further enhance the state role in global nuclear order, eliciting action supplementary to the NPT regime.[9] As suggested, a shift in approach by the 1540 Committee that focuses on legislative compliance rather than reporting could be critical in this respect, forcing the issue of nonstate proliferation atop the agendas of all UN member states. The ability of the Security Council to enact sanctions as means of enforcement would support this endeavor. Meanwhile, a similar resolution in nuclear security could provide an alternative, state-centric means of tackling that issue.

Still, a global nuclear order that promotes individual state responsibility would be more susceptible to politicization, with nonproliferation and disarmament goals linked to the policy preferences of individual leaders and domestic coalitions. The numerous regulatory weaknesses in the Japanese nuclear industry that contributed to the Fukushima Daiichi disaster illustrate the pitfalls of such an approach. Moreover, at a fundamental level, many states in the developing world simply do not have the capacity to tackle proliferation-related concerns effectively. The weak orders in Africa and Southeast Asia are attributable to competing national priorities and limited resources; shifting Resolution 1540 in a more punitive direction, for instance, appears premature and will likely only create more antagonism in an already fraught global landscape. In addition, the challenge of nuclear weapons and related materials, equipment, technologies, and knowledge is one that ultimately transcends state borders. The weaknesses of individual states expand the spectrum of risk across the whole of global nuclear order. As such, a strong order ultimately must emphasize collaborative action, must promote information-sharing, best practices, and regularized dialogue.

Regionalism

As with the preceding paradigms, the role of regionalism in the existing global nuclear order is not hypothetical. In Europe, the European Atomic Energy Community (Euratom) governs the peaceful use of nuclear energy, while the Strategy against Proliferation of WMD establishes principles in that field for European Union member states. The European Council's Committee on Non-Proliferation and the Committee on Nuclear Affairs offer regular venues for discussion of other challenges. Certainly, European patterns of integration—political, economic, sociocultural—far exceed those of any other region in the world. Yet regionalist approaches to nuclear order are not remiss elsewhere, as this book has demonstrated. There exist the five nuclear-weapon-free zones and, in some instances, associated organizations. Regional-level cooperation also takes place within the context of existing multilateral treaties and forums: outreach from the World Nuclear Association on technical and regulatory issues, workshops hosted in conjunction with the Nuclear Security Summit, safety networks that entail dialogue and training.

Yet a regional approach to nuclear order is also not without its pitfalls. Just as states differ in their resources, capabilities, and levels of commitment as it pertains to nuclear challenges, so too do regions. This is expected given the absence of nuclear energy programs—let alone weapons programs—in many areas. Even among states that may share common interests in theory, regional dynamics can present a deterrent to collaborative action. The presence of rivalries can prevent any discussion of security issues, even overshadow existing institutions. For instance, the fact that neither Brazil nor Argentina were involved in OPANAL removed the teeth of the Latin America nuclear order for decades; similarly, a revitalization of that rivalry could threaten the robust order now in existence. The intractable cases of South Asia and the Middle East further demonstrate the elusive nature of particular regional orders in the nuclear sphere. Further, regional nuclear order may be held hostage by global power dynamics. The difficulties of sanctions implementation in North Korea provide just a glimpse of the overriding impact of geopolitics.

REGIONALISM AND NUCLEAR ORDER, REVISITED

This book posited that strengthening regional nuclear orders represented the most effective means of supplementing the existing NPT regime, thus readying global nuclear order to face current and future nuclear proliferation and proliferation-related challenges. It intuited the need for such a reorientation because the most prominent issues on the nuclear agenda appear intertwined with dynamics and conflicts exclusive to individual regions. And it intuited the possibility of such a reorientation because of the patterns of global regionalism that have taken hold in the post–Cold War era.

Indeed, there exist more regional organizations across more issue areas than ever before, with the level and scope of economic integration unprecedented even compared to past regionalist waves. There have even emerged strong common identities linked to such processes. The overall effect, then, should be a convergence of values and interests, with impact on political and security affairs as well. Because states have greater investment at the regional level, they would be expected to have more incentive to overcome difficulties at that level—at least in theory. The inferences that formed the core of the empirical case studies centered on (1) whether these macro-level trends were applicable at the level of the individual region, and (2) whether they pertain to nuclear proliferation and proliferation-related issues. The three components detailed in the analytical framework employed in this book—commonalities in issue definition, patterns of regionalism, and existing nuclear cooperation—provided a barometer for assessment. Table 9.1 provides an overview of the findings from the case studies discussed in this section.

The Nearly Perfect Storm

Indeed, the historical analysis of the Western European and Latin American cases underline the strong link present between regionalism and the initial nuclear orders that emerged in the late 1950s–1960s. States in those two regions were bonded to one another because of environmental conditions and geopolitical dynamics. Each was in the midst of massive integration processes, and while the success of the prolonged project in Latin America did not match that in Western Europe, there was a remarkable breadth and scope of institutions in place for both. Further, each enjoyed a unique common identity, with corresponding shared values and interests: in Latin America, this identity stemmed from the American hegemonic presence and corresponding backlash thereto; in Europe, it was linked to the postwar reconciliation and rebuilding experience.

The patterns of regionalism in those two cases in turn shaped how each came to define the nuclear issue and contributed directly to the shared understandings regarding the need for solutions above the national level. While the final

TABLE 9.1 Case Study Overview

Region	Issue Definition (Proliferation)	Patterns of Regionalism	Existing Nuclear Cooperation	Nuclear Orders and Pathways
Western Europe	Longstanding priority	Matured EU integration	Well incorporated in global regime	Perpetuate "effective multilateralism" principle
	Tension between France and UK vs. other states	Strong security coordination	Euratom and common energy market	E.g., EU *Strategy against Proliferation of WMD*
South America	Longstanding acceptance of norms	Brazil-led order ("consensual hegemony")	Treaty of Tlatelolco	Maintain OPANAL- and ABACC-centered stability
	Frustration with aspects of NPT regime	Strong identity; shared values and interests	Brazil-Argentina safety and technical protocols	Enhance interregional activity
Northeast Asia	North Korea as priority	Economic interdependence	Six-Party Talks on hold	China, Japan, South Korea–centric
	Post-Fukushima nuclear safety concerns	Evolving U.S. "hub-and-spoke" vs. China-Russia vision	Forum for Nuclear Cooperation; Safeguards Network	Expand technical cooperation, create linkage to political realm
Southeast Asia	Deprioritized post-NWFZ	ASEAN dominated	Bangkok Treaty	Institutionalize ASEANTOM further
	Energy security concerns	Competing identities (East Asia, Asia Pacific)	ASEANTOM technical activities	Ensure energy security through nuclear safety
Middle East	Divisive effects of Israel and Iran	Arab and non-Arab divide	Stunted WMD–free zone process	Isolate nuclear issue
	Fears of ISIS's nuclear potential	Emerging subregionalisms		Coalesce on nonstate proliferation; GCC and Arab led

Africa	Deprioritized post-NWFZ	African Union and "nonindifference"	Treaty of Pelindaba and AFCONE	External push for 1540 engagement
	Limited nuclear security concerns	Human security	Forum of Nuclear Regulatory Bodies in Africa	Link to development and establish culture through peaceful use
South Asia	India-Pakistan perception gap	Limited SAARC integration	India-Pakistan non–nuclear aggression agreement	Expand measures to prevent accidental nuclear war
	Post–A. Q. Khan nuclear security concerns	Identity clash; Kashmir conflict	Lahore Agreement framework	Target weapons that upend stability

component of the framework employed in this book—existing nuclear cooperation—was largely absent, this was simply a product of the relative nascence of the nuclear issue. Indeed, the vacuum only resulted in the strong character of the Euratom and Tlatelolco treaties and the expansive nature of the nuclear orders they respectively anchored. Even as the nature of nuclear threat has shifted, states in both instances have continued to pursue primarily regional solutions—bolstering existing orders versus the pursuit of alternative approaches. This underscores the lingering impact of strong foundations, both within the context of the nuclear issue and beyond.

The regionalisms and consequent nuclear orders of Western Europe and Latin America are inextricably linked to the particular world time in which they emerged. Notably, the latest wave of regionalism, the one examined in depth by this book, sparked a second life for each. This manifested with a strong nonproliferation focus within the context of the European Union and with the bolstering of Tlatelolco and OPANAL through the integration of Brazil and Argentina. The two provide a blueprint for functioning, stable orders. However, the applicability of that blueprint has limitations. Indeed, integration processes across the rest of the world have simply not reached the levels attained by Western Europe and, to a lesser extent, Latin America. None of the other cases in this book have enjoyed anything resembling a perfect storm of conditions conducive to the construction of encompassing regional nuclear order.

Assessing the Landscape

At the same time, it is abundantly clear that the new regionalism that has defined the post–Cold War era has had significant—if differential—effects across each of the regions examined, including the three identified as crucial case studies for nonproliferation: Northeast Asia, Southeast Asia, and the Middle East. Southeast Asia enjoys the most formalized patterns of regionalism, linked to the durable presence of the Association of Southeast Asian Nations (ASEAN). Yet despite much effort in recent decades, integrative security processes lag behind precisely because of ASEAN principles, with an elusive common identity the outcome of the association's substantial membership expansion in the mid-1990s. In Northeast Asia, great power politics inform competing and often divisive visions of security regionalism. There remain fundamental antagonisms across states linked to historical grievances and territorial disputes as well. Yet, economic patterns of regionalism have taken firm hold as part of the new wave, inspiring cooperation—if modest in character—elsewhere. Meanwhile in the Middle East, the economic structure that upholds the region has long stood as an obstacle to regionalisms. Still, propped by the identity politics that permeate the region, subregional arrangements have made noticeable inroads.

The patterns of regionalism in each case have then had clear impacts on the degree to which commonalities in the definition of the proliferation issue exist, reflected also in the character of existing nuclear cooperation. The incompatibility of ASEAN principles with hard security issues has limited the reach of ASEANTOM to date, with Southeast Asian nations coalescing on energy security concerns rather than proliferation. In Northeast Asia, there exists a fair degree of convergence around the North Korea nuclear program. Yet the country's strategic value to China, given great power rivalries in the region, has prevented consensus on how states define and perceive the solution to the issue. Nuclear safety and security issues have proven less divisive, with technical cooperation in particular offering common ground for economies with massive and growing nuclear energy sectors. Finally, for the countries of the Middle East, identity politics clearly inform how states perceive the threat posed by Israel and Iran, with how states define not only the nature of the solution required (including a WMD-free zone) but the very sequence in which that solution must take place.

An Uphill Battle?

The overview above appears discouraging at first glance. Patterns of regionalism in each case fall far short of the standards set by Western Europe and Latin America. There is no comparable integrative drive, certainly not across political and security issue areas. Inclusive regional organizations in hard security areas are either lacking (as in Northeast Asia and the Middle East) or toothless (as in Southeast Asia). In addition, there is a paucity of shared values and interests, let alone common identity, across those regions. Levels of existing nuclear cooperation are similarly inconsistent, both in terms of engagement with the global nuclear order and intra-regionally. The obstacles to regional nuclear orders in the three cases are myriad, ranging from the preponderance of power politics to absence of trust and transparency to sheer apathy concerning proliferation issues.

Yet this book does not seek as its outcome comprehensive nuclear orders in each region. Rather, it identifies the possibility for and likely pathway toward strengthened regional nuclear orders that would supplement the existing NPT regime. In other words, the expectations for each region must be commensurate with the conditions outlined by the analytical framework. Indeed, even the elusive orders in Africa and South Asia offer some semblance of hope for strengthened cooperation moving forward. In Africa, a strategy that highlights the contributions of nuclear technology to economic development can lead to the fostering of safety and security culture. In South Asia, India and Pakistan can enhance cooperation at their most basic shared interest: the desire to avoid accidental nuclear war. Such policies in those two cases would provide a tremendous boon to global nuclear order. In the same vein, then, obstacles in

Northeast Asia, Southeast Asia, and the Middle East do not preclude the possibility of strengthened orders. On the contrary, because of the new regionalism and the character of the international order, these obstacles can be mitigated in a more realistic manner than those associated with the globalism, multilateralism, and nationalism paradigms.

A REGIONAL APPROACH TO NUCLEAR NONPROLIFERATION

The perpetuation of the new regionalism and the maturation of integration processes across the world suggest that nuclear cooperation is likely to continue—even expand—at the regional level, holding all other variables constant. This might echo the steady process that witnessed the spread of nuclear-weapon-free zones over the course of decades, accompanying the rise of the region itself as political unit.[10] However, the shortcomings of the existing global nuclear order and the urgent and varied nature of the nuclear threat necessitate a more proactive, concerted effort in existing, if imperfect, conditions. Indeed, the intensification of regional nuclear cooperation and the strengthening of regional nuclear orders are essential to upholding the longstanding NPT regime. Such an approach requires the conditions discussed in the remainder of this section.

Deepening Technical Cooperation

Technical cooperation on issues such as nuclear safety and security has heretofore managed to avoid the complicated politics of nonproliferation and disarmament, even if they are inextricably linked to those issues. States have formed safety and safeguards networks that build capacity through training exercises, best practices, and focused seminars. Nuclear Security Centers of Excellence engage in similar activities. These provide a promising foundation for regional cooperation. At the same time, there is room for improvement. Existing dialogues tend to be circumscribed around Asian and European states, with membership further reflecting a competitive multilateralism. Increased cooperation on technical issues through ASEAN and AFCONE, for instance, would be of particular use for states planning or building nuclear power plants.

Technical forums also tend to operate rather loosely and independently. The IAEA could initiate a move toward standardizing training exercises and workshops. Furthermore, states could formalize their activities through the incorporation of peer review processes, joint risk assessment exercises, and, in certain cases, accounting and verification mechanisms. While ambitious, the Brazilian-Argentine Agency for Accounting and Control of Nuclear Materials (ABACC) provides a model of collaboration, especially in less sensitive areas such as emergency response procedures and power plant accident notification. In addition, technical forums would benefit from greater interaction with domestic nuclear operators and regulatory bodies. It is rather revealing that Japan modeled its newly established and independent Nuclear Regulation Authority after the U.S. Nuclear Regulatory Commission in the aftermath of Fukushima. There certainly appears room for more varied and deeper forms of technical cooperation.

Expanding Subregional Activity

There appears to be a certain "all or nothing" mentality as it pertains to the construction of regional nuclear order. This is perhaps because of the precedent set by Euratom and the existing nuclear-weapon-free zones. Subregional zones, while acknowledged in the 1975 Comprehensive Study of the Question of Nuclear-Weapon-Free Zones in All Its Aspects, have not been pursued. On the contrary, the 1998 General Assembly declaration that permitted Mongolia to declare itself a single-state zone lacked discussion of subregional zones altogether. According to the country's permanent representative to the UN, this was precisely "intended to avoid setting a precedent (at least for the moment) on the establishment or recognition of such zones."[11] The preference for total inclusiveness in regional nuclear affairs perhaps reflects strategic considerations as well. This helps explain why China continues with its push for a return to Six-Party Talks, or why Arab states insist on denuclearizing Israel prior to any WMD-free zone in the Middle East.

Returning to the framework deployed in this book, a strengthened nuclear order requires the presence of shared understandings (regarding both the nature of the threat and the necessity of action above the national level) and the development of mature regionalism processes (in the form of institutional architecture and shared identity). As the case studies have demonstrated, convergence of these factors is far more likely to exist at a subregional level. Regional nuclear order, therefore, must move beyond the nuclear-weapon-free zone paradigm. Technical cooperation presents one means through which subregional cooperation can take place without placing states at a comparative disadvantage. In Northeast Asia, the triumvirate of China, Japan, and South Korea presents a natural base for activity. In the Middle East, with multiple members considering nuclear energy programs, the Gulf Cooperation Council states can start a process that will eventually extend to the greater Arab community. Even in Southeast Asia, the concrete plans of Indonesia and Malaysia should inspire closer cooperation within the context of a flagging ASEANTOM.

Amplifying Regional Outreach

There is no shortage of regional outreach in the context of existing nonproliferation instruments and campaigns. As discussed in chapter 2, parties to the NPT have progressively devoted more space to nuclear-weapon-free zones in the outcome documents, expressing their support for particular proposals, highlighting obstacles to progress, and—in the case of the Middle East—mandating concrete action (albeit with less-than-ideal results). The IAEA hosts regular regional training exercises and workshops to help member states put safety measures into place. Meanwhile, UN Regional Centres for Peace and Disarmament partner with regional and subregional organizations on matters of nonproliferation and disarmament. Security Council Resolution 1977, which extended the mandate of 1540 for ten years, requested relevant regional and subregional organizations to designate a point of contact for implementation purposes. It also urged the 1540 Committee to engage with those groups and recommended strengthening the regional capacity of the UN Office for Disarmament Affairs.[12]

Problematically, however, existing regional outreach continues to be informal, messy, and ad hoc, requiring far too much initiative from inexperienced or overwhelmed parties. Certainly, the plethora of regional organizations with overlapping memberships and jurisdictions makes it difficult for the UN or other caretakers of multilateral instruments to designate "official" entities. Yet, there are other means with which they can draw out the regional dimensions of nonproliferation. It is necessary for such groups to promulgate more regional-centric data, for instance, with the reporting rates of Resolution 1540, or the implementation rates of the IAEA Additional Protocol. Rather than simply listing the regional and subregional workshops conducted, the IAEA and the 1540 Committee could present a qualitative picture of progress across regions. Inter-regional dialogues too must be expanded, with the establishment of formal mechanisms that link organizations to one another. Overall, outreach efforts must evolve to take into account the unique needs of particular regions.

RETHINKING NUCLEAR NONPROLIFERATION

The existing global nuclear order emerged under Cold War conditions, at a time when a select group of industrialized states neared the capability for nuclear weapons development. This was a product of the "Atoms for Peace" era, which ushered in the dramatic expansion of civilian nuclear assistance and trade. The near miss of the 1962 Cuban Missile Crisis, however, along with China's 1964 test explosion, raised concerns about the possibility of catastrophe in a world with too many nuclear weapon states. The international community thus moved quickly to freeze the number in existence. They did so through the NPT, which sought to prevent the diversion of materials and technologies from peaceful nuclear programs to weapons use. Since the treaty entered into force in 1970, it has become the centerpiece of the global nuclear nonproliferation regime and the backbone of global nuclear order.

Yet the nature of the nuclear proliferation threat has evolved in these nearly five decades, and especially so in the last twenty-five years. The collapse of the Soviet Union raised a number of questions regarding the command and control of its nuclear stockpile. Tests by Pakistan in 1998 and North Korea in 2006 expanded the membership of the nuclear club to two unstable regimes. The events of September 11, 2001, highlighted the possibility of terrorism involving nuclear or radiological materials. The unraveling of the A. Q. Khan network underscored the existence of the black market trade of nuclear components. Because of the shortcomings of the global nuclear order, and in particular the need to address the nonstate threat, "states have added a diverse array of other cooperative initiatives to the nonproliferation tool kit."[13] The Proliferation Security Initiative, Resolution 1540, the International Convention for the Suppression of Acts of Nuclear Terrorism, and the Nuclear Security Summit series, among others, reflect the flurry of activity—and alternative multilateral approaches—that the international community has employed.

Still, a truly effective global nuclear order must both reflect and engage the world in which it exists. The nuclear issue certainly remains rife with global impact. Yet the particular nature of proliferation threat has become far more divergent, linked to regional security, energy, and economic dynamics and policies. More specialized, decentralized, and localized nuclear orders with which to supplement the NPT regime would help disaggregate the spectrum of threat more effectively in the contemporary era. Most important, it would take advantage of the institutional foundations that have resulted from the remarkable wave of regionalism that has taken place over the past three decades. Fostering a regional reorientation—however modest—of the nuclear nonproliferation regime is not only possible and desirable but also critical to the preservation of global nuclear order.

NOTES

Chapter 1. Nuclear Frustrations

Epigraph: Dr. Mohamed ElBaradei, "Treaty on the Non-Proliferation of Nuclear Weapons," 2005 Review Conference of the Treaty on the Non-Proliferation of Nuclear Weapons, May 2, 2005, http://www.iaea.org/NewsCenter/Statements/2005/ebsp2005n006.html.

1. Agence France-Presse, "North Korea Ends Missile-Test Moratorium, Raising Nuclear Stakes," Space War: Your World at War, March 3, 2005, http://www.spacewar.com/2005/050303133800.odute9s2.html.

2. Glenn Kessler, "North Korea May Have Sent Libya Nuclear Material, U.S. Tells Allies," *Washington Post*, February 2, 2005, sec. A1, http://www.washingtonpost.com/wp-dyn/articles/A55947-2005Feb2.html; David E. Sanger and William J. Broad, "Tests Said to Tie Deal on Uranium to North Korea," *New York Times*, February 2, 2005, http://www.nytimes.com/2005/02/02/washington/tests-said-to-tie-deal-on-uranium-to-north-korea.html.

3. Dr. Mohamed ElBaradei, "Introductory Statement to the Board of Governors," International Atomic Energy Agency, February 28, 2010, https://www.iaea.org/newscenter/statements/introductory-statement-board-governors-14.

4. Goldschmidt, "Exposing Nuclear Non-Compliance," 155.

5. H. E. Sebastian Kurz, Federal Minister for Europe, Integration and Foreign Affairs, "Joint Statement on the Humanitarian Consequences of Nuclear Weapons," 2015 Review Conference of the Parties to the Treaty on the Non-Proliferation of Nuclear Weapons, April 28, 2015, http://www.mofa.go.jp/files/000079082.pdf; Statement by H. E. Gillian Bird, Ambassador and Permanent Representative of Australia to the United Nations, "Statement on the Humanitarian Consequences of Nuclear Weapons," Australia Mission to the United Nations, April 30, 2015, http://www.mofa.go.jp/files/000079078.pdf.

6. Arka Biswas, "Iran Deal, NPT and the Norms of Nuclear Non-Proliferation," *Diplomat*, February 18, 2016, http://thediplomat.com/2016/02/iran-deal-npt-and-the-norms-of-nuclear-non-proliferation/.

7. Drawing upon the notion of regimes as "principles, norms, rules, and decision-making procedures around which actor expectations converge in a given issue-area," from Krasner, "Structural Causes and Regime Consequences," 185.

8. Global nuclear order is thus composed of institutional arrangements such as the NPT as well as the system of deterrence. For more, see Walker, "Nuclear Order and Disorder," 703–24; Biswas, *Nuclear Desire*; Dalton, Kassenova, and Williams, *Perspectives on the Evolving Nuclear Order*.

9. There exists some disagreement about what precisely constitutes a region. This book opts for a fluid definition that incorporates "both material and ideational dimensions." It acknowledges that a region is generally a grouping of states in close geographic proximity but allows for a degree of flexibility given geopolitical considerations—for instance, as with the central role of the United States in Northeast Asia. See Katzenstein, *World of Regions*, 6.

10. R. Johnson, "Rethinking the NPT's Role," 429.

11. Hecker, "Lessons Learned," 44–56; Mearsheimer, "False Promise," 5–49; Paul, *Power versus Prudence*.

12. Tannenwald, *Nuclear Taboo*, 334.

13. Rublee, *Nonproliferation Norms*; Tannenwald, "Stigmatizing the Bomb," 5–49.

14. Fuhrmann, *Atomic Assistance*; Jo and Gartzke, "Determinants of Nuclear Weapons Proliferation," 167–94.

15. Chakma, *Politics of Nuclear Weapons*; Leventhal and Tanzer, *Averting a Latin American Nuclear Arms Race*; Moore, *North Korean Nuclear Operationality*.

16. Narang, *Nuclear Strategy*; Potter and Mukhatzhanova, *Forecasting Nuclear Proliferation*; Paul, *Power versus Prudence*.

17. Cho, *Global Rogues*; Solingen, *Nuclear Logics*.

18. Exceptions include Meier and Daase, *Arms Control*; Müller and Wunderlich, *Norm Dynamics*; Fields, *State Behavior*.

19. Keohane, "Demand for International Regimes," 325–55; Koremenos, Lipson, and Snidal, "Rational Design," 761–99; Lipson, "International Cooperation," 1–23.

20. As discussed in Rublee, "Taking Stock," 420–50; Sagan, "Causes of Nuclear Weapons Proliferation," 225–44.

21. Boulden, Thakur, and Weiss, *United Nations*; Knopf, *Security Assurances*; Njolstad, ed., *Nuclear Proliferation*.

22. Acharya, "Nuclear Proliferation," 248–72; Hamel-Green, "Cooperating Regionally," 206–28.

23. Giovannini, "Understanding the 'Proliferation,'" 250–70.

24. A collection of essays that perhaps most thoroughly encompasses these topics comes from Thakur, *Nuclear Weapons and International Security*. But his writings are stand-alone selections, with some dating back to 1995.

25. Sokova, "Non-State Actors," 83.

26. Previous arrangements had prohibited nuclear weapons in nonpopulated zones: this included the 1959 Antarctic Treaty and the 1967 Outer Space Treaty. Subsequently, the 1971 Seabed Treaty and the 1979 Moon Agreement would fall into this category as well.

27. Text of the Treaty for the Prohibition of Nuclear Weapons in Latin America and the Caribbean (Treaty of Tlatelolco), February 14, 1967 (opened for signatures), *United Nations Treaty Series*, vol. 634, no. 9068, Article 1, http://www.opanal.org/en/text-of-the-treaty-of-tlatelolco/.

28. Treaty on the Non-Proliferation of Nuclear Weapons, July 1, 1968 (opened for signatures), *United Nations Treaty Series*, vol. 729, no. 10485, Article III, https://www.un.org/disarmament/wmd/nuclear/npt/.

29. "Final Document of the Review Conference of the Parties to the Treaty on the Non-Proliferation of Nuclear Weapons, Part I," NPT/CONF/35/I, May 30, 1975, Annex I, p. 9, http://undocs.org/NPT/CONF/35/I.

30. United Nations General Assembly, "Comprehensive Study of the Question of Nuclear-Weapon-Free Zones in All its Aspects: Report of the Conference of the Committee on Disarmament," A/10027/Add.1, 1976, p. 40, http://undocs.org/A/10027/Add.1(SUPP).

31. This fell by the wayside in 1993 following IAEA revelations about noncompliance by the North Koreans with the terms of its safeguards agreement.

32. Roberts, "From Nonproliferation to Antiproliferation," 173.

33. "1995 Review and Extension Conference of the Parties to the Treaty on the Non-Proliferation of Nuclear Weapons: Final Document; Part I, Organization and Work of the Conference," NPT/CONF.1995/32, May 11, 1995, p. 10, http://undocs.org/NPT/CONF.1995/32 (PARTI).

34. Each treaty has laid out different spaces captured by the zone, with some including continental shelves and Economic Exclusive Zones, and others using longitudinal and latitudinal coordinates.

35. Thakur and Van Langenhove, "Enhancing Global Governance," 235.

36. A sample of newspapers used include the *Guardian, Japan Times, Los Angeles Times, Mainichi, New York Times, Telegraph, Wall Street Journal,* and *Washington Post,* among others. Stories were also gleaned online from news agencies such as the Agence France-Press, Associated Press, MercoPress, Reuters, RIA Novosti, Xinhua News Agency, and Yonhap News Agency. Sources were judged on a case-by-case, story-by-story basis but were generally weighed in terms of access to officials, direct quotations and objective summary of relevant events, and lack of editorializing.

37. For more on case study methodologies see Eckstein, "Case Study and Theory," 79–137; Bennett and Elman, "Qualitative Research," 455–76.

38. George and Bennett, *Case Studies and Theory Development*, 121.

39. While Donald J. Trump during his 2016 presidential campaign did allow the possibility of Japan and South Korea developing their own stockpiles, he has since walked back those remarks.

40. Including Buzan and Waever, *Regions and Powers*; Hurrell, "Explaining the Resurgence," 331–58; Lake and Morgan, *Regional Orders*; Mansfield and Milner, "New Wave of Regionalism," 589–627.

Chapter 2. Global Nuclear Order at a Crossroads

1. Barack Obama, "Remarks by President Barack Obama in Prague as Delivered," April 5, 2009, https://obamawhitehouse.archives.gov/the-press-office/remarks-president-barack-obama-prague-delivered.

2. Hans Blix, "Time for Disarmament," Finnish Institute of International Affairs, March 26, 2008, http://www.fiia.fi/assets/events/Full_Speech_by_Dr_Hans_Blix_(PDF).pdf.

3. The Zangger Committee emerged through a series of meetings beginning in 1971, with fifteen NPT parties eventually establishing conditions of supply for specific items when they were transferred to nonparties. The Nuclear Suppliers Group (also the London Club), established in 1975, reached agreement on even more stringent controls to be adopted by nuclear suppliers. Its Guidelines for Nuclear Transfers included details on physical protection measures, required safeguards on facilities and materials, and called for regular consultations between members. As of 2017, the Zangger membership stands at thirty-nine states, while the Nuclear Suppliers Group is at forty-eight. SAGSI, also established in 1975 but by the IAEA director general, was composed of technical experts who would interpret and standardize terms from the model agreement, while setting forth specific timeframes and efficiency goals.

4. Programme 93+2 included questionnaires on a State's System of Accounting and Control, requests regarding closed or decommissioned facilities, and use of no-notice routine inspections and advanced surveillance and monitoring technologies. The 1996 establishment of the Information Review Committee and the 1997 creation of a Security of Material Programme underscored the enhanced IAEA role. The model Additional Protocol (INFCIRC/540) was voluntary, but states parties would provide broad-based information—including descriptions, maps, and development plans—that went far beyond quantitative indicators. In addition, the notion of complementary access allowed the agency to verify information and resolve issues via short-notice special inspections. See Moyland, *IAEA's Programme "93+2."*

5. This includes Security Council Resolution 1540 and the Proliferation Security Initiative.

6. Among many others, see Nye, "Maintaining a Nonproliferation Regime," 15–38; Pilat and Pendley, *Beyond 1995*; Paul, "Strengthening the Non-Proliferation Regime," 440; Fields and Enia, "Health of the Nuclear Nonproliferation Regime," 173–96; Fields, *State Behavior*.

7. This was furthered by the absence of China and France in the negotiating process. Any concrete disarmament commitments would place the United States, Soviet Union, and UK at a severe strategic disadvantage.

8. United Nations General Assembly, "Resolutions Adopted on the Reports of the First Committee," A/RES/2028(XX), November 23, 1965, point 1.a, http://undocs.org/A/RES/2028(XX).

9. Treaty on the Non-Proliferation of Nuclear Weapons, Article III, para. 1.

10. Its full title was "The Structure and Content of Agreements between the Agency and States Required in Connection with the Treaty on the Non-Proliferation of Nuclear Weapons."

11. Treaty on the Non-Proliferation of Nuclear Weapons, Article IV, para. 2.

12. Ibid., Article VI.

13. Hearing before the Senate Committee on Armed Services, "Military Implications of the Treaty on the Non-Proliferation of Nuclear Weapons," February 27–28, 1969, p. 121, as quoted in Ford, "Debating Disarmament," 407.

14. For more on the significance of India and Iraq, see Wan, "Firewalling Nuclear Diffusion."

15. Richter, "Testimony from a Former Safeguards Inspector," 29.

16. Israel was subject only to a limited safeguards agreement with the IAEA (based on Information Circular 66, which preceded the NPT).

17. This was also true with the 1992 noncompliance ruling in Romania, as the postcommunist government invited the IAEA in for special inspections.

18. On the complexities of "noncompliance," see Carlson, "Defining Noncompliance," and Goldschmidt, "Exposing Nuclear Non-Compliance."

19. Dr. Mohamed ElBaradei, "Introductory Statement to the Board of Governors," International Atomic Energy Agency, February 12, 2003, https://www.iaea.org/newscenter/statements/introductory-statement-board-governors-45.

20. International Atomic Energy Agency, "Report by the Director General on the Implementation of the Resolution Adopted by the Board on 6 January 2003 and the Agreement between the IAEA and the Democratic People's Republic of Korea," GOV/2003/3, January 6, 2003. https://www.iaea.org/sites/default/files/gov2003-4.pdf.

21. James Sterngold, "Experts Fear Nuke Genie's Out of Bottle / Arms Technology Spreading beyond Iran, North Korea," *San Francisco Chronicle*, November 22, 2004, sec. A.

22. Dhanapala and Rydell, *Multilateral Diplomacy and the NPT*.

23. Conference on Disarmament, Decision on Agenda Item 1 "Nuclear Test Ban," CD/1212, August 10, 1993, http://undocs.org/CD/1212. See R. Johnson, *Unfinished Business*, for a detailed chronology leading up to the Comprehensive Test Ban Treaty.

24. "1995 Review and Extension Conference of the Parties to the Treaty on the Non-Proliferation of Nuclear Weapons: Final Document; Part I, Organization and Work of the Conference," NPT/CONF.1995/32, May 11, 1995, p. 10, http://undocs.org/NPT/CONF.1995/32 (PARTI).

25. "2000 Review Conference of the Parties to the Treaty on the Non-Proliferation of Nuclear Weapons: Final Document; Volume I, Part I and Part II," NPT/CONF.2000/28, May 19, 2000, http://undocs.org/NPT/CONF.2000/28%20(Parts%20I%20and%20II).

26. "2010 Review Conference of the Parties to the Treaty on the Non-Proliferation of Nuclear Weapons: Final Document; Volume I, Part I and Part II," NPT/CONF.2010/50, May 28, 2010, p. 19, http://undocs.org/NPT/CONF.2010/50%20(VOL.I).

27. The comprehensive test ban always represented "a litmus test of the [NWS] commitment to fulfill their obligations under Article VI" (Mendelsohn and Lockwood, "Nuclear-Weapon States," 14).

28. France shied away from the 13 Steps over the topic of tactical nuclear weapons (a concern shared by Russia), and because it expressed a desire to relink "nuclear disarmament" to "general and complete disarmament" (objecting to the exclusive focus on the nuclear weapon states). China had concerns over the transparency measures requested. Meanwhile, in the aftermath of the September 11 attacks, the United States pursued a number of policies that rolled back items expressly listed in the 13 Steps, weighing the development and use of nuclear-tipped bunker busters, a limited missile defense system, and preemptive nuclear attacks. For more on the deterioration from 2000 to 2005, see R. Johnson, "2000 NPT Review Conference," 2–21, and Ogilvie-White and Simpson, "NPT and Its 2003 PrepCom Session," 40–58.

29. See, for instance, statements issued at the three Preparatory Committees sessions in the lead-up to the 2015 NPT Review Conference.

30. In a Joint Statement issued July 7, 2017, following the adoption of the treaty, the United States, UK, and France noted that they "do not intend to sign, ratify or ever become part to it" and attacked the treaty as potentially "undermining the existing international security architecture."

31. Treaty on the Non-Proliferation of Nuclear Weapons, Article IV, para. 2.

32. Tate, "Regime-Building," 400.

33. Yudin, *Multilateralization*.

34. India also was granted a trade exemption by the Nuclear Suppliers Group.

35. Small Quantities Protocols were modified in the post–A. Q. Khan atmosphere.

36. R. Johnson, "Rethinking the NPT's Role," 435.

37. Bunn, "Preventing a Nuclear 9/11," 55–62.

38. "2000 Review Conference of the Parties to the Treaty on the Non-Proliferation of Nuclear Weapons: Final Document; Volume I, Part I," 19. At the time, the states in question also included Cuba, which acceded in 2002.

39. Treaty on the Non-Proliferation of Nuclear Weapons, Article VII.

Chapter 3. Foundations for Regional Nuclear Order

1. See, for instance, Fishlow and Haggard, "United States and the Regionalisation"; Mansfield and Milner, "New Wave of Regionalism"; Mansfield and Solingen, "Regionalism," 145–63.

2. Preusse, *New American Regionalism*; Thakur and Van Langenhove, "Enhancing Global Governance"; Telò, *European Union and New Regionalism*.

3. There is reference to four regionalist waves in total. The first came in the second half of the nineteenth century; the second occurred shortly after the conclusion of World War I. See Mansfield and Milner, "New Wave of Regionalism."

4. Harold Macmillan, "The Winds of Change (the Original Text)," February 3, 1960, http://www.africanrhetoric.org/pdf/ayor%206.2%205%20Harold%20MacMillan%20-%20The%20wind%20of%20change.pdf.

5. Hall, "New North-South Dealignment," 97.

6. United Nations General Assembly, "Comprehensive Study of the Question of Nuclear-Weapon-Free Zones in All Its Aspects: Report of the Conference of the Committee on Disarmament," A/10027/Add.1, 1976, p. 40, http://undocs.org/A/10027/Add.1(SUPP).

7. The plenary meeting records of the 1980 NPT Review Conference reveal widespread discord with the additional export controls imposed. The Group of 77 circulated a docu-

ment that claimed states had "unilaterally imposed restrictive measures beyond safeguards required under the pretext of preventing horizontal proliferation" ("Working Paper Containing Formulations for the Final Declaration on Articles III and IV of the Treaty," NPT/CONF. II/C.II/34, August 27, 1980, p. 4, https://unoda-web.s3-accelerate.amazonaws.com/wp-content/uploads/assets/WMD/Nuclear/pdf/finaldocs/1980%20-%20Geneva%20-%20NPT%20Review%20Conference%20-%20Final%20Document%20Part%20I.pdf).

8. Geldart and Lyon, "Group of 77," 93.

9. Gross, "On the Degradation," 569–84.

10. "Final Document of the Review Conference of the Parties to the Treaty on the Non-Proliferation of Nuclear Weapons Part I," NPT/CONF/35/I, May 30, 1975, Annex I, p. 4, http://undocs.org/NPT/CONF/35/I.

11. Ghana et al., "Working Paper: Containing a Draft Additional Protocol to the Treaty on the Non-Proliferation of Nuclear Weapons Regarding the Implementation of Its Article VI," NPT/CONF/18, May 12, 1975, p. 2, http://undocs.org/NPT/CONF/35/II.

12. "Working Paper Containing Some Basic Elements for the Sections of the Final Document of the Conference Dealing with Items Allocated to Main Committee I," NPT/CONF. II/C.I/2, August 26, 1980, p. 2. https://unoda-web.s3-accelerate.amazonaws.com/wp-content/uploads/assets/WMD/Nuclear/pdf/finaldocs/1980%20-%20Geneva%20-%20NPT%20Review%20Conference%20-%20Final%20Document%20Part%20I.pdf.

13. "Final Document of the Review Conference of the Parties to the Treaty on the Non-Proliferation of Nuclear Weapons Part I," NPT/CONF/35/I, May 30, 1975, Annex I, p. 8, http://undocs.org/NPT/CONF/35/I.

14. United Nations General Assembly, "Resolutions and Decisions Adopted by the General Assembly during Its Tenth Special Session: 23 May–30 June 1978," Supplement no. 4 (A/S-10/4), http://undocs.org/en/A/S-10/4.

15. The first half of the 1970s marked a period of détente between the United States and the Soviet Union, with the Strategic Arms Limitation Talks (1969) providing the framework that resulted in the Anti-Ballistic Treaty, the Interim Agreement, and others.

16. Sampson, introduction to *Regionalism, Multilateralism*, 3–4.

17. Ronald Reagan, "Remarks at a Luncheon Hosted by the New Jersey Chamber of Commerce in Somerset," October 13, 1987, http://www.presidency.ucsb.edu/ws/?pid=33543.

18. Mansfield and Milner, "New Wave of Regionalism."

19. The group eventually took shape as a caucus within the APEC. For more, see Hurrell, "Explaining the Resurgence."

20. Organisation of African Unity, "Lagos Plan of Action," Preamble, point 14 vi.

21. Other arrangements emerged, including the West African Economic and Monetary Union and the Economic and Monetary Union of Central Africa. See Salami, *Financial Regulation in Africa*.

22. Devlin and Estevadeordal, "What's New."

23. Hettne and Inotai, "New Regionalism."

24. Fawcett, "Regionalism in Historical Perspective," 9–36.

25. Hurrell, "Explaining the Resurgence," 52.

26. Börzel and Risse, "Rise of (Inter-) Regionalism"; Telò, *European Union and New Regionalism*.

27. For discussion of the process leading up to Maastricht, see Ludlow, "European Integration in the 1980s," 11–22.

28. European Union, Treaty on European Union (Consolidated Version), Treaty of Maastricht, February 7, 1992, http://www.refworld.org/docid/3ae6b39218.html.

29. For an extensive list, see Fawcett, "Regionalism in World Politics," 1–14.
30. Stremlau, "Clinton's Dollar Diplomacy," 24.
31. Baker, "America in Asia," 1–18.
32. "Clinton in Korea: A Call for a Pacific Community Based on 'Shared Strength,'" *New York Times*, July 11, 1993, sec. World, http://www.nytimes.com/1993/07/11/world/clinton-in-korea-a-call-for-a-pacific-community-based-on-shared-strength.html.
33. United Nations Secretary-General, "An Agenda for Peace: Preventive Diplomacy and Related Matters," June 17, 1992, A/47/277, para. 11, http://undocs.org/A/47/277.
34. Ibid., para. 64.
35. Notably, Boutros-Ghali wrote his PhD thesis on the topic of regional organizations.
36. Bellamy, Williams, and Griffin, *Understanding Peacekeeping*.
37. United Nations Secretary-General, "Support by the United Nations System of the Efforts of Governments to Promote and Consolidate New or Restored Democracies" [also known as "An Agenda for Democratization"], A/51/761, December 20, 1996, paras. 80, 81, 82, http://undocs.org/A/51/761.
38. Alagappa, "Regional Institutions," 421.
39. For more, see Baldwin, "Security Studies," 117–41; Buzan, "Rethinking Security," 5–28.
40. Stadtmuller, "Regional Dimensions of Security," 106.
41. There is a larger debate on how to define institutions, hinging on formality, the nature of specificity and obligation, and hard versus soft law. See Keohane, *International Institutions*; C. Joyner, "International Regimes," 212–13; Duffield, "What Are International Institutions?", 1–22.
42. United Nations Secretary-General, "An Agenda for Peace: Preventive Diplomacy and Related Matters," June 17, 1992, A/47/277, para. 61, http://undocs.org/A/47/277.
43. Breslin and Croft, "Researching Regional Security Governance," 7.
44. Keohane and Martin, "Promise of Institutionalist Theory," 42.
45. Keohane, "Institutional Theory"; Lake, "Beyond Anarchy," 129–60; Lindley, *Promoting Peace with Information*.
46. Lipson, "International Cooperation."
47. In fact, institutional ideologies based on ambitious unification goals have acted as "a force for division and consequently ... ineffectiveness." See Acharya and Johnston, "Conclusion," 266.
48. One notable typology of security institutions refers to the presence of great powers. See Lake, "Beyond Anarchy."
49. Solingen, *Nuclear Logics*.
50. Sagan, "Perils of Proliferation," 55.
51. Some scholars have toyed with the idea that the spread of nuclear weapons may be beneficial for global order—notably Waltz, *Spread of Nuclear Weapons*. Policymakers have not.
52. Walker, "Nuclear Order and Disorder."
53. Tannenwald, *Nuclear Taboo*.
54. For more on security communities, see Adler and Barnett, *Security Communities*.
55. Koremenos, Lipson, and Snidal, "Rational Design," 762.
56. Lake and Morgan, *Regional Orders*.
57. Solingen, "Political Economy," 126–69.
58. Väyrynen, "Regionalism," 25–51.
59. Campbell, *Institutional Change and Globalization*.
60. Streeck and Thelen, introduction to *Institutional Change*, 24.

Chapter 4. Established Orders: Western Europe and Latin America

1. Shanks, "Economic Integration," 27.
2. Fursdon, *European Defence Community*, 153.
3. Gavin, "Power through Europe?," 69–87.
4. Fueling these concerns, the EDC Treaty became intertwined later in 1952 with a proposed European Political Community that would combine components from both it and the European Coal and Steel Community.
5. Mallard, "Can the Euratom Treaty Inspire," 462.
6. Spiering and Wintle, *European Identity*.
7. O'Driscoll and Lake, "European Parliament," 1.
8. See J. G. Johnson, "European Atomic Community," 801–12; O'Driscoll and Lake, "European Parliament," for a breakdown and analysis of the treaty provisions.
9. Krige, *Sharing Knowledge, Shaping Europe*, 67.
10. Mallison, "United States Bilateral Agreements," 142–49.
11. Mallard, *Fallout*.
12. Single European Act, February 17, 1986, para. 6, http://eur-lex.europa.eu/legal-content/EN/TXT/PDF/?uri=CELEX:11986U/TXT&from=EN.
13. Portela, "EU's Use of 'Targeted' Sanctions."
14. United Nations Security Council, "Note by the President of the Security Council," S/23500, January 31, 1992, http://undocs.org/S/23500.
15. One exception was a 1994 joint action centered on the harmonization of European controls on dual-use exports.
16. Grand, "European Union," 30.
17. Valasek, "European Union's Role," 43–50.
18. This approach became the centerpiece of the European Union's strategy toward the Iranian safeguards noncompliance case over the course of the next decade.
19. Similar proposals were introduced across a number of venues by the end of the decade, most notably by Poland and Sweden in the UN General Assembly.
20. United Nations General Assembly, "Adopted on the Reports of the First Committee," A/RES/2028(XX), November 23, 1965, point 1.e, http://undocs.org/A/RES/2028(XX)
21. Redick, "Tlatelolco Regime," 103.
22. Treaty for the Prohibition of Nuclear Weapons in Latin America (Tlatelolco Treaty), Article 1, http://www.opanal.org/texto-del-tratado-de-tlatelolco/.
23. Ibid., Article 3. The United States and the UK signed the second protocol by 1968; France and China in 1973 (long before they acceded to the NPT, though France declared it would adhere to that treaty de facto), and the Soviet Union in 1978.
24. Dominguez, "International Cooperation," 83.
25. George, Reiling, and Scaperlanda, "Short-Run Trade Effects," 618–36.
26. Wionczek, "Central American Common Market," 237–40.
27. Chanona, "Regional Security Governance," 109.
28. Dawood and Herz, "Nuclear Governance," 497–535.
29. Acharya, "Ideas, Norms, and Regional Orders," 183–209.
30. Oelsner, *International Relations*.
31. Allyn, Blight, and Welch, "Essence of Revision," 136–72; Dobbs, *One Minute to Midnight*.
32. Epstein, "Making of the Treaty of Tlatelolco," 156.

33. United Nations, "Urgent Need for Suspension of Nuclear and Thermo-nuclear Tests," A/RES/1911 (XVIII), November 27, 1963, http://undocs.org/A/RES/1911(XVIII).
34. Epstein, "Making of the Treaty of Tlatelolco."
35. Redick, "Nuclear Illusions."
36. Grossi, "Latin America's Road," 320.
37. "Argentina provided Brazil uranium concentrate and zirconium used for fabrication of nuclear reactor fuel elements, and a Brazilian-German company (based in Brazil) assumed responsibility for construction of a major portion of the pressure vessel for the third Argentine power reactor vessel" (Redick, "Nuclear Illusions," 20).
38. Sotomayor Velazquez, "Civil-Military Affairs," 29–60.
39. Carasales, "Argentine-Brazilian Nuclear Rapprochement," 39–48.
40. Argentine-Brazilian Declaration on Common Nuclear Policy, November 28, 1990, https://www.iaea.org/sites/default/files/infcirc388.pdf.
41. The IAEA was trusted over OPANAL because of its technical expertise and general resources. Meanwhile, the Treaty of Tlatelolco came into full force when Cuba signed the treaty in 1995 and ratified it in 2002.
42. For more on ending fissile material production, see Simpson, "Nuclear Non-Proliferation," 17–39.
43. Grossi, "Latin America's Road," 322.
44. Solingen, *Regional Orders*; Sotomayor Velazquez, "Civil-Military Affairs."
45. The Tlatelolco Treaty was also updated with the words "and the Caribbean" in the official title in 1990 and was made to include independent states that resided within the zone of application in May 1991; these adjustments further expanded the jurisdiction of the zone.
46. Togzhan Kassenova, "Brazil's Nuclear Kaleidoscope: An Evolving Identity," Brief (Carnegie Endowment for International Peace, March 2014), http://carnegieendowment.org/files/Brief-Togzhan-Brazil.pdf.
47. Herz, Dawood, and Lage, "Nuclear Submarine," 329–50.
48. Rublee, "Threshold States," 151–87.
49. Kutchesfahani, "Bilateral Cooperation on Nonproliferation," 229–49.
50. Associated Press, "Brazil Spending $160M on Nuclear Sub," *NY Daily News*, August 29, 2008, http://www.nydailynews.com/latino/brazil-spending-160m-nuclear-propelled-submarine-article-1.318900.
51. Kaplow, "Canary in the Nuclear Submarine," 185–202.
52. Grant Christopher, "A Nuclear Powered Argentine Submarine?", *ICSA_Kings*, International Centre for Security Analysis, King's College, July 21, 2015, https://blogs.kcl.ac.uk/icsa/2015/07/21/a-nuclear-powered-argentine-submarine/.
53. Kassenova, "Brazil and the Global Nuclear Order," 117–42.
54. Battaglino, "Post-Hegemonic Regional Agenda," 82.
55. Trinkunas, "Reordering Regional Security," 83–99.
56. Burges, "Consensual Hegemony," 65–84.
57. MercoPress, "Brazil Strongly Supports Argentina Falklands' Claim at Defence Ministers' Summit," October 9, 2012, http://en.mercopress.com/2012/10/09/brazil-strongly-supports-argentina-falklands-claim-at-defence-ministers-summit.
58. Trinkunas, "Brazil's Global Ambitions."
59. Rublee, "Threshold States," 172. This is a reference to May 2010, when Brazil—at the encouragement of Washington—reached out to Tehran and brokered an ill-fated fuel swap deal.

Chapter 5. Northeast Asia

1. See Calder and Ye, *Making of Northeast Asia*; Seliger and Pascha, *Northeast Asian Security Community*; Lee and Pempel, "Northeast Asian Security Complex," 3–22.

2. The Six-Party Talks involved North Korea, South Korea, China, Japan, Russia, and the United States.

3. Joint Statement of the Fourth Round of the Six-Party Talks, Beijing, September 19, 2005. https://www.state.gov/p/eap/regional/c15455.htm.

4. Lee and Pempel, "Northeast Asian Security Complex," 8.

5. Casarini, "Visions of North-East Asia."

6. The law is known as the "Permanent International Peace Support Law" and the "Legislation for Peace and Security."

7. Government of Japan, Ministry of Foreign Affairs, "National Security Strategy," December 17, 2013. http://japan.kantei.go.jp/96_abe/documents/2013/__icsFiles/afieldfile/2013/12/17/NSS.pdf.

8. Wallace, "Japan's Strategic Pivot South," 484.

9. Choe Sang-Hun, "South Korea's New President, Moon Jae-In, Promises New Approach to North," *New York Times*, May 10, 2017, sec. Asia Pacific, https://www.nytimes.com/2017/05/10/world/asia/moon-jae-in-president-south-korea.html; Motoko Rich, "North Korea Fires More Missiles as Seoul Puts Off U.S. Defense System," *New York Times*, June 7, 2017, sec. Asia Pacific, https://www.nytimes.com/2017/06/07/world/asia/south-korea-thaad-missile-defense-us.html.

10. Russian Federation and Chinese People's Republic Joint Statement on Comprehensive Deepening of Sino-Russian Partnership and Strategic Cooperation, September 27, 2010, http://news.kremlin.ru/ref_notes/719 (Russian).

11. Xi Jinping, "New Asian Security Concept for New Progress in Security Cooperation," remarks presented at Fourth Summit of the Conference on Interaction and Confidence Building Measures in Asia, Shanghai, May 21, 2014, http://www.fmprc.gov.cn/mfa_eng/zxxx_662805/t1159951.shtml.

12. Yi Wang, "Stay Committed to the Six-Party Talks for Lasting Peace," remarks presented at "Retrospect & Outlook: A Decade of the Six-Party Talks," Diaoyutai State Guesthouse, Beijing, September 19, 2013.

13. Radchenko, "Multilateralism in Northeast Asia."

14. Putin, as expressed in an interview with several Chinese media outlets; see "Russia-China Ties at Highest Level in History—Putin", RT News Channel, May 18, 2014, http://rt.com/news/159804-putin-china-visit-interview/.

15. Bob Savic, "Behind China and Russia's 'Special Relationship,'" *Diplomat*, December 7, 2016, http://thediplomat.com/2016/12/behind-china-and-russias-special-relationship/.

16. Lu, "Reflections on Strategic Stability," 135.

17. Medeiros, as quoted in Eisenman, "Rethinking U.S. Strategy."

18. In categorizing the substance of trilateral meetings from 1999 to 2011, "politics and security" issues accounted for just 16 percent of the total. Further, the Trilateral Cooperation Secretariat's own database lists just two counterterrorism meetings under the "security" label (Yeo, "China, Japan, South Korea").

19. Mongolia is uninvolved directly but has played the role of peacemaker with North Korea. President Tsakhiagiin Elbegdorj visited the country in 2013; Ulaanbaatar has served as an intermediary in talks about the abduction of Japanese citizens, including in March 2014, and hosted a secret Track 1.5 meeting between North Korea and the United States in May 2014.

20. Chairman's Statement for the Second Round of Six-Party Talks, February 28, 2004, http://www.mofa.go.jp/region/asia-paci/n_korea/state0402.html; Chairman's Statement for the Third Round of Six-Party Talks, June 28, 2004, http://www.china.org.cn/english/3rd/99447.htm.

21. Joint Statement of the Fourth Round of the Six-Party Talks, Beijing, September 19, 2005, para. 4, https://www.state.gov/p/eap/regional/c15455.htm.

22. Initial Actions to Implement Six-Party Joint Statement, Beijing, February 13, 2007, https://2001-2009.state.gov/r/pa/prs/ps/2007/february/80508.htm.

23. Lukin, "Emerging Institutional Order," 232.

24. Six-Party Talks—Second-Phase Actions for the Implementation of the September 2005 Joint Statement, Beijing, October 3, 2007, https://2001-2009.state.gov/r/pa/prs/ps/2007/oct/93217.htm; Press Communique of the Heads of Delegation Meeting of the Sixth Round of the Six-Party Talks, Beijing, July 12, 2008, http://www.mofa.go.jp/region/asia-paci/n_korea/6party/press0807.html.

25. Sungnam Lim, Remarks by Ambassador for North Korean Nuclear Issue, Sixth ROK-UN Joint Conference on Disarmament and Non-Proliferation Issues, Seoul, December 4, 2007, http://www.mofa.go.kr/webmodule/htsboard/template/read/korboardread.jsp?typeID=12&boardid=315&seqno=305242.

26. See Streeck and Thelen, introduction to *Institutional Change*.

27. Chun, "Building a Mechanism."

28. RIA Novosti, "Russia, China to Try to Prevent Conflict on Korean Peninsula—Lavrov," Sputnik News, June 4, 2010, http://sputniknews.com/world/20100604/159304757.html.

29. Joint Statement of the Russian Federation and the People's Republic of China, May 20, 2014, http://kremlin.ru/supplement/1642.

30. Clary, "A. Q. Khan," 33–42.

31. Bunn, "Preventing a Nuclear 9/11."

32. International Atomic Energy Agency, "International Legal Framework."

33. Karen DeYoung, "Russia to Skip Nuclear Security Summit Scheduled for 2016 in Washington," *Washington Post*, November 5, 2014.

34. As ranked by the 2016 Nuclear Threat Initiative index.

35. Cirincione, Wolfsthal, and Rajkumar, *Deadly Arsenals*.

36. Park Geun-Hye, "Opening Remarks at the Opening Ceremony of the Nuclear Security Summit 2014," March 25, 2014, https://www.youtube.com/watch?v=1LjXXpXPj_I.

37. See UN, Event List and Related Documents, http://www.un.org/en/sc/1540/transparency-and-outreach/past-outreach-events/event-list-and-related-documents.shtml#2014.

38. For instance, see IAEA, "Voluntary Contributions to IAEA Nuclear Security Fund," https://www.iaea.org/newscenter/news/table-voluntary-contributions-iaea-nuclear-security-fund.

39. Thakur and Evans, *Nuclear Weapons*, 170.

40. This includes Codes of Conduct on the Safety and Security of Radioactive Sources (2003) and on the Safety of Research Reactors (2004).

41. North Korea has signed the Conventions on Early Notification and on Assistance in Case of a Nuclear Accident, while Mongolia is party to those two conventions; neither has signed nor ratified the other conventions listed.

42. With Russia's thirty-three and ten reactors, respectively, the region will be home to 33 percent of reactors in the world. These numbers are on the Nuclear Energy Institute website, dated May 2016, http://www.nei.org/Knowledge-Center/Nuclear-Statistics/World-Statistics.

However, South Korean president Moon expressed in June 2017 a desire to halt plans for construction.

43. For instance, Mack, "Potential, Not Proliferation," 48–53; Manning, "PACATOM, 214–32; S. Lee, "Nuclear Energy Cooperation"; S. Lee and Ginting, "Nuclear Security Cooperation," 93–118.

44. Suzuki, "Lessons from EURATOM."

45. A process of institutional translation. See Campbell, *Institutional Change and Globalization*.

46. Park, "Address by President Park Geun-Hye."

47. United Nations General Assembly, "Comprehensive Study of the Question of Nuclear-Weapon-Free Zones in All Its Aspects: Special Report of the Conference of the Committee on Disarmament," A/10027/Add.1, 1976, p. 41, http://undocs.org/A/10027/Add.1(SUPP).

48. Ibid., p. 43.

49. Kihl and Hayes, *Peace and Security*.

50. Koo, "Northeast Asian," 123–39.

51. United Nations General Assembly, "Work of the Advisory Board on Disarmament Matters: Report of the Secretary-General," A/68/206, July 26, 2013, p. 6, http://undocs.org/A/68/206.

52. For instance, Elbegdorj Tsakhia, "Statement at the High-Level Meeting on Nuclear Disarmament," September 26, 2013, http://www.president.mn/eng/newsCenter/viewNews.php?newsId=970.

53. Statement of Support for a Northeast Asia Nuclear Weapon Free Zone, convened by Peace Depot Inc., Peace Network, and People's Solidarity for Participatory Democracy, April 22, 2009, http://archive.pnnd.org/docs/update23/NEA-NWFZ%20Statement%20_as%20of%2009.4.22_.pdf.

54. See Park, "Address by President Park Geun-Hye."

55. United Nations General Assembly, "Report of the Disarmament Commission," A/54/42, December 1, 1999, p. 8, http://undocs.org/A/54/42(SUPP).

56. Seana K. Magee, "Hiraoka Calls for Nuke-Free Zones," *Japan Times Online*, May 21, 2009, http://www.japantimes.co.jp/news/2009/05/21/national/hiraoka-calls-for-nuke-free-zones/.

57. Davenport and Kimball, "Nuclear-Weapon-Free Zones."

58. Evans, "Constructing Multilateralism," 109.

59. Snyder, "Northeast Asian Security Architecture."

Chapter 6. Southeast Asia

1. Katsumata, "Norms and Regional Institutions," 35–48.

2. Weber, "ASEAN Regional Forum," 220.

3. Finlay, *Southern Flows*, 128.

4. Selth, "Burma and Weapons of Mass Destruction," 52–70.

5. This left only East Timor (an observer state) as a nonmember in the geographic area.

6. Koga, "Explaining the Transformation," 1–27.

7. Yamamoto, "Asia and Regional Integration Theory," 20.

8. Declaration of ASEAN Concord (Bali Concord), Bali, Indonesia, February 24, 1976, Part E, http://asean.org/?static_post=declaration-of-asean-concord-indonesia-24-february-1976.

9. Narine, "Institutional Theory," 33–47.
10. Almonte, "Ensuring Security," 81.
11. Katsumata, "ASEAN Regional Forum," 181–98.
12. Haacke, *ASEAN's Diplomatic and Security Culture*.
13. Chairman's Statement: The First ASEAN Regional Forum Ministerial Meeting, Bangkok, July 25, 1994, https://2001-2009.state.gov/t/ac/csbm/rd/4377.htm.
14. 1995 Treaty on the Southeast Asia Nuclear Weapon-Free Zone (Bangkok Treaty), December 15, 1995, http://asean.org/?static_post=treaty-on-the-southeast-asia-nuclear-weapon-free-zone.
15. Buszynski, "Southeast Asia," 830–47; Chalmers, "ASEAN and Confidence Building," 36–56.
16. None of the five have signed onto their separate protocol.
17. Campbell, *Institutional Change and Globalization*.
18. This stood in contrast to the Treaty of Tlatelolco in Latin America and the Caribbean, which had created a wholly separate institutional arrangement.
19. 1995 Treaty on the Southeast Asia Nuclear Weapon-Free Zone, December 15, 1995, Articles 4, 12, 13, http://asean.org/?static_post=treaty-on-the-southeast-asia-nuclear-weapon-free-zone.
20. Ibid., Article 21.
21. Acharya, *Constructing a Security Community*; Goh, "'ASEAN Way,'" 113–18.
22. Narine, "ASEAN in the Aftermath," 179–94.
23. ASEAN Vision 2020, December 15, 1997, para. 6, http://asean.org/?static_post=asean-vision-2020.
24. 1998 Hanoi Plan of Action, December 15, 1998, Hanoi, Vietnam, http://asean.org/?static_post=hanoi-plan-of-action.
25. Caballero-Anthony, "Evolving Regional Governance," 32–65.
26. Stubbs, "ASEAN Plus Three," 440–55.
27. Matsuoka, "Institutional Approaches," 85.
28. ASEAN, Declaration of ASEAN Concord II (Bali Concord II), October 7, 2003, part A2, http://asean.org/?static_post=declaration-of-asean-concord-ii-bali-concord-ii.
29. ASEAN, Vientiane Action Programme (VAP) 2004–2010, November 29, 2004, pp. 6–8, http://www.asean.org/storage/images/archive/VAP-10th%20ASEAN%20Summit.pdf.
30. Shoji, "ASEAN Security Community."
31. Joint Declaration of the ASEAN Defence Ministers on Enhancing Regional Peace and Stability, Singapore, November 14, 2007, para. 7, http://asean.org/?static_post=joint-declaration-of-the-asean-defence-ministers-on-enhancing-regional-peace-and-stability-singapore-14-november-2007.
32. Nair, "Regionalism," 110–42.
33. ASEAN Secretariat, "Kuala Lumpur Declaration on the East Asia Summit," December 14, 2005, http://asean.org/?static_post=kuala-lumpur-declaration-on-the-east-asia-summit-kuala-lumpur-14-december-2005.
34. Tan, "ASEAN Charter," 171–98.
35. The ASEAN Security Community was renamed the ASEAN Political-Security Community in 2009.
36. Koga, *Reinventing Regional Security Institutions*.
37. Narine, "ASEAN into the Twenty-First Century," 357–80; Acharya, *Constructing a Security Community*.
38. Pempel, "Race to Connect," 239.

39. H. J. Kim and Lee, "Changing Role of Dialogue," 953–70.
40. Weatherbee, *International Relations*.
41. Peou, "Security Community-Building," 144–66.
42. A critical juncture is a period characterized by the relaxing of the "'normal' structural and institutional constraints on action." See Capoccia and Kelemen, "Study of Critical Junctures," 355.
43. Acharya, *Constructing a Security Community*, 140.
44. Acharya, *Whose Ideas Matter?*
45. Cheong, "Evaluation of Recent Progress," 37–56.
46. Nesadurai, "Global Politics of Regionalism," 155.
47. Framework Agreements on Enhancing ASEAN Economic Cooperation, January 28, 1992, Singapore, http://www.asean.org/storage/images/2012/Economic/AFTA/Common_Effective_Preferential_Tariff/Framework%20Agreements%20on%20Enhancing%20ASEAN%20Economic%20Cooperation%20.pdf.
48. Weatherbee, *International Relations*.
49. Stubbs, "ASEAN Plus Three."
50. Kawai, "Chiang Mai Initiative."
51. Kraft, "ASEAN and Intra-ASEAN Relations," 453–72; Narine, "ASEAN into the Twenty-First Century."
52. Stubbs, "ASEAN Plus Three," 444.
53. Ibid.
54. Ravenhill, "Three Bloc World?," 167–95.
55. China has also prioritized the Conference on Interaction and Confidence Building Measures—where neither Japan nor the United States are full members.
56. Interview with Tang Siew Mun, senior fellow at the Institute of Southeast Asian Studies, March 25, 2015.
57. As an example of the former, see Xinhua News Agency, "ASEAN Political-Security Community Blueprint Fully Implemented: Malaysian Official," November 19, 2015, http://www.globaltimes.cn/content/953664.shtml.
58. The Ministry of Trade, Industry, and Energy of Korea recently funded a three-year program aimed at building ASEAN capacity for civilian nuclear power development.
59. As mentioned, this feature marks a departure from all other nuclear-weapon-free zones.
60. South Pacific Nuclear Free Zone Treaty and Protocols (Treaty of Rarotonga), August 6, 1985, Article I, para. C, http://disarmament.un.org/treaties/t/rarotonga/text.
61. Hamel-Green, "Nuclear-Weapon-Free Zone Developments," 239–52.
62. 1995 Treaty on the Southeast Asia Nuclear Weapon-Free Zone (Bangkok Treaty), December 15, 1995, Article 9, para. 3b, http://asean.org/?static_post=treaty-on-the-southeast-asia-nuclear-weapon-free-zone.
63. The treaty requires parties to join the 1986 Convention on Early Notification of a Nuclear Accident and includes provision against the disposal of radioactive wastes.
64. See list at IAEA, Status of the Additional Protocol, https://www.iaea.org/safeguards/safeguards-legal-framework/additional-protocol/status-of-additional-protocol.
65. Since 2010, 74 of the 193 UN member states have submitted updated national reports.
66. Malley and Ogilvie-White, "Nuclear Challenges," 4, 8.
67. Summary of 1st Meeting of ASEAN Network of Regulatory Bodies on Atomic Energy (ASEANTOM), September 3–4, 2013, Phuket, Thailand, http://www.iaea.org/inis/collection/NCLCollectionStore/_Public/45/075/45075439.pdf.

68. Ibid.
69. Interview with Mely Caballero Anthony, head of Centre for Non-Traditional Security Studies, Nanyang Technological University, Singapore, March 27, 2015.
70. The energy demand in the region is expected to grow 2.5 percent annually from 2007 to 2035, nearly doubling and well outpacing the growth in the global demand. See Kutani, "Energy Outlook for Asia," 87–94.
71. International Centre for Security Analysis, "Nuclear Security."
72. James Martin Center for Nonproliferation Studies, "Prospects for Nuclear Security Partnership."

Chapter 7. The Middle East

1. Slackman, "Session Four."
2. Habib Toumi, "Calls for GCC Union Intensify ahead of Summit," *Gulf News*, November 21, 2016, http://gulfnews.com/news/gulf/calls-for-gcc-union-intensify-ahead-of-summit-1.1932912.
3. Monier, "Arabness of Middle East Regionalism," 421.
4. Patrick, "Future of Middle East Regionalism"; Fawcett, "Alliances and Regionalism," 185–204; Talani, *Arab Spring*.
5. Solingen, *Nuclear Logics*.
6. Legrenzi and Calculli, "Regionalism and Regionalization."
7. Brock, "Regional Cooperation," 4.
8. Rouis and Tabor, "Regional Economic Integration."
9. Abdmoulah, "Arab Trade Integration," 39–66.
10. Rouis and Tabor, "Regional Economic Integration."
11. Ibid.
12. Albareda and Barba, "Sub-Regionalism in North Africa," 7.
13. Ehteshami, "MENA Region," 130–53.
14. Salamé, "Integration in the Arab World," 256.
15. Barnett and Solingen, "Designed to Fail," 193.
16. Legrenzi and Calculli, "Regionalism and Regionalization." Notably, Saudi Arabia houses 61 percent of the GCC population and 45 percent of its gross domestic product.
17. Charter of the Gulf Cooperation Council (GCC), May 25, 1981. http://www.gccsg.org/en-us/AboutGCC/Pages/Primarylaw.aspx.
18. Tripp, "Regionalism," 283–308.
19. Especially between the Saudi Arabia–led faction within the GCC and Qatar, which led to the isolation of the latter in June 2017. See David Roberts, "Qatar Row: What's Caused the Fall-out between Gulf Neighbours?," BBC News, June 5, 2017, http://www.bbc.com/news/world-middle-east-40159080.
20. Treaty Instituting the Arab Maghreb Union, February 17, 1989.
21. Hufbauer and Brunel, *Maghreb Regional and Global Integration*.
22. Albareda and Barba, "Sub-Regionalism in North Africa," 15.
23. Legrenzi and Calculli, "Regionalism and Regionalization."
24. Beck, "End of Regional Middle Eastern Exceptionalism?," 190–207.
25. Rishmawi, "League of Arab States."
26. League of Arab States Council Resolution 7438, Extraordinary Session, November 12, 2011.

27. Lebanon and Yemen voted against the resolution.
28. Isaac, "Resurgence in Arab Regional Institutions?," 151–67.
29. Hamel-Green, "Peeling the Orange," 3–14.
30. Pakistan's proposal for a South Asian nuclear-weapon-free zone, for instance, immediately followed India's 1974 peaceful nuclear explosion, suggesting the normalcy of a regional-centric response to threats.
31. United Nations General Assembly, Comprehensive Study of the Question of Nuclear-Weapon-Free Zones in All Its Aspects, A/10027/Add.1(SUPP), 1976; the study was conducted by experts from twenty-one countries and presented at the Conference of the Committee on Disarmament.
32. IAEA, "Modalities of Application of Agency Safeguards in the Middle East," GC(XXXIII)/887, August 29, 1989, https://www.iaea.org/About/Policy/GC/GC33/GC33Documents/English/gc33-887_en.pdf.
33. IAEA, "Application of IAEA Safeguards in the Middle East," GC(XXXV)/RES/571, September 20, 1991, https://www.iaea.org/About/Policy/GC/GC59/GC59Documents/English/gc59-15_en.pdf.
34. Baumgart and Müller, "Nuclear Weapons–Free Zone," 45–58.
35. United Nations Security Council, Resolution 687, S/RES/687, April 3, 1991, para. 14, http://undocs.org/S/RES/687(1991). This included the destruction of Kuwait's biological and chemical stocks and longer-range ballistic missiles, and the confirmation of its NPT obligations, with all weapons-grade nuclear materials to be placed under IAEA control for destruction or removal.
36. Yaffe, "Promoting Arms Control," 9–25.
37. Simpson and Howlett, "NPT Renewal Conference," 41–71. Simpson and Howlett even suggest that UN Security Council Resolutions 687, 707, and 175 on Iraqi noncompliance provided a "basis for long-term verification and monitoring proposals . . . [for a] regional arms control agreement" (52–53). The crux of their article notes the "discernible shift from global to regional solutions" in the post–Cold War era (54).
38. "1995 Review and Extension Conference of the Parties to the Treaty on the Non-Proliferation of Nuclear Weapons: Final Document Part I Organization and Work of the Conference," NPT/CONF.1995/32, May 11, 1995, Decision 2, para. 6, http://undocs.org/NPT/CONF.1995/32(PARTI).
39. Ibid.
40. Baumgart and Müller, "Nuclear Weapons–Free Zone."
41. "1995 Review and Extension Conference of the Parties to the Treaty on the Non-Proliferation of Nuclear Weapons, Report of Main Committee 1," NPT/CONF.1995/MC.II/1, May 5, 1995, para. 44, http://undocs.org/NPT/CONF.1995/32%20(Part%20II).
42. "2000 Review Conference of the Parties to the Treaty on the Non-Proliferation of Nuclear Weapons, Report of Main Committee II," NPT/CONF.2000/28, Article VII, para 16.7, http://undocs.org/NPT/CONF.2000/28%20(Part%20III).
43. United Nations General Assembly, "Establishment of a Nuclear-Weapon-Free Zone in the Region of the Middle East," A/RES/58/34, December 19, 2003, http://undocs.org/A/RES/58/34.
44. "2010 Review Conference of the Parties to the Treaty on the Non-Proliferation of Nuclear Weapons, Final Document Volume I," NPT/CONF.2010/50, May 28, 2010, p. 19, http://undocs.org/NPT/CONF.2010/50%20(VOL.I).
45. Ibid., Section IV, para. 7b.
46. Kubbig and Weidlich, "WMD/DVs Free Zone," 4.

47. Wilfred Wan, "Why the 2015 NPT Review Conference Fell Apart—United Nations University Centre for Policy Research," United Nations University Centre for Policy Research, May 28, 2015, https://cpr.unu.edu/why-the-2015-npt-review-conference-fell-apart.html.

48. Ibid.

49. "Bahrain (on behalf of the Arab Group), "Implementation of the 1995 Resolution and 2010 Outcome on the Middle East," NPT/CONF.2015/WP.33, April 22, 2015, http://undocs.org/NPT/CONF.2015/WP.33.

50. This has been a longstanding concern. See Landau, "Egypt and Israel in ACRS."

51. Kubbig and Fikenscher, *Arms Control*.

52. Kubbig et al., "Overall Military Asymmetries," 66–88.

53. Bar-Joseph, "Israel's Security Interests," 99.

54. Peter Beaumont, "Israel Will Not Accept Iran Nuclear Deal, Says Binyamin Netanyahu," *Guardian*, April 3, 2015, sec. World news, https://www.theguardian.com/world/2015/apr/03/iran-deal-threatens-israels-existence-benjamin-netanyahu-tells-obama.

55. Fitzpatrick, "Overwhelming Global Vote," 71–75.

56. Solingen, *Sanctions, Statecraft*.

57. IAEA, Implementation of the NPT Safeguards Agreement in the Islamic Republic of Iran, GOV/2003/40, June 6, 2003, https://www.iaea.org/sites/default/files/gov-2015-34.pdf.

58. United Nations Security Council, Resolution 1737 (2006), S/RES/1737, December 23, 2006, http://www.undocs.org/S/RES/1737(2006).

59. For more on the chronology that follows, see Reynolds and Wan, "Empirical Trends," 56–124.

60. United Nations Security Council, Resolution 1747 (2007), A/RES/1747, March 24, 2007, http://www.undocs.org/S/RES/1747(2007), and United Nations Security Council, Resolution 1803 (2008), S/RES/1803, March 3, 2008, http://www.undocs.org/S/RES/1803(2008).

61. United Nations Security Council, Resolution 1929 (2010), S/RES/1929, June 9, 2010, www.undocs.org/S/RES/1929%20(2010).

62. Iran: Nuclear Intentions and Capabilities, National Intelligence Council, November 2007, point E, https://graphics8.nytimes.com/packages/pdf/international/20071203_release.pdf.

63. David E. Sanger and William J. Broad, "Nuclear Agency Says Iran Worked on Weapons Design until 2009," *New York Times*, December 2, 2015, https://www.nytimes.com/2015/12/03/world/middleeast/iran-nuclear-report-atomic-agency.html.

64. Reynolds and Wan, "Empirical Trends," 56–124.

65. Interview with former Panel of Experts member, conducted in New York, May 20, 2015.

66. Leverett, "Iranian Nuclear Issue," 245.

67. Jonathan Schanzer and Mark Dubowitz, "It Just Got Easier for Iran to Fund Terrorism," *Foreign Policy*, July 17, 2015, https://foreignpolicy.com/2015/07/17/it-just-got-easier-for-iran-to-fund-terrorism-swift-bank/.

68. Helene Cooper, "Saudi Arabia Approves of Iran Nuclear Deal, U.S. Defense Chief Says," *New York Times*, July 22, 2015, https://www.nytimes.com/2015/07/23/world/middleeast/iran-nuclear-deal-saudi-arabia.html; Jay Solomon, "Egypt Says Iran Deal Provides New Opening for a Nuclear Weapons–Free Mideast," *Wall Street Journal*, February 8, 2016, sec. World, http://www.wsj.com/articles/egypt-says-iran-deal-provides-new-opening-for-a-nuclear-weapons-free-mideast-1454975799.

69. Lt. Gen. Gadi Eisenkot, remarks at the Ninth Institute for National Security Studies International Conference, Tel Aviv, Israel, January 18, 2016, https://www.youtube.com/watch?v=BFC9pdAaSiM.

70. Ben Caspit, "New IDF Strategy Dismisses Iran Nuclear Threat—Al-Monitor: The Pulse of the Middle East," trans. Sandy Bloom, *Al-Monitor*, August 17, 2015, para. 3, http://www.al-monitor.com/pulse/originals/2015/08/israel-new-strategy-eizenkot-terror-hezbollah-hamas-is-iran.html.

71. Thaler et al., *Mullahs, Guards, and Bonyads*.

72. George Perkovich, "Nuclear Quagmire with Iran," interview by Bernard Gwertzman, November 23, 2009, http://www.carnegieendowment.org/publications/index.cfm?fa=view&id=24223. The fuel exchange agreement between Iran, the United States, France, and Russia collapsed in February 2010 as a result, with Iran increasing its enrichment level. Perhaps in an Iranian effort to prevent further sanctions from the Security Council, Iran then agreed to a diplomatic initiative by Brazil and Turkey that would involve exporting part of its low-enriched uranium stockpile. The trilateral fuel exchange agreement was rejected by France, Russia, and the United States.

73. Monshipouri and Dorraj, "Iran's Foreign Policy," 133–47.

74. Leverett, "Iranian Nuclear Issue," 264.

75. Dan De Luce, "Trump Keeps the Iran Deal Alive, For Now," Foreign Policy, *Cable*, May 17, 2017, https://foreignpolicy.com/2017/05/17/trump-keeps-the-iran-deal-alive-for-now/.

76. Reuters, "Qatar Willing to Listen to Gulf Concerns, Kuwait Says," *New York Times*, June 11, 2017, sec. Business Day, available at https://www.reuters.com/article/us-gulf-qatar/qatar-willing-to-listen-to-gulf-concerns-kuwait-says-idUSKBN1920P2.

77. David E. Sanger, "John Kerry Confronts Concerns of Arab States after Iran Nuclear Deal," *New York Times*, April 7, 2016, http://www.nytimes.com/2016/04/08/world/middleeast/year-after-iran-nuclear-deal-kerry-confronts-concerns-of-arab-states.html.

Chapter 8. Elusive Orders: Africa and South Asia

1. United Nations General Assembly, "Implementation of the Declaration on the Denuclearization of Africa," A/RES/45/56, December 4, 1990, point 9, http://www.undocs.org/A/RES/45/56; see also Nwogugu, "Treaty of Pelindaba," 227–48.

2. South Africa did not accede to the Nuclear Non-Proliferation Treaty (NPT) until 1991, and its dismantlement process was not concluded until 1993.

3. United Nations General Assembly, "Implementation of the Declaration on the Denuclearization of Africa," A/RES/47/76, December 15, 1992, http://www.undocs.org/A/RES/47/76.

4. Stumpf, "South Africa's Nuclear Weapons Program," 5.

5. Burgess, "South Africa's Nuclear Weapons Policies," 519–26.

6. Ohaegbulam, "United States and Africa," 19–34.

7. Kutchesfahani and Lombardi, "South Africa," 289–306. While the traditional narrative refers to the thawing of Cold War relations for the overall change of direction in U.S. policy, an alternative interpretation posits that anti-apartheid and racial equality norms at the global level led the United States to enact sanctions on the National Party (see Klotz, "Norms Reconstituting Interests," 451–78). In any case, the results were the same.

8. Villiers, Jardine, and Reiss, "Why South Africa Gave Up," 98–109.

9. Goldblat, "Denuclearization of Africa," 169–72.

10. Nwogugu, "Treaty of Pelindaba."

11. Herbst, "Crafting Regional Cooperation," 129.

12. Jackson, "Regional Security," 113–30.

13. Conflict regularly spanned the entirety of the Cold War era, from border wars with Algeria and Morocco, Somalia and Ethiopia, Tanzania and Uganda, to civil wars in Liberia and Sierra Leone.

14. Protocol Relating to the Establishment of the Peace and Security Council of the African Union, July 9, 2002, Article 3, paras. a and e, https://au.int/sites/default/files/treaties/7781-file-protocol_peace_and_security.pdf.

15. For instance, Madagascar in 2009, Mali in 2012, Egypt in 2013, and Burkina Faso in 2015.

16. Burgess and Kassenova, "Rollback States," 85–117.

17. Underlining the impressive level of institutionalization and independence, AFCONE contains a chairman, vice-chairman, and executive secretary. Its membership is elected by the parties for three-year terms, and its annual sessions were wholly separate from any existing OAU ministerial meetings or sessions.

18. Clary, "A. Q. Khan," 36.

19. Polner, "Authorized Economic Operator (AEO) Programmes." This was linked to the World Customs Organization's adoption of a SAFE Framework of Standards in 2005, which introduced the concept of approved Authorized Economic Operators (AEOs) aimed to streamline processing of goods for these businesses and create one set of international standards.

20. See United Nations, Multilateral Treaties Deposited with the Secretary-General, https://treaties.un.org/Pages/ParticipationStatus.aspx?clang=_en.

21. See United Nations Security Council, National Reports, http://www.un.org/en/sc/1540/national-implementation/national-reports.shtml.

22. United Nations Security Council, "Letter Dated 9 December 2016 from the Chair of the Security Council," Document S/2016/1038, December 9, 2016, http://www.undocs.org/S/2016/1038.

23. Adala, "Nonproliferation in Eastern Africa," 79.

24. Charter of the South Asian Association for Regional Cooperation, December 8, 1985, http://www.saarc-sec.org/SAARC-Charter/5/.

25. Svensson, "Regional Security Governance," 94–112.

26. Sally, "Regional Economic Integration."

27. Pitigala, "Regional Trade in South Asia."

28. Saez, *South Asian Association*.

29. Bandara and McGillivray, "Trade Policy Reforms," 881–96.

30. Weerakoon, "SAFTA," 72.

31. Ibid.

32. In this manner, South Asia appears almost as a counterfactual for South America, had the Brazil-Argentina rivalry persisted throughout the Cold War.

33. Saez, *South Asian Association*.

34. Wagner, "Security Cooperation," 18, 7.

35. Dash, "Political Economy," 185–209.

36. Kapur, "Indian Nuclear Program," 13–25.

37. Chakma, "Pakistan's Nuclear Weapons Programme," 26–38.

38. Hagerty, "Nuclear Deterrence," 95.

39. Ibid.; Wirsing, *Kashmir in the Shadow*.

40. Morgan et al., "India and the United States," 155–79.

41. Wagner, "Security Cooperation."

42. Buzan, "South Asian Security Complex," 5.

43. Kapur, "Ten Years of Instability," 71–94; Narang, *Nuclear Strategy*.

44. India has taken unilateral actions to reduce that risk, including a voluntary moratorium on nuclear testing; it has also expressed support for negotiations for a Fissile Material Cut-Off Treaty. In that latter instance, however, given Pakistan's opposition, this could be construed as a political move.

45. "A nuclear-weapon State is one which has manufactured and exploded a nuclear weapon or other nuclear explosive device prior to 1 January 1967," as stated in Article IX of the NPT.

46. "2010 Review Conference of the Parties to the Treaty on the Non-Proliferation of Nuclear Weapons, Final Document Volume I," NPT/CONF.2010/50, May 28, 2010, p. 19, http://undocs.org/NPT/CONF.2010/50%20(VOL.I).

47. Krepon, "Looking Back," 51–55.

48. Khan, "South Asia," 86–96.

49. Nuclear Threat Initiative, "NTI Nuclear Materials Security Index."

50. Ibid.

51. Proponents suggest that these deals allowed the nuclear weapon states to enhance their minimal regulation of the Indian and Pakistani nuclear programs. Each has increased its cooperation with the IAEA since those civilian agreements, employing additional facility-specific safeguards agreements (Fields and Enia, "Health of the Nuclear Nonproliferation Regime"). Meanwhile, the domestic Hyde Act attached to the U.S.-India deal imposes more obligations upon the United States to report on significant nuclear activities by India; to some, it "opened a new chapter in the international nonproliferation regime" and "strengthens existing nonproliferation principles" (Gupta and Patil, "India and the Global Nuclear Nonproliferation," 105).

52. Karim, "Future of South Asian Security," 7.

53. Lahore Declaration, Governments of India and Pakistan, February 21, 1999, point 1, http://mea.gov.in/in-focus-article.htm?18997/Lahore+Declaration+February+1999.

54. Parthemore, "Unique Risks of Nuclear-Armed Cruise Missiles," 46.

Chapter 9. *The Future of Nonproliferation*

1. Julian Borger, "Nuclear Weapons Risk Greater Than in Cold War, Says Ex-Pentagon Chief," *Guardian*, January 7, 2016, sec. World news, https://www.theguardian.com/world/2016/jan/07/nuclear-weapons-risk-greater-than-in-cold-war-says-ex-pentagon-chief.

2. Lack of information about Russia's historical production prevents more precise numbers, but it is estimated that the five nuclear weapon states combined account for 99 percent of highly enriched uranium stocks and 98 percent of the separated plutonium stocks. See International Panel on Fissile Materials, "Global Fissile Material Report 2015."

3. Jack Kim and James Pearson, "North Korea Ramps Up Uranium Enrichment, Enough for Six Nuclear Bombs a Year: Experts," *Reuters*, September 14, 2016, http://www.reuters.com/article/us-northkorea-nuclear-fuel-idUSKCN11K07Y.

4. Elizabeth Roche, "India in NSG Could Fuel Nuclear Arms Race, Warns Chinese Media," *Livemint* (Delhi), June 14, 2016, http://www.livemint.com/Politics/cOwdE5RBMSVPcqBOk2XJSI/Indias-NSG-membership-bid-to-touch-raw-nerve-in-Pakistan-C.html.

5. Science and Security Board, "It Is 2 Minutes to Midnight."

6. Richard Stone, "Russia Suspends Nuclear R&D Pact with United States," *Science*, October 7, 2016, http://www.sciencemag.org/news/2016/10/russia-suspends-nuclear-rd-pact-united-states.

7. For a volume that studies many of these, see Knopf, *International Cooperation*.

8. Logan, "Proliferation Security Initiative," 253–74; Cotton, "Proliferation Security Initiative," 193–211; D. H. Joyner, "Proliferation Security Initiative," 507–48.

9. Asada, "Security Council Resolution 1540," 303–32.

10. And becoming "a separate level of analysis . . . between the state and the globe." See Kelly, "Security Theory," 198.

11. Enkhsaikhan, "Mongolia's Nuclear-Weapon-Free Status," 353.

12. United Nations Security Council, Resolution 1977 (2011), S/RES/1977, April 20, 2011, http://www.undocs.org/S/RES/1977(2011).

13. Knopf, "Conclusions," 294.

BIBLIOGRAPHY

Abdmoulah, Walid. "Arab Trade Integration: Evidence from Zero-Inflated Negative Biomial Model." *Journal of Economic Cooperation and Development* 32, no. 2 (2011): 39–66.
Acharya, Amitav. *Constructing a Security Community in Southeast Asia: ASEAN and the Problem of Regional Order.* 3rd ed. New York: Routledge, 2014.
———. "Ideas, Norms, and Regional Orders." In *International Relations Theory and Regional Transformation*, edited by T. V. Paul, 183–209. New York: Cambridge University Press, 2012.
———. "Nuclear Proliferation and Regional Security Orders: Comparing North Korea and Iran." In *The United Nations and Nuclear Orders*, edited by Jane Boulden, Ramesh Thakur, and Thomas G. Weiss, 248–72. New York: United Nations University Press, 2009.
———. *Whose Ideas Matter?: Agency and Power in Asian Regionalism.* Ithaca: Cornell University Press, 2011.
Acharya, Amitav, and Alastair Iain Johnston. "Conclusion: Institutional Features, Cooperation Effects, and the Agenda for Further Research on Comparative Regionalism." In *Crafting Cooperation: Regional International Institutions in Comparative Perspective*, edited by Amitav Acharya and Alastair Iain Johnston, 244–78. Cambridge: Cambridge University Press, 2007.
Adala, Ochieng. "Nonproliferation in Eastern Africa." In *Southern Flows: WMD Nonproliferation in the Developing World*, edited by Brian Finlay, 66–80. Washington, D.C.: The Stanley Foundation and Stimson, 2014.
Adler, Emanuel, and Michael Barnett, eds. *Security Communities.* Cambridge: Cambridge University Press, 1998.
African Union. Protocol Relating to the Establishment of the Peace and Security Council of the African Union. July 9, 2002. https://au.int/en/treaties/protocol-relating-establishment-peace-and-security-council-african-union.
Alagappa, Muthiah. "Regional Institutions, the UN and International Security: A Framework for Analysis." *Third World Quarterly* 18, no. 3 (September 1, 1997): 421–42.
Albareda, Adria, and Oriol Barba. "Sub-Regionalism in North Africa and the Middle East: Lessons Learned and New Opportunities." Barcelona: European Institute of the Mediterranean, 2011.
Allyn, Bruce J., James G. Blight, and David A. Welch. "Essence of Revision: Moscow, Havana, and the Cuban Missile Crisis." *International Security* 14, no. 3 (1989): 136–72.
Almonte, Jose T. "Ensuring Security the 'ASEAN Way.'" *Survival* 39, no. 4 (1997): 80–92.
Argentine-Brazilian Declaration on Common Nuclear Policy. November 28, 1990. https://www.iaea.org/sites/default/files/infcirc388.pdf.
Asada, Masahiko. "Security Council Resolution 1540 to Combat WMD Terrorism: Effectiveness and Legitimacy in International Legislation." *Journal of Conflict and Security Law* 13, no. 3 (December 21, 2008): 303–32.
Association of Southeast Asian Nations (ASEAN). ASEAN Vision 2020. December 15, 1997.

———. Declaration of ASEAN Concord II (Bali Concord II). October 7, 2003. http://asean.org/?static_post=declaration-of-asean-concord-ii-bali-concord-ii.

———. "Kuala Lumpur Declaration on the East Asia Summit." December 14, 2005. http://asean.org/?static_post=kuala-lumpur-declaration-on-the-east-asia-summit-kuala-lumpur-14-december-2005.

———. 1976 Declaration of ASEAN Concord (Bali Concord). February 24, 1976. http://asean.org/?static_post=declaration-of-asean-concord-indonesia-24-february-1976.

———. 1995 Treaty on the Southeast Asia Nuclear Weapon-Free Zone (Bangkok Treaty). December 15, 1995. http://asean.org/?static_post=treaty-on-the-southeast-asia-nuclear-weapon-free-zone.

———. 1998 Ha Noi Action Plan. December 16, 1998. http://asean.org/?static_post=hanoi-plan-of-action.

———. Vientiane Action Programme (VAP) 2004–2010. November 29, 2004. http://www.asean.org/storage/images/archive/VAP-10th%20ASEAN%20Summit.pdf.

Baker, James A. "America in Asia: Emerging Architecture for a Pacific Community." *Foreign Affairs* 70, no. 5 (1991): 1–18.

Baldwin, David A. "Security Studies and the End of the Cold War." *World Politics* 48, no. 1 (October 1995): 117–41.

Bandara, Jayatilleke S., and Mark McGillivray. "Trade Policy Reforms in South Asia." *World Economy* 21, no. 7 (September 1, 1998): 881–96.

Bar-Joseph, Uri. "Taking Israel's Security Interests into Account: Deterrence Policy in a Changing Strategic Environment." In *Arms Control and Missile Proliferation in the Middle East*, edited by Bernd W. Kubbig and Sven-Eric Fikenscher, 89–105. New York: Routledge, 2012.

Barnett, Michael, and Etel Solingen. "Designed to Fail or Failure of Design? The Origins and Legacy of the Arab League." In *Crafting Cooperation: Regional International Institutions in Comparative Perspective*, edited by Amitav Acharya and Alastair Iain Johnston, 180–220. Cambridge: Cambridge University Press, 2007.

Battaglino, Jorge. "Defence in a Post-Hegemonic Regional Agenda: The Case of the South American Defence Council." In *The Rise of Post-Hegemonic Regionalism*, edited by Pía Riggirozzi and Diana Tussie, 81–100. United Nations University Series on Regionalism 4. Dordrecht, Netherlands: Springer, 2012.

Baumgart, Claudia, and Harald Müller. "A Nuclear Weapons–Free Zone in the Middle East: A Pie in the Sky?" *Washington Quarterly* 28, no. 1 (2004): 45–58.

Beck, Martin. "The End of Regional Middle Eastern Exceptionalism? The Arab League and the Gulf Cooperation Council after the Arab Uprisings." *Democracy and Security* 11, no. 2 (June 15, 2015): 190–207.

Bellamy, Alex J., Paul D. Williams, and Stuart Griffin. *Understanding Peacekeeping*. Cambridge: Polity, 2010.

Bennett, Andrew, and Colin Elman. "Qualitative Research: Recent Developments in Case Study Methods." *Annual Review of Political Science* 9 (2006): 455–76.

Biswas, Shampa. *Nuclear Desire: Power and the Postcolonial Nuclear Order*. Minneapolis: University of Minnesota Press, 2014.

Börzel, Tanja, and Thomas Risse. "The Rise of (Inter-) Regionalism: The EU as a Model of Regional Integration." SSRN Scholarly Paper. Rochester, NY: Social Science Research Network, 2009. https://papers.ssrn.com/abstract=1450391.

Boulden, Jane, Ramesh Thakur, and Thomas G. Weiss, eds. *The United Nations and Nuclear Orders*. New York: United Nations University Press, 2009.

Breslin, Shaun, and Stuart Croft. "Researching Regional Security Governance: Dimensions, Debates and Discourses." In *Comparative Regional Security Governance*, edited by Shaun Breslin and Stuart Croft, 1–22. New York: Routledge, 2013.
Brock, Alexander. "Regional Cooperation in a New Middle East." Summary Report. Washington, D.C.: Council on Foreign Relations, 2012.
Bunn, Matthew. "Preventing a Nuclear 9/11." *Issues in Science and Technology*, 21, no. 2 (Winter 2005): 55–62.
Burges, Sean W. "Consensual Hegemony: Theorizing Brazilian Foreign Policy after the Cold War." *International Relations* 22, no. 1 (March 1, 2008): 65–84.
Burgess, Stephen F. "South Africa's Nuclear Weapons Policies." *Nonproliferation Review* 13, no. 3 (November 1, 2006): 519–26.
Burgess, Stephen F., and Togzhan Kassenova. "The Rollback States: South Africa and Kazakhstan." In *Slaying the Nuclear Dragon: Disarmament Dynamics in the Twenty-First Century*, edited by Tanya Ogilvie-White and David Santoro, 85–117. Athens: University of Georgia Press, 2012.
Buszynski, Leszek. "Southeast Asia in the Post–Cold War Era: Regionalism and Security." *Asian Survey* 32, no. 9 (1992): 830–47.
Buzan, Barry. "Rethinking Security after the Cold War." *Cooperation and Conflict* 32, no. 1 (March 1, 1997): 5–28.
———. "The South Asian Security Complex in a Decentring World Order: Reconsidering Regions and Powers Ten Years On." *International Studies* 48, no. 1 (January 1, 2011): 1–19.
Buzan, Barry, and Ole Waever. *Regions and Powers: The Structure of International Security*. Cambridge: Cambridge University Press, 2003.
Caballero-Anthony, Mely. "Evolving Regional Governance in East Asia: From ASEAN to an East Asian Community." In *Governance and Regionalism in Asia*, edited by Nicholas Thomas, 32–65. New York: Routledge, 2009.
Calder, Kent, and Min Ye. *The Making of Northeast Asia*. Stanford, Calif.: Stanford University Press, 2010.
Campbell, John L. *Institutional Change and Globalization*. Princeton: Princeton University Press, 2004.
Capoccia, Giovanni, and R. Daniel Kelemen. "The Study of Critical Junctures: Theory, Narrative, and Counterfactuals in Historical Institutionalism." *World Politics* 59, no. 3 (2007): 341–69.
Carasales, Julio C. "The Argentine-Brazilian Nuclear Rapprochement." *Nonproliferation Review* 2, no. 3 (1995): 39–48.
Carlson, John. "Defining Noncompliance: NPT Safeguards Agreements." *Arms Control Today* 39 (May 2009). http://www.armscontrol.org/print/3642.
Casarini, Nicola. "Visions of North-East Asia—China, Japan, Korea and the EU." Issue Brief. Paris: European Union Institute for Security Studies, 2014.
Chakma, Bhumitra. "Pakistan's Nuclear Weapons Programme: Past and Future." In *Nuclear Proliferation and International Order: Challenges to the Non-Proliferation Treaty*, edited by Olav Njolstad, 26–38. New York: Routledge, 2010.
———. *The Politics of Nuclear Weapons in South Asia*. Farmham, Surrey, UK: Ashgate, 2011.
Chalmers, Malcolm. "ASEAN and Confidence Building: Continuity and Change after the Cold War." *Contemporary Security Policy* 18, no. 1 (1997): 36–56.
Chanona, Alejandro. "Regional Security Governance in the Americas: The Organization of American States." In *The Security Governance of Regional Organizations*, edited by Emil J. Kirchner and Roberto Dominguez, 107–35. New York: Routledge, 2011.

Charter of the Gulf Cooperation Council (GCC). May 25, 1981. http://www.gccsg.org/en-us/AboutGCC/Pages/Primarylaw.aspx.

Charter of the South Asian Association for Regional Cooperation. December 8, 1985. http://www.saarc-sec.org/SAARC-Charter/5/.

Cheong, Inkyo. "Evaluation of Recent Progress of FTAs in East Asia—A Korean Perspective." In *East Asian Economic Regionalism: Feasibilities and Challenges*, edited by Choong Yong Ahn, Richard E. Baldwin, and Inkyo Cheong, 37–56. Dordrecht, Netherlands: Springer Science & Business Media, 2005.

Cho, Il Hyun. *Global Rogues and Regional Orders: The Multidimensional Challenge of North Korea and Iran*. New York: Oxford University Press, 2015.

Chun, Yung-Woo. "Building a Mechanism for Multilateral Security Cooperation in Southeast Asia." Paper presented at the Northeast Asia Cooperation Dialogue, Seoul, October 18, 2010.

Cirincione, Joseph, Jon B. Wolfsthal, and Miriam Rajkumar. *Deadly Arsenals: Nuclear, Biological, and Chemical Threats*. Washington, D.C.: Carnegie Endowment for International Peace, 2011.

Clary, Christopher. "A. Q. Khan and the Limits of the Non-Proliferation Regime." *Disarmament Forum*, no. 4 (2004): 33–42.

Cotton, James. "The Proliferation Security Initiative and North Korea: Legality and Limitations of a Coalition Strategy." *Security Dialogue* 36, no. 2 (2005): 193–211.

Dalton, Toby, Togzhan Kassenova, and Lauryn Williams, eds. *Perspectives on the Evolving Nuclear Order*. Washington, D.C.: Carnegie Endowment for International Peace, 2016.

Dash, Kishore C. "The Political Economy of Regional Cooperation in South Asia." *Pacific Affairs* 69, no. 2 (1996): 185–209.

Davenport, Kelsey, and Daryl G. Kimball. "Nuclear-Weapon-Free Zones (NWFZ) at a Glance." Fact Sheets & Briefs. Washington, D.C.: Arms Control Association, 2012. http://www.armscontrol.org/factsheets/nwfz.

Dawood, Layla, and Mônica Herz. "Nuclear Governance in Latin America." *Contexto Internacional* 35, no. 2 (December 2013): 497–535.

Devlin, Robert, and Antoni Estevadeordal. "What's New in the New Regionalism in the Americas?" Working Paper no. 6. Washington, D.C.: Inter-American Development Bank, 2001.

Dhanapala, Jayantha, and Randy Rydell. *Multilateral Diplomacy and the NPT: An Insider's Account*. Geneva: United Nations Institute for Disarmament Research, 2005.

Dobbs, Michael. *One Minute to Midnight: Kennedy, Khrushchev, and Castro on the Brink of Nuclear War*. New York: Alfred A. Knopf, 2008.

Dominguez, Jorge I. "International Cooperation in Latin America: The Design of Regional Institutions by Slow Accretion." In *Crafting Cooperation: Regional International Institutions in Comparative Perspective*, edited by Amitav Acharya and Alastair Iain Johnston, 83–128. Cambridge: Cambridge University Press, 2007.

Duffield, John. "What Are International Institutions?" *International Studies Review* 9, no. 1 (2007): 1–22.

Eckstein, Harry. "Case Study and Theory in Political Science." In *Handbook of Political Science*, edited by Fred J. Greenstein and Nelson W. Polsby, 7:79–137. Reading, Mass.: Addison-Wesley, 1975.

Ehteshami, Anoushiravan. "MENA Region: Security and Regional Governance." In *Comparative Regional Security Governance*, edited by Shaun Breslin and Stuart Croft, 130–53. New York: Routledge, 2013.

Eisenman, Joshua. "Rethinking U.S. Strategy towards China." *Carnegie Council for Ethics in International Affairs*, January 21, 2016. http://www.carnegiecouncil.org/publications/articles _papers_reports/756.
ElBaradei, Dr. Mohamed. "Treaty on the Non-Proliferation of Nuclear Weapons." 2005 Review Conference of the Treaty on the Non-Proliferation of Nuclear Weapons, New York, May 2, 2005. http://www.iaea.org/NewsCenter/Statements/2005/ebsp2005n006 .html.
Enkhsaikhan, J. "Mongolia's Nuclear-Weapon-Free Status: Concept and Practice." *Asian Survey* 40, no. 2 (2000): 342–59.
Epstein, William. "The Making of the Treaty of Tlatelolco." *Journal of the History of International Law* 3, no. 2 (2001): 153–79.
European Union. Treaty on European Union (Consolidated Version), Treaty of Maastricht, February 7, 1992. http://www.refworld.org/docid/3ae6b39218.html.
Evans, Paul. "Constructing Multilateralism in an Anti-Region: From Six Party Talks to a Regional Security Framework in Northeast Asia?" In *Cross Currents: Regionalism and Nationalism in Northeast Asia*, edited by Gi-Wook Shin and Daniel C. Sneider, 99–116. Washington, D.C.: Brookings Institution Press, 2007.
Fawcett, Louise. "Alliances and Regionalism in the Middle East." In *International Relations of the Middle East*, edited by Louise Fawcett, 3rd ed., 185–204. Oxford: Oxford University Press, 2013.
―――. "Regionalism in Historical Perspective." In *Regionalism in World Politics: Regional Organization and International Order*, edited by Louise Fawcett and Andrew Hurrell, 9–36. Oxford: Oxford University Press, 1996.
―――. "Regionalism in World Politics: Past and Present." In *Elements of Regional Integration: A Multidimensional Approach*, edited by Ariane Kosler and Martin Zimmek, 1–14. Baden-Baden: Nomos, 2008.
Fields, Jeffrey R., ed. *State Behavior and the Nuclear Nonproliferation Regime*. Athens: University of Georgia Press, 2014.
Fields, Jeffrey, and Jason S. Enia. "The Health of the Nuclear Nonproliferation Regime." *Nonproliferation Review* 16, no. 2 (2009): 173–96.
Finlay, Brian, ed. *Southern Flows: WMD Nonproliferation in the Developing World*. Washington, D.C.: Stanley Foundation and Stimson, 2014.
Fishlow, Albert, and Stephan Haggard. "The United States and the Regionalisation of the World Economy." Paris: Organisation for Economic Co-operation and Development, 1992.
Fitzpatrick, Mark. "Overwhelming Global Vote for the Iran Nuclear Deal." *Survival* 56, no. 1 (January 2, 2014): 71–75.
Ford, Christopher A. "Debating Disarmament: Interpreting Article VI of the Treaty on the Non-Proliferation of Nuclear Weapons." *Nonproliferation Review* 14, no. 3 (2007): 401–28.
Framework Agreements on Enhancing ASEAN Economic Cooperation. January 28, 1992. http://www.asean.org/storage/images/2012/Economic/AFTA/Common_Effective_Pref erential_Tariff/Framework%20Agreements%20on%20Enhancing%20ASEAN%20Eco nomic%20Cooperation%20.pdf.
Fuhrmann, Matthew. *Atomic Assistance: How "Atoms for Peace" Programs Cause Nuclear Insecurity*. Ithaca: Cornell University Press, 2012.
Fursdon, Edward. *The European Defence Community: A History*. London: Macmillan, 1980.
Gavin, Victor. "Power through Europe? The Case of the European Defence Community in France (1950–1954)." *French History* 23, no. 1 (March 1, 2009): 69–87.

Geldart, Carol, and Peter Lyon. "The Group of 77: A Perspective View." *International Affairs* 57, no. 1 (1980–81): 79–101.
George, Alexander L., and Andrew Bennett. *Case Studies and Theory Development in the Social Sciences*. Cambridge, Mass.: MIT Press for Belfer Center for Science and International Affairs, Harvard University, 2004.
George, Robert, Eldon Reiling, and Anthony Scaperlanda. "Short-Run Trade Effects of the LAFTA." *Kyklos* 30, no. 4 (November 1, 1977): 618–36.
Giovannini, Francesca. "Understanding the 'Proliferation' of Nuclear Cooperation: An Alternative Theoretical Framework and Its Implications for Regional Efforts." In *International Cooperation on WMD Nonproliferation*, edited by Jeffrey W. Knopf, 250–70. Athens: University of Georgia Press, 2016.
Goh, Gillian. "The 'ASEAN Way': Non-Intervention and ASEAN's Role in Conflict Management." *Stanford Journal of East Asian Affairs* 3, no. 1 (2003): 113–18.
Goldblat, Jozef. "Denuclearization of Africa." *Security Dialogue* 23, no. 2 (June 1, 1992): 169–72.
Goldschmidt, Pierre. "Exposing Nuclear Non-Compliance." *Survival* 51, no. 1 (2009): 143–64.
Government of Japan, Ministry of Foreign Affairs. "National Security Strategy." December 17, 2013. http://japan.kantei.go.jp/96_abe/documents/2013/__icsFiles/afieldfile/2013/12/17/NSS.pdf.
Governments of India and Pakistan. Lahore Declaration. February 21, 1999. http://mea.gov.in/in-focus-article.htm?18997/Lahore+Declaration+February+1999.
Grand, Camille. "The European Union and the Non-Proliferation of Nuclear Weapons." Chaillot Papers. Paris: Institute for Security Studies of Western European Union, 2000. https://www.iss.europa.eu/content/european-union-and-non-proliferation-nuclear-weapons.
Gross, Leo. "On the Degradation of the Constitutional Environment of the United Nations." *American Journal of International Law* 77, no. 3 (1983): 569–84.
Grossi, Rafael Mariano. "Latin America's Road to a Region Free of Nuclear Weapons." In *Routledge Handbook of Nuclear Proliferation and Policy*, edited by Joseph F. Pilat and Nathan E. Busch, 317–27. New York: Routledge, 2015.
Gupta, Arvind, and Kapil Patil. "India and the Global Nuclear Nonproliferation Regime: An Assessment." In *Routledge Handbook of Nuclear Proliferation and Policy*, edited by Joseph F. Pilat and Nathan E. Busch, 97–107. New York: Routledge, 2015.
Haacke, Jürgen. *ASEAN's Diplomatic and Security Culture: Origins, Development and Prospects*. New York: Routledge, 2013.
Hagerty, Devin T. "Nuclear Deterrence in South Asia: The 1990 Indo-Pakistani Crisis." *International Security* 20, no. 3 (1995): 79–114.
Hall, Gregory O. "The New North-South Dealignment in International Relations and the Impact on Regional and Global Affairs." In *Eternal Colonialism*, edited by Russell Benjamin and Gregory O. Hall, 89–118. Lanham, Md.: University Press of America, 2010.
Hamel-Green, Michael. "Cooperating Regionally, Denuclearizing Globally: Multilateral Nuclear-Weapon-Free-Zone Initiatives." In *International Cooperation on WMD Nonproliferation*, edited by Jeffrey W. Knopf, 206–28. Athens: University of Georgia Press, 2016.
———. "Nuclear-Weapon-Free Zone Developments in Asia: Problems and Prospects." *Global Change, Peace & Security* 17, no. 3 (2005): 239–52.
———. "Peeling the Orange: Regional Paths to a Nuclear-Weapon-Free-World." *Disarmament Forum*, no. 2 (2011): 3–14.
Hecker, Siegfried S. "Lessons Learned from the North Korean Nuclear Crises." *Daedalus* 139, no. 1 (January 1, 2010): 44–56.

Herbst, Jeffrey. "Crafting Regional Cooperation in Africa." In *Crafting Cooperation: Regional International Institutions in Comparative Perspective*, edited by Amitav Acharya and Alastair Iain Johnston, 129–44. Cambridge: Cambridge University Press, 2007.

Herz, Mônica, Layla Dawood, and Victor Coutinho Lage. "A Nuclear Submarine in the South Atlantic: The Framing of Threats and Deterrence." *Contexto Internacional* 39, no. 2 (2017): 329–50.

Hettne, Bjorn, and Andras Inotai. "The New Regionalism: Implications for Global Development and International Security." Research for Action. Helsinki: UNU World Institute for Development Economics Research, 1994.

Hufbauer, Gary Clyde, and Claire Brunel, eds. *Maghreb Regional and Global Integration: A Dream to Be Fulfilled*. Washington, D.C.: Peterson Institute for International Economics, 2008.

Hurrell, Andrew. "Explaining the Resurgence of Regionalism in World Politics." *Review of International Studies* 21, no. 4 (1995): 331–58.

International Atomic Energy Agency. "The International Legal Framework for Nuclear Security." IAEA International Law Series no. 4. Vienna: IAEA, 2011.

———. "Modalities of Application of Agency Safeguards in the Middle East." GC(XXXIII)/887. August 29, 1989. https://www.iaea.org/About/Policy/GC/GC33/GC33Documents/English/gc33-887_en.pdf.

———. "Application of IAEA Safeguards in the Middle East." GC(XXXV)/RES/571. September 20, 1991. https://www.iaea.org/About/Policy/GC/GC35/GC35Resolutions/English/gc35res-571_en.pdf.

———. "Report by the Director General on the Implementation of the Resolution Adopted by the Board on 6 January 2003 and of the Agreement Between the IAEA and the Democratic People's Republic of Korea for the Application of Safeguards in Connection with the Treaty on the Non-Proliferation of Nuclear Weapons." GOV/2003/3. January 6, 2003. https://www.iaea.org/sites/default/files/gov2003-4.pdf.

———. "Implementation of the NPT Safeguards Agreement in the Islamic Republic of Iran." GOV/2003/40. June 6, 2003. https://www.iaea.org/sites/default/files/gov2003-40.pdf.

International Centre for Security Analysis. "Nuclear Security in Southeast Asia." New York: Carnegie Corporation, 2012. http://www.kcl.ac.uk/sspp/policy-institute/icsa/Southeast-Asia-Nuclear-Security-KCL-(ICSA)-Jan-12.pdf.

International Panel on Fissile Materials. "Global Fissile Material Report 2015: Nuclear Weapon and Fissile Material Stockpiles and Production." Princeton: International Panel on Fissile Materials, 2015. http://fissilematerials.org/publications/2015/12/global_fissile_material_report_7.html.

Isaac, Sally Kahlifa. "A Resurgence in Arab Regional Institutions? The Cases of the Arab League and the Gulf Cooperation Council Post-2011." In *Regional Insecurity after the Arab Uprisings: Narratives of Security and Threat*, edited by Elizabeth Monier, 151–67. London: Palgrave Macmillan, 2015.

Jackson, Paul. "Regional Security in Sub-Saharan Africa." In *Comparative Regional Security Governance*, edited by Shaun Breslin and Stuart Croft, 113–30. New York: Routledge, 2013.

James Martin Center for Nonproliferation Studies at the Monterey Institute of International Studies, Center for Energy and Security Studies, and Vienna Center for Disarmament and Non-Proliferation. "Prospects for Nuclear Security Partnership in Southeast Asia." Monterey: CNS, CENESS, VCDNP, 2012. http://www.nonproliferation.org/wp-content/uploads/2013/12/120515_seasia_nuclear_security_partnership.pdf.

Jo, Dong-Joon, and Erik Gartzke. "Determinants of Nuclear Weapons Proliferation." *Journal of Conflict Resolution* 51, no. 1 (2007): 167–94.

Johnson, James G. "An Introduction to the European Atomic Community (EURATOM)." *Business Lawyer* 13, no. 4 (1958): 801–12.

Johnson, Rebecca. "Rethinking the NPT's Role in Security: 2010 and Beyond." *International Affairs* 86, no. 2 (2010): 429–45.

———. "The 2000 NPT Review Conference." *Disarmament Diplomacy*, no. 46 (May 2000): 2–21.

———. *Unfinished Business: The Negotiation of the CTBT and the End of Nuclear Testing*. New York: United Nations, 2009. http://www.unidir.org/files/publications/pdfs/unfinished-business-the-negotiation-of-the-ctbt-and-the-end-of-nuclear-testing-346.pdf.

Joyner, Christopher C. "International Regimes and International Relations Theorists." *Proceedings of the Annual Meeting (American Society of International Law)* 94 (2000): 212–13.

Joyner, Daniel H. "The Proliferation Security Initiative: Nonproliferation, Counterproliferation, and International Law." *Yale Journal of International Law* 30 (2005): 507–48.

Kaplow, Jeffrey. "The Canary in the Nuclear Submarine: Assessing the Nonproliferation Risk of the Naval Nuclear Propulsion Loophole." *Nonproliferation Review* 22, no. 2 (2015): 185–202.

Kapur, S. Paul. "The Indian Nuclear Program: Motivations, Effects, and Future Trajectories." In *Nuclear Proliferation and International Order: Challenges to the Non-Proliferation Treaty*, edited by Olav Njolstad, 13–25. New York: Routledge, 2010.

———. "Ten Years of Instability in a Nuclear South Asia." *International Security* 33, no. 2 (September 30, 2008): 71–94.

Karim, Mahin. "The Future of South Asian Security: Prospects for a Nontraditional Regional Security Architecture." NBR Project Report. Seattle: National Bureau of Asian Research, 2013. http://www.nbr.org/downloads/pdfs/PSA/NTS_projectreport_April2013.pdf.

Kassenova, Togzhan. "Brazil and the Global Nuclear Order." In *Brazil on the Global Stage*, edited by Oliver Stuenkel and Matthew M. Taylor, 117–42. New York: Palgrave Macmillan, 2015.

Katsumata, Hiro. "Establishment of the ASEAN Regional Forum: Constructing a 'Talking Shop' or a 'Norm Brewery'?" *Pacific Review* 19, no. 2 (June 1, 2006): 181–98.

———. "Norms and Regional Institutions: Towards an East Asian Community." In *Regional Integration in East Asia: Theoretical and Historical Perspectives*, edited by Satoshi Amako, Shunji Matsuoka, and Kenji Horiuchi, 35–48. Tokyo: United Nations University Press, 2013.

Katzenstein, Peter J. *A World of Regions: Asia and Europe in the American Imperium*. Ithaca: Cornell University Press, 2005.

Kawai, Masahiro. "From the Chiang Mai Initiative to an Asian Monetary Fund." ADBI Working Paper Series. Tokyo: Asian Development Bank Institute, 2015. https://www.adb.org/sites/default/files/publication/160056/adbi-wp527.pdf.

Kelly, Robert E. "Security Theory in the 'New Regionalism.'" *International Studies Review* 9, no. 2 (2007): 197–229.

Keohane, Robert O. "The Demand for International Regimes." *International Organization* 36, no. 2 (1982): 325–55.

———. "Institutional Theory and the Realist Challenge after the Cold War." In *Neorealism and Neoliberalism*, edited by David A. Baldwin. New York: Columbia University Press, 1993.

———. *International Institutions and State Power: Essays in International Relations Theory.* Boulder, Colo.: Westview Press, 1989.

Keohane, Robert O., and Lisa L. Martin. "The Promise of Institutionalist Theory." *International Security* 20, no. 1 (1995): 39–51.

Khan, Feroz Hassan. "South Asia: Strategic Competition and Nuclear Policies." In *Routledge Handbook of Nuclear Proliferation and Policy*, edited by Joseph F. Pilat and Nathan E. Busch, 86–96. New York: Routledge, 2015.

Kihl, Young Whan, and Peter Hayes. *Peace and Security in Northeast Asia: The Nuclear Issue and the Korean Peninsula.* Armonk, N.Y.: M. E. Sharpe, 1997.

Kim, Hyung Jong, and Poh Ping Lee. "The Changing Role of Dialogue in the International Relations of Southeast Asia." *Asian Survey* 51, no. 5 (September 1, 2011): 953–70.

Klotz, Audie. "Norms Reconstituting Interests: Global Racial Equality and U.S. Sanctions against South Africa." *International Organization* 49, no. 3 (1995): 451–78.

Knopf, Jeffrey W. "Conclusions." In *International Cooperation on WMD Nonproliferation*, edited by Jeffrey W. Knopf, 294–316. Athens: University of Georgia Press, 2016.

———, ed. *International Cooperation on WMD Nonproliferation.* Athens: University of Georgia Press, 2016.

———, ed. *Security Assurances and Nuclear Nonproliferation.* Stanford: Stanford University Press, 2012.

Koga, Kei. "Explaining the Transformation of ASEAN's Security Functions in East Asia: The Cases of ARF and ASEAN+3." *Asian Regional Integration Review* 4 (2012): 1–27.

———. *Reinventing Regional Security Institutions in Asia and Africa: Power Shifts, Ideas, and Institutional Change.* London: Routledge, 2016.

Koo, Bon-Hak. "A Northeast Asian Nuclear-Weapon-Free Zone: A Korean Perspective." In *Nuclear Weapons–Free Zones*, edited by Ramesh Thakur, 123–39. Houndmills, Basingsoke, UK: Macmillan, 1998.

Koremenos, Barbara, Charles Lipson, and Duncan Snidal. "The Rational Design of International Institutions." *International Organization* 55, no. 4 (2001): 761–99.

Kraft, Herman Joseph S. "ASEAN and Intra-ASEAN Relations: Weathering the Storm?" *Pacific Review* 13, no. 3 (January 1, 2000): 453–72.

Krasner, Stephen. "Structural Causes and Regime Consequences: Regimes as Intervening Variables." *International Organization* 36, no. 2 (1982): 185–205.

Krepon, Michael. "Looking Back: The 1998 Indian and Pakistani Nuclear Tests." *Arms Control Today* 38, no. 4 (May 2008): 51–55.

Krige, John. *Sharing Knowledge, Shaping Europe: US Technological Collaboration and Nonproliferation.* Cambridge, Mass.: MIT Press, 2016.

Kubbig, Bernd W., and Sven-Eric Fikenscher, eds. *Arms Control and Missile Proliferation in the Middle East.* New York: Routledge, 2012.

Kubbig, Bernd W., Mohamed Noman Galal, Michael Haas, Murhaf Jouejati, Sabahat Khan, Ahmed Saif, and Mahmood Sariolghalam. "Taking Overall Military Asymmetries into Account: Objections from the Arab World and Iran." In *Arms Control and Missile Proliferation in the Middle East*, edited by Bernd W. Kubbig and Sven-Eric Fikenscher, 66–88. New York: Routledge, 2012.

Kubbig, Bernd W., and Christian Weidlich. "A WMD/DVs Free Zone for the Middle East: Taking Stock, Moving Forward towards Cooperative Security." Academic Peace Orchestra, Middle East. Frankfurt: Peace Research Institute Frankfurt, 2015.

Kutani, Ichiro. "The Energy Outlook for Asia to 2035." *Journal of Energy and Development* 34, no. 1/2 (2008): 87–94.

Kutchesfahani, Sara, and Marcie Lombardi. "South Africa." In *Nuclear Safeguards, Security and Nonproliferation: Achieving Security with Technology and Policy*, edited by James Doyle, 289–306. Burlington, Mass.: Elsevier, 2011.

Kutchesfahani, Sara Z. "Bilateral Cooperation on Nonproliferation: The Role of an Epistemic Community in Argentina and Brazil's Creation of a Joint Safeguards Arrangement." In *International Cooperation on WMD Nonproliferation*, edited by Jeffrey W. Knopf, 229–49. Athens: University of Georgia Press, 2016.

Lake, David A. "Beyond Anarchy: The Importance of Security Institutions." *International Security* 26, no. 1 (2001): 129–60.

Lake, David A., and Patrick M. Morgan, eds. *Regional Orders: Building Security in a New World*. University Park: Pennsylvania State University Press, 1997.

Landau, Emily. "Egypt and Israel in ACRS: Bilateral Concerns in a Regional Arms Control Process." Memorandum no. 59. Tel Aviv: Jaffee Center for Strategic Studies, June 2001.

Lee, Chung-Min, and T. J. Pempel. "The Northeast Asian Security Complex: History, Power, and Strategic Choices." In *Security Cooperation in Northeast Asia: Architecture and Beyond*, edited by T. J. Pempel and Chung-Min Lee, 3–22. New York: Routledge, 2012.

Lee, Sangsoo. "Nuclear Energy Cooperation in Northeast Asia: Implications from the European Experience." Policy Brief. Stockholm: Institute for Security & Development Policy, 2012.

Lee, Sangsoo, and Bernadetta Ginting. "Nuclear Security Cooperation in Northeast Asia: Implications from EURATOM." *Journal of Northeast Asian History* 13, no. 2 (2016): 93–118.

Legrenzi, Matteo, and Marina Calculli. "Regionalism and Regionalization in the Middle East: Options and Challenges." Issue Brief. New York: International Peace Institute, 2013.

Leventhal, Paul, and Sharon Tanzer, eds. *Averting a Latin American Nuclear Arms Race: New Prospects and Challenges for Argentine-Brazil Nuclear Co-operation*. London: Palgrave Macmillan, 1992.

Leverett, Flynt. "The Iranian Nuclear Issue, the End of the American Century, and the Future of International Order." *Penn State Journal of Law and International Affairs* 2, no. 2 (2013): 240–71.

Lindley, Dan. *Promoting Peace with Information*. Princeton: Princeton University Press, 2007.

Lipson, Charles. "International Cooperation in Economic and Security Affairs." *World Politics* 37, no. 1 (1984): 1–23.

Logan, Samuel E. "The Proliferation Security Initiative: Navigating the Legal Challenges." *Journal of Transnational Law & Policy* 14 (2004–5): 253–74.

Lu, Yin. "Reflections on Strategic Stability." In *Understanding Chinese Nuclear Thinking*, edited by Li Bin and Tong Zhao, 127–47. Washington, D.C.: Carnegie Endowment for International Peace, 2016. http://carnegieendowment.org/files/ChineseNuclearThinking_Final.pdf.

Ludlow, N. Piers. "European Integration in the 1980s: On the Way to Maastricht." *Journal of European Integration History* 19, no. 1 (2013): 11–22.

Lukin, Artyom. "The Emerging Institutional Order in the Asia-Pacific: Opportunities for Russia and Russia-US Relations." In *From APEC 2011 to APEC 2012: American and Russian Perspectives on Asia-Pacific Security and Cooperation*, edited by Rouben Azizian and Artyom Lukin, 225–36. Honolulu: Asia-Pacific Center for Security Studies, 2012.

Mack, Andrew. "Potential, Not Proliferation." *Bulletin of the Atomic Scientists* 53, no. 4 (1997): 48–53.

Mallard, Gregoire. "Can the Euratom Treaty Inspire the Middle East? The Political Promises of Regional Nuclear Communities." *Nonproliferation Review* 15, no. 3 (November 1, 2008): 459–77.

———. *Fallout: Nuclear Diplomacy in an Age of Global Fracture*. Chicago: University of Chicago Press, 2014.
Malley, Michael S., and Tanya Ogilvie-White. "Nuclear Challenges in Southeast Asia: Promoting Cooperation and Consensus." Second Southeast Asia Strategic Dialogue, February 15–17, 2011. Christchurch: Center on Contemporary Conflict, 2012. http://www.dtic.mil/dtic/tr/fulltext/u2/a565766.pdf.
Mallison, W. T. "The United States Bilateral Agreements for Co-operation in the Civil Uses of Atomic Energy." *Proceedings of the American Society of International Law at Its Annual Meeting (1921–1969)* 51 (1957): 142–49.
Manning, Robert A. "PACATOM: Nuclear Cooperation in Asia." *Washington Quarterly* 20, no. 2 (1997): 214–32.
Mansfield, Edward D., and Helen V. Milner. "The New Wave of Regionalism." *International Organization* 53, no. 3 (1999): 589–627.
Mansfield, Edward D., and Etel Solingen. "Regionalism." *Annual Review of Political Science* 13, no. 1 (2010): 145–63.
Matsuoka, Shunji. "Institutional Approaches to Asian Regional Integration." In *Regional Integration in East Asia: Theoretical and Historical Perspectives*, edited by Satoshi Amako, Shunji Matsuoka, and Kenji Horiuchi, 70–92. Tokyo: United Nations University Press, 2013.
Mearsheimer, John J. "The False Promise of International Institutions." *International Security* 19, no. 3 (1994): 5–49.
Meier, Oliver, and Christopher Daase, eds. *Arms Control in the 21st Century: Between Coercion and Cooperation*. New York: Routledge, 2013.
Mendelsohn, Jack, and Dunbar Lockwood. "The Nuclear-Weapon States and Article VI of the NPT." *Arms Control Today* 25, no. 2 (1995): 11–16.
Monier, Elizabeth. "The Arabness of Middle East Regionalism: The Arab Spring and Competition for Discursive Hegemony between Egypt, Iran and Turkey." *Contemporary Politics* 20, no. 4 (October 2, 2014): 421–34.
Monshipouri, Mahmood, and Manochehr Dorraj. "Iran's Foreign Policy: A Shifting Strategic Landscape." *Middle East Policy* 20, no. 4 (December 1, 2013): 133–47.
Moore, Gregory J., ed. *North Korean Nuclear Operationality: Regional Security and Nonproliferation*. Baltimore: Johns Hopkins University Press, 2013.
Morgan, M. Granger, K. Subrahmanyam, K. Sundarji, and Robert M. White. "India and the United States." *Washington Quarterly* 18, no. 2 (June 1, 1995): 155–79.
Moyland, Suzanna van. *The IAEA's Programme "93+2."* Verification Matters 10. London: VERTIC, 1997. http://www.vertic.org/media/Archived_Publications/Matters/Verification_Matters_No10.pdf.
Müller, Harald, and Carmen Wunderlich, eds. *Norm Dynamics in Multilateral Arms Control: Interests, Conflicts, and Justice*. Athens: University of Georgia Press, 2013.
Nair, Deepak. "Regionalism in the Asia Pacific/East Asia: A Frustrated Regionalism?" *Contemporary Southeast Asia: A Journal of International and Strategic Affairs* 31, no. 1 (2009): 110–42.
Narang, Vipin. *Nuclear Strategy in the Modern Era: Regional Powers and International Conflict: Regional Powers and International Conflict*. Princeton: Princeton University Press, 2014.
Narine, Shaun. "ASEAN in the Aftermath: The Consequences of the East Asian Economic Crisis." *Global Governance* 8, no. 2 (April 1, 2002): 179–94.
———. "ASEAN into the Twenty-First Century: Problems and Prospects." *Pacific Review* 12, no. 3 (January 1, 1999): 357–80.
———. "Institutional Theory and Southeast Asia: The Case of ASEAN." *World Affairs* 161, no. 1 (1998): 33–47.

National Intelligence Council. *Iran: Nuclear Intentions and Capabilities.* Washington: D.C.: National Intelligence Council, November 2007.

Nesadurai, Helen E. S. "The Global Politics of Regionalism: Asia and the Asia-Pacific." In *Global Politics of Regionalism: Theory and Practice*, edited by Mary Farrell, Bjorn Hettne, and Luk Van Langenhove, 155–70. Ann Arbor, Mich.: Pluto Press, 2005.

Njolstad, Olav, ed. *Nuclear Proliferation and International Order: Challenges to the Non-Proliferation Treaty.* New York: Routledge, 2010.

Nuclear Threat Initiative. "NTI Nuclear Materials Security Index: Building a Framework for Assurance, Accountability, and Action." Washington, D.C.: Nuclear Threat Initiative, 2016.

Nwogugu, E. I. "The Treaty of Pelindaba: An African Nuclear Weapon-Free Zone." In *African Yearbook of International Law*, 4:227–48. Cambridge: Kluwer Law International, 1996.

Nye, Joseph S. "Maintaining a Nonproliferation Regime." *International Organization* 35, no. 1 (1981): 15–38.

O'Driscoll, Mervyn, and Gordon Lake. "The European Parliament and the Euratom Treaty: Past, Present, and Future." Working Paper. Energy and Research Series. Luxembourg: European Union, 2002. http://www.uni-mannheim.de/edz/pdf/dg4/ENER114_EN.pdf.

Oelsner, Andrea. *International Relations in Latin America: Peace and Security in the Southern Cone.* New York: Routledge, 2013.

Ogilvie-White, Tanya, and John Simpson. "The NPT and Its 2003 PrepCom Session: A Regime in Need of Intensive Care." *Nonproliferation Review* 10, no. 1 (2003): 40–58.

Ohaegbulam, F. Ugboaja. "The United States and Africa after the Cold War." *Africa Today* 39, no. 4 (1992): 19–34.

Organisation of African Unity. "Lagos Plan of Action for the Economic Development of Africa, 1980–2000." April 1980. https://www.merit.unu.edu/wp-content/uploads/2015/01/Lagos-Plan-of-Action.pdf.

Parrish, Scott, and Jean Du Preez. "Nuclear-Weapon-Free Zones: Still a Useful Disarmament and Non-Proliferation Tool?" Stockholm: Weapons for Mass Destruction Commission, 2011.

Parthemore, Christine. "The Unique Risks of Nuclear-Armed Cruise Missiles." In *Understanding Nuclear Weapon Risks*, edited by John Borrie, Tim Caughley, and Wilfred Wan, 45–52. Geneva: UNIDIR, 2017.

Patrick, Stewart M. "The Future of Middle East Regionalism: Can an Institutional Desert Bloom?" Council on Foreign Relations, November 12, 2012. https://www.cfr.org/blog/future-middle-east-regionalism-can-institutional-desert-bloom.

Patterson, Ruairi. "EU Sanctions on Iran: The European Political Context." *Middle East Policy* 20, no. 1 (March 1, 2013): 135–46.

Paul, T. V. *Power versus Prudence: Why Nations Forgo Nuclear Weapons.* Montreal: McGill-Queens University Press, 2000.

———. "Strengthening the Non-Proliferation Regime: The Role of Coercive Sanctions." *International Journal* 51, no. 3 (Summer 1996): 440–65.

Pempel, T. J. "The Race to Connect East Asia: An Unending Steeplechase." *Asian Economic Policy Review* 1, no. 2 (December 1, 2006): 239–54.

Peou, Sorpong. "Security Community-Building in the Asia-Pacific." In *Security Politics in the Asia-Pacific: A Regional-Global Nexus?*, edited by William T. Tow, 144–66. New York: Cambridge University Press, 2009.

Pilat, Joseph F., and Robert E. Pendley, eds. *Beyond 1995: The Future of the NPT Regime.* New York: Plenum Press, 1990.

Pitigala, Nihal. "What Does Regional Trade in South Asia Reveal about Future Trade Integration? Some Empirical Evidence." Policy Research Working Papers. Washington, D.C.: World Bank, 2005.
Polner, Mariya. "Compendium of Authorized Economic Operator (AEO) Programmes." WCO Research Paper no. 8. Brussels: World Customs Organization, 2010. http://www.wcoomd.org/en/topics/research/activities-and-programmes/~/media/43AC332690 4F4887925CBB339C135BFE.ashx.
Portela, Clara. "The EU's Use of 'Targeted' Sanctions: Evaluating Effectiveness." CEPS Working Document. Brussels: Centre for European Policy Studies, 2014. https://www.ceps.eu /system/files/WD391%20Portela%20EU%20Targeted%20Sanctions.pdf.
Potter, William C., and Gaukhar Mukhatzhanova, eds. *Forecasting Nuclear Proliferation in the 21st Century*. Vol. 2: *A Comparative Perspective*. Stanford Security Studies. Stanford: Stanford University Press, 2010.
Preusse, Heinz Gert. *The New American Regionalism*. Northampton, Mass.: Edward Elgar, 2004.
Radchenko, Sergey. "Multilateralism in Northeast Asia—1." Topics of the Month, *ASAN Forum*, May 23, 2014.
Ravenhill, John. "A Three Bloc World? The New East Asian Regionalism." *International Relations of the Asia-Pacific* 2, no. 2 (August 1, 2002): 167–95.
Redick, John R. "Nuclear Illusions: Argentina and Brazil." Occasional Paper. Washington, D.C.: Henry L. Stimson Foundation, 1995. http://www.acamedia.info/politics/IRef /StimsonC/redick.pdf.
———. "The Tlatelolco Regime and Nonproliferation in Latin America." *International Organization* 35, no. 1 (1981): 103–34.
Reynolds, Celia L., and Wilfred T. Wan. "Empirical Trends in Sanctions and Positive Inducements in Nonproliferation." In *Sanctions, Statecraft, and Nuclear Proliferation*, edited by Etel Solingen, 56–124. Cambridge: Cambridge University Press, 2012.
Richter, Roger. "Testimony from a Former Safeguards Inspector." *Bulletin of the Atomic Scientists* 37, no. 8 (1981): 29–31.
Rishmawi, Mervat. "The League of Arab States in the Wake of the 'Arab Spring.'" Cairo: Cairo Institute for Human Rights Studies, 2013. http://www.cihrs.org/wp-content/uploads/2013 /09/Arab-Leage.pdf.
Roberts, Brad. "From Nonproliferation to Antiproliferation." *International Security* 18, no. 1 (1993): 139–73.
Rouis, Mustapha, and Steven R. Tabor. "Regional Economic Integration in the Middle East and North Africa: Beyond Trade Reform." Directions in Development. Washington, D.C.: World Bank, 2012. http://documents.worldbank.org/curated/en/813531468052157933/Regional -economic-integration-in-the-Middle-East-and-North-Africa-beyond-trade-reform.
Rublee, Maria Rost. *Nonproliferation Norms: Why States Choose Nuclear Restraint*. Athens: University of Georgia Press, 2009.
———. "Taking Stock of the Nuclear Nonproliferation Regime: Using Social Psychology to Understand Regime Effectiveness." *International Studies Review* 10, no. 3 (2008): 420–50.
———. "The Threshold States: Japan and Brazil." In *Slaying the Nuclear Dragon: Disarmament Dynamics in the Twenty-First Century*, edited by Tanya Ogilvie-White and David Santoro, 151–87. Athens: University of Georgia Press, 2012.
Saez, Lawrence. *The South Asian Association for Regional Cooperation (SAARC): An Emerging Collaboration Architecture*. New York: Routledge, 2012.
Sagan, Scott D. "The Causes of Nuclear Weapons Proliferation." *Annual Review of Political Science* 14, no. 1 (2011): 225–44.

———. "The Perils of Proliferation: Organization Theory, Deterrence Theory, and the Spread of Nuclear Weapons." *International Security* 18, no. 4 (1994): 66–107.
Salamé, Ghassan. "Integration in the Arab World: The Institutional Framework." In *The Politics of Arab Integration*, edited by Giacomo Luciani and Ghassan Salamé, 4:256–79. London: Routledge, 2016.
Salami, Iwa. *Financial Regulation in Africa: An Assessment of Financial Integration Arrangements in African Emerging and Frontier Markets*. Burlington: Ashgate Publishing, Ltd., 2012.
Sally, Razeen. "Regional Economic Integration in Asia: The Track Record and Prospects." ECIPE Occasional Paper. Brussels: European Centre for International Political Economy, 2010. http://ecipe.org/app/uploads/2014/12/regional-economic-integration-in-asia-the-track-record-and-prospects.pdf.
Sampson, Gary P. Introduction to *Regionalism, Multilateralism, and Economic Integration: The Recent Experience*, edited by Gary P. Sampson and Stephen Woolcock, 3–17. Tokyo: United Nations University Press, 2003.
Science and Security Board. "It Is Two Minutes to Midnight: 2018 Doomsday Clock Statement." *Bulletin of the Atomic Scientists*, 2018. http://thebulletin.org/sites/default/files/2018%20Doomsday%20Clock%20Statement.pdf.
Seliger, Bernhard, and Werner Pascha. *Towards a Northeast Asian Security Community: Implications for Korea's Growth and Economic Development*. New York: Springer Science & Business Media, 2011.
Selth, Andrew. "Burma and Weapons of Mass Destruction: Three Unanswered Questions." *Comparative Strategy* 32, no. 1 (2013): 52–70.
Shanks, M. "Economic Integration in Western Europe since 1945." *Acta Oeconomica* 6, no. 1/2 (1971): 27–36.
Shoji Tomotaka. "ASEAN Security Community: An Initiative for Peace and Stability." NIDS Security Reports. Tokyo: National Institute for Defense Studies, 2008. http://www.nids.mod.go.jp/english/publication/kiyo/pdf/2008/bulletin_e2008_3.pdf.
Simpson, John. "Nuclear Non-Proliferation in the Post–Cold War Era." *International Affairs* 70, no. 1 (1994): 17–39.
Simpson, John, and Darryl Howlett. "The NPT Renewal Conference: Stumbling toward 1995." *International Security* 19, no. 1 (1994): 41–71.
Single European Act. February 17, 1986. http://eur-lex.europa.eu/legal-content/EN/TXT/PDF/?uri=CELEX:11986U/TXT&from=EN.
Snyder, Scott. "Northeast Asian Security Architecture: Lessons from European History." Asia Unbound (blog), Council on Foreign Relations, July 17, 2014. http://blogs.cfr.org/asia/2014/07/17/northeast-asian-security-architecture-lessons-from-european-history/.
Sokova, Elena K. "Non-State Actors and Nuclear Weapons." In *Understanding Nuclear Weapon Risks*, edited by John Borrie, Tim Caughley, and Wilfred Wan, 83–90. Geneva: UNIDIR, 2017.
Solingen, Etel. *Nuclear Logics: Contrasting Paths in East Asia and the Middle East*. Princeton: Princeton University Press, 2007.
———. "The Political Economy of Nuclear Restraint." *International Security* 19, no. 2 (1994): 126–69.
———. *Regional Orders at Century's Dawn: Global and Domestic Influences on Grand Strategy*. Princeton: Princeton University Press, 1998.
———, ed. *Sanctions, Statecraft, and Nuclear Proliferation*. Cambridge: Cambridge University Press, 2012.

Sotomayor Velazquez, Arturo C. "Civil-Military Affairs and Security Institutions in the Southern Cone: The Sources of Argentine-Brazilian Nuclear Cooperation." *Latin American Politics and Society* 46, no. 4 (2004): 29–60.
South Pacific Nuclear Free Zone Treaty and Protocols (Treaty of Rarotonga), August 6, 1985. http://disarmament.un.org/treaties/t/rarotonga/text.
Spiering, Menno, and Michael Wintle, eds. *European Identity and the Second World War*. New York: Palgrave Macmillan, 2011.
Stadtmuller, Elzbieta. "Regional Dimensions of Security." In *Global Politics of Regionalism: Theory and Practice*, edited by Mary Farrell, Bjorn Hettne, and Luk Van Langenhove, 104–19. Ann Arbor, Mich.: Pluto Press, 2005.
Streeck, Wolfgang, and Kathleen Thelen. "Introduction: Institutional Change in Advanced Political Economies." In *Institutional Change in Advanced Political Economies*, 1–39. New York: Oxford University Press, 2005.
Stremlau, John. "Clinton's Dollar Diplomacy." *Foreign Policy*, no. 97 (1994): 18–35.
Stubbs, Richard. "ASEAN Plus Three: Emerging East Asian Regionalism?" *Asian Survey* 42, no. 3 (2002): 440–55.
Stumpf, Waldo. "South Africa's Nuclear Weapons Program: From Deterrence to Dismantlement." *Arms Control Today* 25, no. 10 (December 1995/January 1996): 4–7.
Summary of 1st Meeting of ASEAN Network of Regulatory Bodies on Atomic Energy (ASEANTOM). September 3–4, 2013, Phuket, Thailand. http://www.iaea.org/inis/collection/NCLCollectionStore/_Public/45/075/45075439.pdf.
Suzuki, Tatsujuiro. "Lessons from EURATOM for Possible Regional Nuclear Cooperation in the Asia Pacific Region (ASIATOM)." Policy Paper. Energy and Security in Northeast Asia. La Jolla: Institute on Global Conflict and Cooperation, 1996.
Svensson, Ted. "Regional Security Governance: The Case of South Asia." In *Comparative Regional Security Governance*, edited by Shaun Breslin and Stuart Croft, 94–112. New York: Routledge, 2013.
Talani, Leila Simona. *The Arab Spring in the Global Political Economy*. London: Palgrave Macmillan, 2014.
Tan, Eugene K. B. "ASEAN Charter as 'Legs to Go Places': Ideational Norms and Pragmatic Legalism in Community Building in Southeast Asia." *Singapore Year Book of International Law* 12 (2008): 171–98.
Tannenwald, Nina. *The Nuclear Taboo: The United States and the Non-Use of Nuclear Weapons since 1945*. New York: Cambridge University Press, 2007.
———. "Stigmatizing the Bomb: Origins of the Nuclear Taboo." *International Security* 29, no. 4 (2005): 5–49.
Tate, Trevor McMorris. "Regime-Building in the Non-Proliferation System." *Journal of Peace Research* 27, no. 4 (1990): 399–414.
Telò, Mario. *European Union and New Regionalism: Competing Regionalism and Global Governance in a Post-Hegemonic Era*. New York: Routledge, 2016.
———, ed. *European Union and New Regionalism: Regional Actors and Global Governance in a Post-Hegemonic Era*. Aldershot, UK: Ashgate, 2013.
Thakur, Ramesh. *Nuclear Weapons and International Security: Collected Essays*. London: Routledge, 2015.
Thakur, Ramesh, and Gareth Evans, eds. *Nuclear Weapons: The State of Play*. Canberra: Centre for Nuclear Non-Proliferation and Disarmament, 2013.
Thakur, Ramesh, and Luk Van Langenhove. "Enhancing Global Governance through Regional Integration." *Global Governance* 12, no. 3 (2006): 233–40.

Thaler, David E., Alireza Nader, Shahram Chubin, Jerrold D. Green, Charlotte Lynch, and Frederic Wehry. *Mullahs, Guards, and Bonyads: An Exploration of Iranian Leadership Dynamics*. Santa Monica: RAND Corporation, 2010.
Treaty for the Prohibition of Nuclear Weapons in Latin America and the Caribbean (Treaty of Tlatelolco), February 14, 1967 (opened for signatures), *United Nations Treaty Series*, vol. 634, no. 9068, http://www.opanal.org/en/text-of-the-treaty-of-tlatelolco/.
Treaty Instituting the Arab Maghreb Union, February 17, 1989 (concluded), *United Nations Treaty Series*, vol. 1546, no. 26844, http://www.diplomatie.gov.tn/index.php?id=303&L=2.
Treaty on the Non-Proliferation of Nuclear Weapons, July 1, 1968 (opened for signatures), *United Nations Treaty Series*, vol. 729, no. 10485, Article III, https://www.un.org/disarmament/wmd/nuclear/npt/.
Trinkunas, Harold. "Brazil's Global Ambitions." *Americas Quarterly*, Winter 2015. http://www.americasquarterly.org/content/brazils-global-ambitions.
———. "Reordering Regional Security in Latin America." *Journal of International Affairs* 66, no. 2 (Spring/Summer 2013): 83–99.
Tripp, Charles. "Regionalism in the Arab Middle East." In *Regionalism in World Politics: Regional Organization and International Order*, edited by Louise Fawcett and Andrew Hurrell, 283–308. Oxford: Oxford University Press, 1996.
United Nations General Assembly. "Comprehensive Study of the Question of Nuclear-Weapon-Free Zones in All Its Aspects: Report of the Conference of the Committee on Disarmament." A/10027/Add.1. 1976. http://undocs.org/A/10027/Add.1(SUPP).
United Nations Secretary-General. "An Agenda for Peace: Preventive Diplomacy and Related Matters." June 17, 1992, A/47/277. http://undocs.org/A/47/277.
United Nations Secretary-General. "Support by the United Nations System of the Efforts of Governments to Promote and Consolidate New or Restored Democracies" [also known as "An Agenda for Democratization"], A/51/761, December 20, 1996. http://undocs.org/A/51/761.
Valasek, Tomas. "The European Union's Role in Nonproliferation." In *US-European Nonproliferation Perspectives: A Transatlantic Conversation*, 43–50. Washington, D.C.: Center for Strategic and International Studies, 2009.
Väyrynen, Raimo. "Regionalism: Old and New." *International Studies Review* 5, no. 1 (March 1, 2003): 25–51.
Villiers, J. W de, Roger Jardine, and Mitchell Reiss. "Why South Africa Gave Up the Bomb." *Foreign Affairs* 72, no. 5 (1993): 98–109.
Wagner, Christian. "Security Cooperation in South Asia: Overview, Reasons, Prospects." SWP Research Paper. Berlin: German Institute for International and Security Affairs, 2014. https://www.swp-berlin.org/fileadmin/contents/products/research_papers/2014_RP06_wgn.pdf.
Walker, William. "Nuclear Order and Disorder." *International Affairs* 76, no. 4 (2000): 703–24.
Wallace, Corey J. "Japan's Strategic Pivot South: Diversifying the Dual Hedge." *International Relations of the Asia-Pacific* 13, no. 3 (September 1, 2013): 479–517.
Waltz, Kenneth N. *The Spread of Nuclear Weapons: More May Be Better*. Adelphi Papers. London: International Institute for Strategic Studies, 1981.
Wan, Wilfred. "Firewalling Nuclear Diffusion." *International Studies Review* 16, no. 2 (2014).
Weatherbee, Donald E. *International Relations in Southeast Asia: The Struggle for Autonomy*. Lanham, Md.: Rowman & Littlefield, 2014.
Weber, Katja. "Lessons from the ASEAN Regional Forum: Transcending the Image of Paper Tiger?" In *The Security Governance of Regional Organizations*, edited by Emil J. Kirchner and Roberto Dominguez, 219–42. New York: Routledge, 2011.

Weerakoon, Dushni. "SAFTA: Current Status and Prospects." In *Promoting Economic Cooperation in South Asia: Beyond SAFTA*, edited by Sadiq Ahmed, Saman Kelegama, and Ejaz Ghani, 71–88. New Delhi: SAGE Publications India, 2010.

Wionczek, Miguel S. "The Central American Common Market." *Intereconomics* 3, no. 8 (1968): 237–40.

Wirsing, Robert G. *Kashmir in the Shadow of War: Regional Rivalries in a Nuclear Age*. London: M.E. Sharpe, 2003.

Yaffe, Michael D. "Promoting Arms Control and Regional Security in the Middle East." *Disarmament Forum*, no. 2 (2001): 9–25.

Yamamoto, Yoshinobu. "Asia and Regional Integration Theory." In *Regional Integration in East Asia: Theoretical and Historical Perspectives*, edited by Satoshi Amako, Shunji Matsuoka, and Kenji Horiuchi, 3–34. Tokyo: United Nations University Press, 2013.

Yeo, Andrew. "China, Japan, South Korea Trilateral Cooperation: Implications for Northeast Asian Politics and Order." *East Asia Institute Issue Briefing*, no. MASI 2012-07, November 6, 2012. https://www.files.ethz.ch/isn/154972/2012110618151837.pdf.

Yudin, Yury. *Multilateralization of the Nuclear Fuel Cycle: The Need to Build Trust*. Geneva: UNIDIR (United Nations Institute for Disarmament Research), 2010.

INDEX

ABACC. *See* Brazilian-Argentine Agency for Accounting and Control of Nuclear Materials
Abe, Shinzo, 62
Abuja Treaty, 33
ACRS (Arms Control and Regional Security), 102
Additional Protocol: activities associated with, 16, 145n4; implementation of, 140; in Iran, 108; politics of, 12, 19, 55; status of, 2, 90, 128, 130. *See also* Programme 93+2; safeguards
ADMM (ASEAN Defence Ministers' Meeting), 78, 82–83
ADMM-Plus (ASEAN Defence Ministers' Meeting–Plus), 60, 63, 78, 83, 88
Advisory Board on Disarmament Matters, 75
AFCONE (African Commission on Nuclear Energy), 75, 113, 117, 125, 138, 161n17
African Commission on Nuclear Energy, 75, 113, 117, 125, 138, 161n17
African National Congress (South Africa), 115
African nuclear-weapon-free zone. *See* Treaty of Pelindaba
African Peace and Security Architecture, 116, 119, 125
African Regional Cooperative Agreement for Research, Development and Training Related to Nuclear Science and Technology, 119
African Union, 14–15, 35, 116–19, 125
Agadir Agreement, 97, 100
Agency for the Prohibition of Nuclear Weapons in Latin America and the Caribbean, 8, 11, 45, 59; features of, 52; and IAEA, 55, 151n41; status of Brazil and Argentina in, 132, 136
Agreed Framework, 75
Agreement on Cooperation for the Development and Application of the Peaceful Uses of Nuclear Energy, 54
Agreement on Information Exchange and Establishment of Communication Procedures, 82
Ahmadinejad, Mahmoud, 108, 109
Alfonsin, Raul, 54
al-Qaeda, 25, 69, 117, 128
Amano, Yukiya, 23
Andean Pact, 52
Annan, Kofi, 36
Anti-Ballistic Missile Treaty, 21
APEC (Asia-Pacific Economic Cooperation), 33, 35, 85–86, 87, 148n19
APT. *See* ASEAN Plus Three
A. Q. Khan network, 1, 117, 128; policy response to, 25, 69, 122–23, 141, 147n35; and Southeast Asia, 78, 90. *See also* black market; illicit trafficking
Arab Economic Summits, 97
Arab League. *See* League of Arab States
Arab Maghreb Union, 33, 97, 99
Arab Spring, 95–96, 100–101, 107
Arab Winter, 11, 95, 100
ARF. *See* ASEAN Regional Forum
Argentina: and Iran, 106; and the nonproliferation regime, 55–56; relations with Brazil, 5, 53–55, 56, 57–59, 151n37; and Treaty of Tlatelolco, 13, 27, 54–55
arms control, 6, 49, 50, 113, 128, 144, 158n37
Arms Control and Regional Security, 102
ASEAN. *See* Association of Southeast Asian Nations
ASEAN Charter, 83, 84
ASEAN Community, 83, 91, 92
ASEAN Declaration on Joint Action to Counter Terrorism, 82
ASEAN Defence Ministers' Meeting, 78, 82–83
ASEAN Defence Ministers' Meeting–Plus, 60, 63, 78, 83, 88
ASEAN Economic Community, 86
ASEAN Free Trade Area, 33, 86
ASEAN Ministerial Meetings, 79, 81, 93
ASEAN Network of Regulatory Bodies on Atomic Energy, 91–92, 94, 112, 137, 139

ASEAN Plus Three, 60, 63, 78, 82; and East Asia identity, 83, 86–88
ASEAN Political-Security Community, 63, 84, 88, 92, 94, 155n35
ASEAN Regional Forum, 63, 84, 88; agenda of, 35, 60, 80; criticism of, 78, 88
ASEAN Regional Haze Action Plan, 82
ASEAN Summit Meetings, 80, 83
ASEAN Vision 2020, 81–82, 84
ASEANTOM. See ASEAN Network of Regulatory Bodies on Atomic Energy
Asian currency crisis. See 1997 Asian Financial Crisis
Asian Nuclear Safety Network, 72, 91
Asia Pacific: as competing regional identity, 79, 86–88; inclusive order in, 33, 83; limits of ASEAN in, 63, 78, 83–85; trade growth of, 33; U.S. role in, 35, 62, 80
Asia-Pacific Economic Cooperation, 33, 35, 85–86, 87, 148n19
Asia-Pacific Safeguards Network, 72, 90
Association of Southeast Asian Nations: emergence of, 29, 79; expansion and disunity, 78, 84, 86–87, 136; intraregional trade in, 33, 82, 85–86, 97; and Northeast Asia, 60, 63; and nuclear energy community (see ASEAN Network of Regulatory Bodies on Atomic Energy); principles of, 14, 80–81, 84–87, 92–94, 136–37; security agenda of, 10, 40, 80–83; and security community ambitions, 82, 83–84, 88, 93 (see also ASEAN Political-Security Community); and the United States, 62, 88
Atoms for Peace, 47, 140

Bali Concord, 80
Bali Concord II, 82–83, 88
Ban, Ki-moon, 75
Bangkok Treaty, 79, 80–81, 89–93, 104
Berlin Plus agreement, 50
Bhutto, Benazir, 121
bipolarity, 74, 114; aftermath of, 35, 37, 38; collapse of, 29, 32
black market, 3, 25, 78, 93, 141; North Korea involvement in, 1, 69, 128. See also A. Q. Khan network
Blix, Hans, 16
blue book. See safeguards: and the NPT
Boutros-Ghali, Boutros, 35–37, 149n35
Brazil: concerns about, 56; consensual hegemony of, 56–58, 134, 151n9, 160n72; and Iran, 58, 151n59; and the nonproliferation regime, 55–56; relations with Argentina, 5, 53–55, 56, 57–59, 151n37; and Treaty of Tlatelolco, 13, 27, 54–55
Brazilian-Argentine Agency for Accounting and Control of Nuclear Materials: creation of, 8, 13, 45, 55; future of, 56, 58; and significance, 57–58, 138
BRICS (Brazil, Russia, India, China, South Africa), 63, 64, 123
Burma. See Myanmar
Bush, George H. W., 35, 74
Bush, George W., 25, 69

Cambodia, 79, 85, 90, 93
Camp David Accords, 98
Caribbean Community, 29
CARICOM (Caribbean Community), 29
Central American Common Market, 33, 52
Central Asian nuclear-weapon-free zone. See Treaty of Semipalatinsk
Central Treaty Organization, 121
Chavez, Hugo, 57
Chernobyl accident, 22, 71
Chiang Mai Initiative, 86
China: and the Asia Pacific, 77, 79, 80, 83, 87; civil cooperation with Pakistan, 23, 123; as global power, 11, 63, 65, 156n55; modernization plans of, 13–14; and neighbors, 74 (see also China-Japan-Korea relations); 1964 nuclear test of, 18, 140; and North Korea, 3, 39, 68, 137, 139; and nuclear multilateralism, 72; as nuclear weapon state, 2, 12, 76, 146n7, 147n28; relations with India, 121; relations with Iran, 95, 106; relations with Russia, 60, 64, 68, 127; relations with United States, 64, 87, 127, 156n55; role in Six-Party Talks, 63, 66, 67, 139. See also ASEAN Plus Three; South China Sea
China-Japan-Korea relations, 60, 61, 65, 70–72, 152n18; promise of, 14, 73, 112, 139
civil nuclear cooperation, 23, 109, 140, 156n58, 162n51
Clinton, Bill, 21, 35
Cold War: détente, 15, 124; effects of, 87, 114; end of, 34, 49; Europe during, 58–59; nuclear concerns during, 38, 127, 140; proxy conflicts during, 29–30, 55, 101, 124–25, 161n13; and regionalism, 28, 32, 80. See also bipolarity; post–Cold War period
Collective Security Treaty Organization, 35
Collor, Fernando, 54–55
Committee on Disarmament, 31. See also Conference on Disarmament

INDEX [185]

Committee on Nuclear Affairs, 49, 132
Common Foreign and Security Policy (European Union), 34, 49
Common Security and Defense Policy (European Union), 50
Common System of Accounting and Control, 55
Commonwealth of Independent States, 35
Comprehensive Study of the Question of Nuclear-Weapon-Free Zones in All Its Aspects, 30, 74, 110, 139, 158n31
Comprehensive Test Ban Treaty, 2, 21–22, 24, 146n23, 147n27
Conference of States Parties and Signatories to Treaties That Establish Nuclear-Weapon-Free Zones, 8, 104
Conference on Disarmament, 21, 24, 26
Conference on Interaction and Confidence Building Measures, 63, 152, 156n55
consensual hegemony. *See* Brazil: consensual harmony of
Convention on Assistance in Case of a Nuclear Accident, 71, 153n41
Convention on Early Notification of a Nuclear Accident, 71
Convention on Mutual Assistance in Criminal Matters, 120
Convention on Nuclear Safety, 71
Convention on the Law of the Sea, 70, 131
Convention on the Physical Protection of Nuclear Materials, 25, 41, 69, 118
Cooperative Threat Reduction Program, 7, 69, 70, 128, 130
Council for Security Cooperation in the Asia Pacific, 60
critical junctures, 85, 156n42
Cuban Missile Crisis, 18, 53, 59, 140

Declaration of ASEAN Concord II. *See* Bali Concord II
Declaration of Zone of Peace, Freedom and Neutrality, 80, 81
Declaration on the Denuclearization of Africa, 114
Defense Forces Strategy (Israel), 108
de Klerk, F. W., 115
disarmament: as concession by nuclear weapon states, 20–22; debate over, 12, 30–31, 55, 103, 128; in the European Union, 50–51; as NPT pillar, 2, 16, 17, 128, 146n4; and nuclear-weapon-free zones, 75, 102; post–Cold War momentum toward, 21, 49, 93, 103; progress toward, 24, 31; by South Africa, 114, 117, 160n2; and treaty obligations, 18–19, 130, 147n28. *See also* Special Session on Disarmament; Treaty on the Prohibition of Nuclear Weapons
Disarmament Commission, 21, 31, 51
diversion: and Euratom, 48, 73; and the NPT, 18, 19, 23, 24, 128, 140; state role in, 9, 16, 90, 117. *See also* safeguards
DPRK. *See* North Korea
Dulles, John Foster, 48

Early Notification of a Nuclear Accident, 71, 153n41, 156n63
East Asia: identity, 62, 86, 87 (*see also* ASEAN Plus Three); trade involving, 30, 35, 85, 119
East Asia Economic Caucus, 85, 86, 148n19. *See also* Asia-Pacific Economic Cooperation
East Asia Summit, 62, 78, 83–84, 87
Economic and Monetary Community of Central Africa, 35, 148n21
Economic Community of West African States, 29, 33, 116
Economic Community of West African States Monitoring Group, 35
ECOWAS (Economic Community of West African States), 29, 33, 116
EDC (European Defence Community), 46–48, 58, 72, 150n4
effective multilateralism, and European Union, 50
Egypt: and Middle East WMD-free zone, 30, 96, 101–5, 108, 110; safeguards noncompliance, 1, 20
Eisenhower, Dwight, 46, 47, 58
Eizenkot, Gadi, 108
ElBaradei, Mohamed, 1, 20, 23
Elbegdorj, Tsakhiagiin, 75, 152n19
Epstein, William, 53
EU. *See* European Union
Euratom. *See* European Atomic Energy Community
Euratom Commission, 48
Euratom Supplies Agency, 47–48
Euratom Treaty, 13, 46–48, 58, 59, 150
European Atomic Energy Community: establishment of, 45, 47–48, 58, 136; jurisdiction of, 8, 13, 59, 132; as model, 42, 72–74, 91, 139; possibility of UK exit from, 51
European Coal and Steel Community, 46, 150n4
European Council, 34, 49, 132
European Defence Community, 46–48, 58, 72, 150n4

European Economic Community, 32, 58, 73
European Political Cooperation, 34, 49
European Reassurance Initiative, 127
European Security Strategy, 50
European Union: and effective multilateralism, 50; foundation of, 34; integrative nature, 40, 49, 50; intraregional trade, 97; and nonproliferation, 49–51, 58, 132, 136; sanctions on Iran of, 106–7, 150n18; tension in, 4, 51, 59. *See also* Maastricht Treaty
export controls, 92, 118, 119, 147–8n7

1540 Committee, 118, 129, 131, 140. *See also* United Nations Security Council Resolution 1540
First Committee of the General Assembly, 21
Fissile Material Cut-Off Treaty, 2, 21, 24, 26, 162n44
Forum for Nuclear Cooperation in Asia, 72, 90
Forum for Nuclear Regulatory Bodies in Africa, 117
Framework Agreement on Enhancing ASEAN Economic Cooperation, 86
France: accession to the NPT, 49, 58; EDC Treaty views of, 46–48, 58; as nuclear supplier state, 19; nuclear tests of, 115, 117, 125; as nuclear weapon state, 2, 12, 51, 74, 146n7, 147n28; proliferation concerns of, 50; relations with ASEAN, 89; relations with Iran, 95, 106, 160n72; on the Treaty for the Prohibition of Nuclear Weapons, 147n30
Fukushima-Daiichi, 38, 72, 73, 77, 129; and Japanese nuclear regulation, 131, 139

G-24 (Group of 24), 29
G-77 (Group of 77), 29, 31, 147–48n7
Gandhi, Rajiv, 121
GCC. *See* Gulf Cooperation Council
General Agreement on Tariffs and Trade. *See* Uruguay Round
General Security of Military Information Agreement, 64
General Treaty of Central American Economic Integration, 52
Germany: and postwar integration, 46, 48; relations with Iran, 2, 51, 95, 106, 107
Global Initiative to Combat Nuclear Terrorism, 69
global nuclear order: change to, 2, 31, 48, 128–29, 141; defined, 3; foundation of, 12, 27, 38, 131–32; impact of India and Pakistan on, 123, 131, 137; Iranian engagement with, 108–9, 111; and NPT, 4, 140 (*see also* nonproliferation regime); and nuclear security, 25, 130; and regional order, 13, 26, 90, 125, 132–33 (*see also* regional nuclear order as concept); shortcomings of, 4, 130; threats to, 1, 15, 117, 122, 127–28; and the West, 92
Global Partnership Against the Spread of Weapons and Materials of Mass Destruction, 7, 70, 128, 130
global supply chain, 15, 117, 119, 125, 131
Global Threat Reduction Initiative, 69
Gorbachev, Mikhail, 33, 35, 74, 115
Group of 24, 29
Group of 77, 29, 31, 147–48n7
Guadalajara Accord for the Use of Nuclear Energy for Peaceful Purposes, 8, 55
Gulf Cooperation Council, 97, 98–99, 157n16, 157n19; evolution of, 96, 101, 110–11; as model, 99–100, 139

Hanoi Plan of Action, 81, 82
Hiraoka, Hideo, 76
horizontal proliferation, 16, 18, 24, 147–48n7
Hussein, Saddam, 107

IAEA. *See* International Atomic Energy Agency
IAEA Board of Governors, 20, 30, 72, 106
IAEA Committee on Assurances of Supply, 22
IAEA Regional Cooperative Agreement for Asia and the Pacific, 72
illicit trafficking, 3, 11, 25, 40, 90, 112. *See also* A. Q. Khan network
India: approach to regionalism of, 113, 120, 123, 125; civil cooperation with United States, 23, 123, 162n51; 1974 nuclear test of, 19, 22–23, 30, 48, 158n30, 162n44; as NPT nonparty, 3, 5, 26, 122, 130; and the Nuclear Suppliers Group, 127, 131, 147n34; as original NPT target, 18. *See also* India-Pakistan relations; South Asian Association for Regional Cooperation
India-Pakistan relations: bilateral trade, 120; deterrence-based order of, 15, 88, 113, 121–23, 127; nuclear cooperation in, 123–24, 137
Indonesia, 14, 78–79, 90, 93, 139
Information Circular 153. *See* safeguards: and the NPT
Intermediate-Range Nuclear Forces Treaty, 124, 128
International Atomic Energy Agency: and AFCONE, 117; approach of, 6, 19, 23, 56,

90; and ASEANTOM, 91; capacity of, 22–23, 102, 138, 140; creation of, 48; in Iran, 1, 106, 108; in Iraq, 19, 158n35; joint mission in Iraq, 19; and non-NPT parties, 146n16, 162n51; in North Korea, 20, 75, 144n31; and the NPT, 1, 9, 18, 103; and nuclear safety, 71–73; and nuclear security, 25, 69, 70; and nuclear-weapon-free zones, 7–8, 52, 55, 75, 81, 89, 151n41; politicization of, 30; in Romania, 146n17; safeguards system, 16, 18, 49–50, 55, 130, 131, 145n4. *See also* Additional Protocol; Programme 93+2; safeguards; Small Quantities Protocol
International Convention for the Suppression of Acts of Nuclear Terrorism, 118, 141
international fuel banks, 23, 27
International Nuclear Fuel Cycle Evaluation, 48–49
Iran: and Argentina, 106; and Brazil, 58, 151n59; civil nuclear cooperation with Russia, 109; European Union sanctions on, 106–7, 150n18; and IAEA safeguards, 1, 20, 106, 108; involvement in proliferation ring, 69, 122 (*see also* A. Q. Khan network); nuclear deal (*see* Joint Comprehensive Plan of Action); nuclear-weapon-free zone support of, 30, 101, 102, 104 (*see also* Middle East WMD-free zone); perceptions of, 5, 6, 105, 137; regional ambition, 105–6, 107, 109–11; relations with Germany, 2, 51, 95, 106, 107; relations with the P5, 95, 106–7, 109–11, 160n72; UN Security Council sanctions on, 106, 107; uranium enrichment activity of, 2, 105, 108
Iranian Revolution, 32
Iranian Revolutionary Guard Corps, 107, 109
Iran-Iraq War, 99, 101
Iraq, 19, 49, 50, 95, 102, 107. *See also* Osirak nuclear reactor
ISIS (Islamic State), 11, 95, 101, 110–12, 117, 128
Israel: ambiguity of and response to, 5, 40, 103, 112; bombing of Osirak, 19; and the JCPOA, 105, 108; and the Middle East WMD-free zone, 108, 110, 139 (*see also* Middle East WMD-free zone); as NPT nonparty, 3, 5, 26, 104–5, 122; Palestinian relations, 11, 95, 102; safeguards agreement of, 146n16

Japan: alliance with United States, 35, 60 (*see also* United States: hub-and-spoke system of); and Article 9, 62; East Asian presence of, 78, 86, 87 (*see also* ASEAN Plus Three);

increased role of, 62, 65; and North Korea, 66, 88, 152n19; and nuclear industry regulation, 131, 139; nuclear multilateralism of, 72, 90; as original NPT target, 18; and South Korea, 64. *See also* China-Japan-Korea relations
JCPOA. *See* Joint Comprehensive Plan of Action
Jenkins, Bonnie, 70
Joint Comprehensive Plan of Action, 2, 3, 51, 95, 105–6; and regional impact, 14, 107–9, 111, 112
Joint Convention on the Safety of Spent Fuel Management and on the Safety of Radioactive Waste Management, 71–72
Joint Declaration of the Denuclearization of the Korean Peninsula, 8, 74–75
Joint Declaration on Nuclear Policy (Argentina and Brazil), 54
Joint Declaration on the Denuclearization of Latin America, 53
Joint Nuclear Control Commission, 8, 75

Kashmir, 121, 123, 124. *See also* India-Pakistan relations
Kerry, John, 69, 111
Khan, Abdul Qadeer. *See* A. Q. Khan network
Kim, Il-Sung, 74
Kim, Jong-Un, 40
Kislyak, Sergey, 70
Korean Peninsula Energy Development Organization, 50, 61
Korean War, 46

Laajava, Jaakko, 104
Lagos Plan of Action, 33, 116
Lahore Agreement (Lahore Declaration), 122, 124
Lahore Declaration, 122, 124
Latin America and the Caribbean nuclear-weapon-free zone. *See* Treaty of Tlatelolco
Latin American Free Trade Association, 52
Lavrov, Sergei, 68
League of Arab States, 63, 96, 98, 102; evolution of, 100–101; and Middle East WMD-free zone, 96, 103–5, 110
Liberal Democratic Party (Japan), 62
Libya: Arab League suspension of, 100, 110; Arab Maghreb Union membership of, 99; black market role of, 1, 69, 122; safeguards noncompliance, 1, 20
Lim, Sungnam, 67
London Club. *See* Nuclear Suppliers Group

Maastricht Treaty, 34, 49–50, 59, 148n17
Macmillan, Harold, 29
Malaysia, 14, 78–79, 82, 90, 93, 139
Mateos, Aldolfo Lopez, 53
Medeiros, Evan, 64
Menem, Carlos, 54–55
Middle East WMD-free zone: Resolution on the Middle East, 27, 102–4, 110; role of Egypt in, 30, 96, 101–5, 108, 110; stagnation of, 76, 103, 139; steps toward, 2, 26, 102, 104
missile defense system. *See* Terminal High Altitude Area Defense
model agreement. *See* safeguards: and the NPT
modernization plans, 22, 31, 88, 127
Mohamad, Mathahir, 33
Mongolia: nuclear multilateralism of, 72, 153n41; role in Northeast Asia, 65, 75, 152n19 (*see also* Ulaanbaatar Dialogue on Northeast Asia); as single-state nuclear-weapon-free zone, 8, 26, 74, 139
Moon, Jae-In, 62, 65
Myanmar, 79, 84, 90

NAM (Non-Aligned Movement), 29, 92
NAPCI (Northeast Asia Peace and Cooperation Initiative), 62, 65
National Party (South Africa), 114–15, 160n7
National Security Strategy (Japan), 62
NATO. *See* North Atlantic Treaty Organization
NEAPSM (Northeast Asia Peace and Security Mechanism), 61, 67
negative security assurances, 8, 27, 31, 32, 52, 89
neoliberal institutionalism, 5–6
neorealism, 5, 6
Netanyahu, Benjamin, 3, 105, 108
New Pacific Community (United States), 35
new regionalism: economic dimension of, 32–33; foundation of, 32, 34; permanence of, 12, 28, 141; security dimension of, 35–37; signs of, 34–35, 40–41, 44, 136–37; supporters of, 35, 36
1997 Asian Financial Crisis, 81, 86, 87
Non-Aligned Movement, 29, 92
nonindifference (African Union), 116
noninterference, 53, 100, 116, 119. *See also* Association of Southeast Asian Nations: principles of
non-nuclear weapon states (NPT): on disarmament progress, 2, 22, 30–31, 103, 128; on India and the Nuclear Suppliers Group, 123; and rights to peaceful use, 30, 123; role in the Treaty on the Prohibition of Nuclear Weapons, 22, 130; safeguards obligations, 18, 30
nonproliferation regime: components of, 7, 16–18, 131, 140 (*see also* Nuclear Non-Proliferation Treaty); defined, 17–18, 143n7; and disarmament, 22; engagement with, 55, 90, 162n51; expansion of, 24, 38; failures of, 4, 13–14; future of, 88; impact of, 5, 6, 115; and the JCPOA, 2, 95, 108; limitations of, 9, 20, 27, 128; norms perpetuated by, 5 (*see also* nuclear taboo); and regional orders, 38, 41, 51, 113, 133, 137; rigidity of, 23–24, 25; scope of, 9, 12, 18, 19, 26, 129–30; in turmoil, 1–3, 16, 23, 127–28
nonstate actors: instruments targeting, 25, 69, 90; proliferation challenge of, 16, 24, 79, 111, 128, 131. *See also* A. Q. Khan network; nuclear terrorism; United Nations Security Council Resolution 1540
North American Free Trade Agreement, 32, 35
North Atlantic Treaty Organization, 38, 50, 127
Northeast Asia nuclear-weapon-free zone, 8, 9, 26–27, 32, 74–76
Northeast Asia Peace and Cooperation Initiative, 62, 65
Northeast Asia Peace and Security Mechanism, 61, 67
North Korea: aversion to multilateralism, 68, 70, 153n41; black market involvement of, 1, 25, 69, 122–23, 128 (*see also* black market); global response to, 61, 64; inter-Korean relations, 8, 74–75; NPT status of, 5, 12, 20, 66–67, 130; nuclear development of, 2, 127, 141; nuclear regulation of, 70; relations to Myanmar, 79; safeguards noncompliance, 20, 75, 144n31; and Six-Party talks, 1, 61, 66–67 (*see also* Six-Party talks); threat of, 3, 39, 68, 76–77, 112, 137
NPT. *See* Nuclear Non-Proliferation Treaty
NPT Preparatory Committees, 16, 76, 147n29
NPT Review and Extension Conference, 21, 50, 103. *See also* Middle East WMD-free zone; Nuclear Non-Proliferation Treaty
NPT Review Conferences: agendas of, 24, 27, 31, 76, 130; outcomes of, 1–2, 8, 21–22, 31, 104. *See also* 13 Steps; 2010 Action Plan
nuclear deterrence; and global order 37, 38, 143n8; in the Middle East, 105; in Southeast Asia, 15, 113, 121–25. *See also* United States: extended nuclear deterrence
nuclear nonproliferation regime. *See* nonproliferation regime
Nuclear Non-Proliferation Treaty: common

obligations with nuclear-weapon-free zones; 7, 27, 79, 89; disarmament in, 20, 31; discord with, 4, 24, 30–31, 92, 128, 147n7; impact of JCPOA on, 95, 108; implementation of, 48, 131, 147n27; inalienable right of, 22–23, 30, 40 (*see also* peaceful use); indefinite extension of, 22, 50, 102–3; late accession to, 49, 55, 58, 115, 150n23, 160n2; limitations of, 3–4, 16–17, 24–25, 56, 90, 127–28; noncompliance with, 12, 20, 75; nonparties, 19, 26, 102, 122; nuclear weapon states as defined by, 162n45; pillars of (*see* scope of); and regime, 4, 12, 16–17, 24, 28, 127–28, 129–30, 140–41 (*see also* nonproliferation regime); scope of, 2, 12, 17–18, 24, 50, 130; support for nuclear-weapon-free zones, 8, 26, 30, 110, 139–40; 2020 review cycle of, 105, 128–29; withdrawal from, 20, 66, 130. *See also* NPT Preparatory Committees; NPT Review and Extension Conference; NPT Review Conferences; Nuclear Suppliers Group; nuclear weapon states

nuclear safety: in Africa, 117, 119, 125, 137; as confidence-building issue, 14, 41, 55, 73, 137–39; in Europe, 73 (*see also* European Atomic Energy Community); IAEA activities in, 71, 140, 153n40; and nexus with security, 74; in Northeast Asia, 72–74, 77–78 (*see also* China-Japan-Korea relations); in nuclear-weapon-free zone treaties, 9, 75, 90; in Pakistan, 123; post-Chernobyl, 22, 71–72; post-Fukushima focus on, 38, 129; and proliferation link, 6, 24; in Southeast Asia, 3, 78, 88, 91–94 (*see also* ASEAN Network of Regulatory Bodies on Atomic Energy)

nuclear security: capacity-building, 118; defined, 69; framework, 25, 42, 69–71; IAEA role in, 25, 70 (*see also* Nuclear Security Fund; Office of Nuclear Security); and nexus with safety, 74; in Northeast Asia, 70–71 (*see also* Nuclear Security Centers of Excellence); Russian withdrawal from, 70, 77, 128; in Southeast Asia, 40, 78–79, 90; U.S. leadership in, 92 (*see also* Nuclear Security Summit series)

Nuclear Security Centers of Excellence, 71, 138
Nuclear Security Fund, 25, 69, 71, 153n37
Nuclear Security Index, 123
Nuclear Security Summit series, 7, 42, 70, 90, 109, 132; establishment of, 25, 69, 130–31; future of, 70, 71, 128–29

Nuclear Suppliers Group, 30, 48, 145n3; and India, 123, 127, 131, 147n34; and the NPT, 16, 24, 130
nuclear supplier states, 19, 22, 30, 31, 54. *See also* Zangger Committee
nuclear taboo, 38
nuclear terrorism, 25, 50, 69, 117
nuclear waste, 6, 9, 73, 130, 156n63
nuclear waste disposal, 9, 70, 156n63
nuclear-weapon-free zones: in Africa (*see* Treaty of Pelindaba); boundaries of, 80–81, 145n34; in Central Asia (*see* Treaty of Semipalatinsk); establishment of, 51, 75; forms of, 9, 42, 45, 146; in Latin America (*see* Treaty of Tlatelolco); in the Middle East (*see* Middle East WMD-free zone); Mongolia's status as, 8, 26, 74, 139; in Northeast Asia (*see* Northeast Asia nuclear-weapon-free zone); NPT support for, 8, 26, 30, 110, 139–40; and nuclear weapon states, 76, 81; as reinforcing the NPT; 7, 27, 79, 89; relationship to regional nuclear order, 3, 7, 9–10, 44, 139; scope of, 8, 9, 27, 31, 156n59; significance of, 75, 89, 101, 103, 104; in Southeast Asia (*see* Bangkok Treaty); in the South Pacific (*see* Treaty of Rarotonga); subregional zones, 26, 74, 76, 103; UN General Assembly study of, 30, 74, 110, 139, 158n31; in unpopulated areas, 144n26. *See also* Conference of States Parties and Signatories to Treaties That Establish Nuclear-Weapon Free Zones

nuclear weapons ban treaty. *See* Treaty on the Prohibition of Nuclear Weapons
nuclear weapon states (NPT): defined, 122; disarmament obligations, 20–22, 24, 30–31, 109, 147n28 (*see also* 13 Steps; 2010 Action Plan); and nuclear-weapon-free zones, 26, 52, 75–76, 89; resentment against, 2; role in peaceful use, 12, 23; and the Treaty on the Prohibition of Nuclear Weapons, 129–30

OAU (Organisation of African Unity), 114, 115–16, 125
Obama, Barack, 16, 62, 64, 69, 77
Office of Nuclear Security, 25, 69
OPANAL (Agency for the Prohibition of Nuclear Weapons in Latin America and the Caribbean), 8, 11, 45, 59; features of, 52; and IAEA, 55, 151n41; status of Brazil and Argentina in, 132, 136
Organisation of African Unity, 114, 115–16, 125

Organization of American States, 35, 53–54, 56
Osirak nuclear reactor, 19

P5 (permanent members of UN Security Council), 108, 109, 150n23
P5+1 (P5 plus Germany), 2, 95, 105, 107, 108. *See also* Joint Comprehensive Plan of Action
Pacific Community (United States), 35
Pakistan: civil cooperation with China, 23, 123, 162n51; geopolitical significance of, 121; as NPT nonparty, 3, 5, 26, 122, 130; nuclear and missile tests of, 124, 141; as proliferation threat, 123; relations with India (*see* India-Pakistan relations); and South Asian nuclear-weapon-free zone, 30, 158n30. *See also* A. Q. Khan network
Palestine, 11, 107
Pan Arab Free Trade Area, 97, 100
Park, Geun-Hye, 62, 70, 72
path dependence, 59
Peaceful Nuclear Explosions Treaty, 21
peaceful use: IAEA initiatives in, 22–23; infringements on, 30; as NPT obligation, 4, 17, 18, 22, 50; politics of, 12, 128, 130. *See also* diversion
Perry, William, 127
Plutonium Disposition and Management Agreement, 70, 128
post–Cold War period: extended deterrence in, 37; global order in, 7, 24, 55, 80; nonproliferation and disarmament momentum during, 8, 21, 80, 93, 103; and the NPT, 23–24, 89; and peaceful use, 23; proliferation pathways, 6, 16–17, 44; regionalism, 3, 13, 33, 85, 136, 158n37 (*see also* new regionalism); security concepts in, 36–37, 38, 113; security cooperation during, 41
Practical Steps. *See* 13 Steps
Program for Integration and Economic Cooperation, 54
Programme 93+2, 16, 19, 49–50, 145n4. *See also* Additional Protocol
proliferation pathways, 17, 24, 25, 90, 131. *See also* diversion; horizontal proliferation
proliferation ring. *See* A. Q. Khan network; black market
Proliferation Security Initiative, 42, 71, 90, 130, 141; controversy regarding, 70, 131; U.S. role in, 25, 69
Putin, Vladimir, 64, 65

Quartet Cooperation Council, 96, 100

rational-choice analysis, 39
Reagan, Ronald, 33
Regional Convention on the Suppression of Terrorism, 120
regional fuel cycle centers, 8, 32
regionalism: absence of, 125; competing, 79, 84–88, 93 (*see also* subregionalism); new (*see* new regionalism); 1970s, 29–32; post–Cold War patterns of, 3, 13, 34, 133, 141; study of, 6–7, 34; waves of, 28, 44, 133, 147n3
regional nuclear order as concept: emphasis on, 8; foundations of, 3, 38–43, 58, 98, 112–13; Latin America as model for, 8, 57; and nuclear-weapon-free zones, 7, 9–10, 44, 139; obstacles to, 10, 50, 77, 112, 137; utility of, 4
Republic of Korea. *See* South Korea
Resolution on the Middle East, 27, 102–4, 110. *See also* Middle East WMD-free zone
Rice, Condoleezza, 67
Richter, Roger, 19
Rouhani, Hassan, 107, 108
Russia: ambitions of, 63, 64, 65, 83; in the Middle East, 102, 104; nuclear multilateralism of, 70, 72, 77, 128; in nuclear security, 70; as nuclear weapon state, 2, 12, 74, 147n28; relations with China, 60, 64, 68, 127; relations with Iran, 109, 160n72; relations with the United States, 69, 70, 127, 128; and the Six-Party Talks, 67, 68; tensions with the West, 4, 77, 127

SAARC (South Asian Association for Regional Cooperation), 15, 33, 113, 119–21, 123, 125
Sadat, Anwar, 98
safeguards: application in North Korea of, 20, 26, 75, 144n31; costs of, 30; enforcement of, 19–20; exemptions from, 23, 56; as foundation for suppliers networks, 30, 130, 145n3; link with nuclear safety and security of, 6, 92; and noncompliance, 1, 19–20, 112, 150n18, and non-NPT parties, 102–3, 146n16, 162n51; and the NPT, 7–8, 18, 20, 48, 89, 103; and peaceful use, 40, 147–48n7; scope of, 9, 18; strengthening of, 12, 16, 19–20, 49–50, 72; and the Treaty of Tlatelolco, 7, 52, 55. *See also* Additional Protocol; Nuclear Suppliers Group; Programme 93+2
Safeguards Implementation Reports, 16
SAGSI (Standing Advisory Group on Safeguards Implementation), 16, 145n3
Salman bin Abdulaziz Al Saud, 108

sanctions: Arab League use of, 100; and noncompliance, 40, 58, 131, 132; role in Iran, 105–9, 160n72; unilateral U.S. use of, 106, 160n7
Sarney, José, 54
Saudi Arabia, 98, 100–101, 110, 157n16, 157n19
SCCC (Common System of Accounting and Control), 55
SEANWFZ (Southeast Asia nuclear-weapon-free zone). *See* Bangkok Treaty
SEANWFZ Commission, 81
September 11 attacks: and nuclear terrorism, 25, 50, 141; policy impact of, 69, 72, 82, 120, 147n28
Shanghai Cooperation Organization, 35, 60, 63–64
Shangri-La Dialogue, 60
Shoukry, Sameh, 108
Single European Act, 34, 49, 59
Six-Day War, 98
Six-Party Talks: agenda of, 66–67; China's role in, 63, 66, 67, 139; as foundation for regional order, 68; and Northeast Asia Peace and Security Mechanism, 61, 67; September 2005 Joint Statement of, 66, 68, 75; significance of, 65, 75, 76; suspension of, 1, 40, 61
Small Quantities Protocol, 23, 147n35
South Africa: disarmament, 114, 117, 160n2; and regionalism, 29, 33; security environment of, 113–15; and the Treaty of Pelindaba, 27, 75, 114, 124. *See also* African National Congress; National Party
South American Defense Council, 56, 57
South Asian Association for Regional Cooperation, 15, 33, 113, 119–21, 123, 125
South Asian Preferential Trading Area, 33, 120
South China Sea, 14, 79, 80–81, 83, 88, 127
Southeast Asia nuclear-weapon-free zone. *See* Bangkok Treaty
Southeast Asian Treaty Organization, 121
South Korea: alliance with United States, 35, 60, 74 (*see also* Terminal High Altitude Area Defense; United States, hub-and-spoke system of); ambitions of, 62, 65 (*see also* Northeast Asia Peace and Cooperation Initiative); in East Asia, 86, 87, 156n58 (*see also* ASEAN Plus Three); inter-Korean relations, 8, 74–75; nuclear multilateralism, 70–72; relations with Japan, 63; safeguards noncompliance, 1, 20. *See also* China-Japan-Korea relations

South Pacific nuclear-free zone. *See* Treaty of Rarotonga
Soviet Union: collapse of, 35, 55, 141; and European integration, 46; NPT drafting role, 18, 20–21, 146n7; and nuclear-weapon-free zones, 51, 74, 150n23; reforms in, 115; relations with the United States, 21, 49, 53, 124, 148n15; and the Russian Far East, 33; in South Africa, 115; in South Asia, 121, 124–25; threat of, 114
Special Session on Disarmament, 31
SSOD (Special Session on Disarmament), 31
Stalin, Joseph, 46
Standing Advisory Group on Safeguards Implementation, 16, 145n3
START I (Strategic Arms Reduction Treaty), 21
Strategic Arms Reduction Treaty, 21
Strategy against Proliferation of WMD (European Union), 50, 132
subregionalism, in Africa, 116; in the Middle East, 96, 97–100, 110, 111, 136; promise of, 139–40
Suez Crises, 47
Syria, 65, 95, 96, 100, 109, 110

tactical nuclear weapons, 74, 147n28
Taiwan, 65, 77, 87
technical cooperation, 14, 41, 111, 137, 138–39
Terminal High Altitude Area Defense (THAAD), 62, 127
13 Steps, 21, 22, 24, 130, 147n28
Threshold Test Ban Treaty, 21
Top Regulators' Meetings, 72. *See also* China-Japan-Korea relations
Treaty of Amity and Cooperation, 80
Treaty of Montevideo, 52
Treaty of Paris, 46
Treaty of Pelindaba, 27, 75, 114, 116–17, 124–25
Treaty of Rarotonga, 8, 9, 30, 80–81, 89, 156
Treaty of Rome, 49, 58
Treaty of Semipalatinsk, 8, 74, 104
Treaty of Tlatelolco: amendments to, 55, 151n45; as centerpiece of regional order, 13, 45, 57, 58, 136; late accessions, 13, 27, 54–55, 151n41; as model text, 9, 42; negotiation of, 7–8, 26, 51–54; and nuclear weapon states, 26; and OPANAL (*see* Agency for the Prohibition of Nuclear Weapons in Latin America and the Caribbean); safeguards in, 7, 52, 55
Treaty on Integration, Cooperation, and Development, 54

Treaty on the European Union. *See* Maastricht Treaty
Treaty on the Non-Proliferation of Nuclear Weapons. *See* Nuclear Non-Proliferation Treaty
Treaty on the Prohibition of Nuclear Weapons, 4, 22, 28, 128, 129–30
Trilateral Cooperation Secretariat. *See* China-Japan-Korea relations
Trilateral Coordination and Oversight Group, 61
Trump, Donald J.: and isolationism, 4, 62, 65, 110; and the JCPOA, 106, 109; and nuclear policy, 70, 145n39
2010 Action Plan, 2, 21–22, 24, 105, 129–30

Ulaanbaatar Dialogue on Northeast Asia, 65, 75
Union of South American Nations, 56, 57
United Kingdom: economic reform in, 32; as nuclear weapon state, 2, 12, 51, 147n30; proliferation concerns of, 18, 48, 50; and regionalism, 29, 46; relations with Iran, 95, 106, 109
United Nations, 10, 30, 35–36
United Nations General Assembly Resolution 2028, 18, 26, 51
United Nations Regional Centre for Peace and Disarmament Affairs, 118, 151
United Nations Security Council: discord within, 122; and Libya, 100; membership, 108; and North Korea, 25, 67; role in international peace and security, 36, 49; and safeguards noncompliance rulings, 20; sanctions in Iran, 106, 107
United Nations Security Council Resolution 1540, 7, 42, 111, 129, 131–32; implementation of, 71, 90; regional role of, 42, 71, 118, 140–41, and United States, 25, 69, 70. *See also* United Nations Security Council Resolution 1977
United Nations Security Council Resolution 1977, 140
United States: and Asia-Pacific regionalism, 35; backlash against, 29, 53, 64, 131, 133;

Bangkok Treaty reservations of, 89; civil cooperation with India, 23, 123, 162n51; Cold War relations, 21, 49, 122, 124, 125, 148n15; economic regionalism of, 32–33, 34, 35; and European integration, 46, 48, 58, 73; European Reassurance Initiative, 127; extended nuclear deterrence, 12, 76; hub-and-spoke system of, 60, 62–64, 65; Middle East involvement of, 102, 104, 107, 111; Northeast Asia role, 11, 62, 74, 77, 143n9; and North Korea nuclear program, 3, 66, 67, 152n19; NPT drafting role, 18, 20, 146n7; nuclear multilateralism of, 25, 69, 70, 92, 130; nuclear tests of, 21; as nuclear weapon state, 2, 18–19, 147n28; pivot to Asia, 62, 64, 77; presence in Western Hemisphere, 52–53, 57; relations with ASEAN, 80, 83, 85; relations with China, 64, 87, 127, 156n55; relations with Iran, 95, 106–7, 109–11, 160n72; relations with Russia, 69, 70, 127, 128; safeguards, 72; South African policy, 114–15, 160n7; support of Pakistan, 121; on the Treaty on the Prohibition of Nuclear Weapons, 147n30. *See also* Terminal High Altitude Area Defense
United States Nuclear Regulatory Commission, 139
uranium stockpiles, 23, 127, 160n27, 162n2
Uruguay Round, 32, 34, 85

verification. *See* safeguards
Vientiane Action Programme, 82
Vietnam, 79, 93
Vietnam War, 87

World Institute for Nuclear Security, 25, 71
World Nuclear Association, 132

Xi, Jinping, 63
Xiangshan Forum, 63

Yongbyon complex, 66–67

Zangger Committee, 16, 30, 130, 145n3. *See also* nuclear supplier states

www.ingramcontent.com/pod-product-compliance
Lightning Source LLC
Chambersburg PA
CBHW030653230426
43665CB00011B/1079